ISLAMIC FUNDAMENTALIST TERRORISM, 1979–95

Also by Edgar O'Ballance

ARAB GUERILLA POWER
CIVIL WAR IN BOSNIA: 1993–94
CIVIL WAR IN YUGOSLAVIA
NO VICTOR, NO VANQUISHED: The Middle East War, 1973
TERROR IN IRELAND: The Story of the IRA
TERRORISM IN THE 1980s
THE ARAB-ISRAELI WAR: 1948–49
THE ALGERIAN INSURRECTION: 1954–62
THE ELECTRONIC WAR IN THE MIDDLE EAST: 1968–70
THE CYANIDE WAR
THE FRENCH FOREIGN LEGION
THE GREEK CIVIL WAR: 1944–49
THE GULF WAR
THE INDO-CHINA WAR: 1946–54
THE KURDISH REVOLT: 1961–70
THE KURDISH STRUGGLE: 1920–94
THE LANGUAGE OF VIOLENCE
THE MALAYAN INSURRECTION: 1948–60
THE RED ARMY OF CHINA
THE RED ARMY OF RUSSIA
THE SECOND GULF WAR: The Liberation of Kuwait
THE SECRET WAR IN SUDAN: 1955–72
THE SINAI CAMPAIGN: 1956
THE THIRD ARAB–ISRAELI WAR: 1967
TRACKS OF THE BEAR: US–USSR Relations in the 1970s
WAR IN YEMEN: 1962–69
WARS IN AFGHANISTAN: 1839–1992
WARS IN VIETNAM (1954–60)

Islamic Fundamentalist Terrorism, 1979–95

The Iranian Connection

Edgar O'Ballance

NEW YORK UNIVERSITY PRESS
Washington Square, New York

© Edgar O'Ballance 1997

First published in the U.S.A. in 1997 by
NEW YORK UNIVERSITY PRESS
Washington Square
New York, N.Y. 10003

This book is printed on paper suitable for recycling and
made from fully managed and sustained forest sources.

Library of Congress Cataloging-in-Publication Data
O'Ballance, Edgar.
Islamic fundamentalist terrorism, 1979–95 : the Iranian connection
/ Edgar O'Ballance.
p.   cm.
Includes bibliographical references (p.   ) and index.
ISBN 0–8147–6191–7
1. State-sponsored terrorism—Iran.   2. Iran—Foreign
relations—1979–   3. Terrorism—Islamic countries.   4. Islamic
countries—Politics and government.   I. Title.
DS318.825.O23   1996
955.05'4—dc20   96–12962
                                                          CIP

Printed in Great Britain

Contents

Preface

During the 1980s a dreaded bogeyman of the West was Islamic fundamentalism, as expounded and practised by Iran, with its exported terrorism. This was especially so when the USSR began to crumble and new enemies were sought. It was visualised that Islamic fundamentalism would swamp the Muslim world and threaten the West, politically, economically and perhaps militarily. Iranian-instigated terrorism was already reaching out to scar some Western nations, with Israel as the catalyst. Islamic fundamentalist terrorist activity in Egypt, Sudan and Algeria gave credence to this fear. In the Muslim world a civil war was in progress between Islamic fundamentalists who wanted to govern according to the Koran and Islamic custom, and 'moderates' or semisecularists who wanted a more tolerant regime.

The 'Iranian Connection' is a network of embassies and diplomatic missions spread across the world, staffed with intelligence personnel who shelter terrorists, store their weaponry and monitor their prey, while diplomatic couriers carry explosives, arms and ammunition with impunity through national customs barriers. The Tehran government flatly denies all such allegations, but Western intelligence agencies insist they are true and Western governments continue to expel Iranian diplomats for subversive activities. The Iranian Connection is a secret, underground organisation that is authorised by a government fascinated with the use of terrorism as an arm of its foreign policy.

Iran is placed high on the US 'List of Countries Supporting Terrorism'. Its aim is ultimately to march to Jerusalem and destroy the state of Israel. Iran also uses terrorism as a substitute for its weak military capability, to strike at unfriendly powers, especially Western ones, and those supporting Israel.

If there is a Paradise, and Hassan Ben Sabbah, a Persian born in 1003 AD, managed to reach it, he must be smiling down approvingly on the Iranian government, which is emulating his methods. From the remote Alamut Valley in northern Persia this 'Old Man of the Mountains' dispatched assassins on murder missions. Sultans, emirs and governors of provinces slept in chain-mail vests, fearing the assassins' daggers. The difference between Ben Sabbah and Ayatollah Khomeini is that one used daggers, while the other used bullets and bombs.

In 1982 a detachment of the Iranian Hezbollah (Party of God), originally a dubious street gang that distinguished itself in revolutionary street fighting to become the military wing of the official Iranian Islamic Revolutionary Party, descended on the Lebanese Bekaa Valley. Directed and funded by the Tehran government, it developed into a terrorist coalition that has been striking at Israeli and Western targets ever since.

Islamic fundamentalist terrorism has turned westwards during the present decade. This was vividly illustrated in March 1992, when an explosion wrecked the Israeli embassy in Buenos Aires, killing 28 people and injuring 252, followed in February 1993 by an explosion in the World Trade Centre in New York that killed six people and injured 1042. The alleged godfather in the latter case was Sheikh Omar Abdul Rahman, who had been involved in plotting the assassination of President Anwar Sadat of Egypt in October 1981.

An explosion at a Jewish building in Buenos Aires in 1994 killed 96 people and injured over 200. Another, at the Israeli embassy in London, injured 14 people; and a few hours later yet another, at Balfour House in north London, injured six people. An explosion in an aircraft flying over Panama killed 21 people.

In all cases the finger of suspicion pointed to Hezbollah as the perpetrator and Iran as the godfather, Hezbollah's intention being to disrupt the Middle East peace talks. Iranian embassies and diplomats were harnessed into a terrorist network that was controlled by 'Department 15' of the Iranian Intelligence and Security Ministry. Circumstantial evidence abounded, but direct proof was elusive. The Iranian government continually denied any involvement.

When Ayatollah Khomeini and his leadership team arrived in Iran in February 1979 to effect the Islamic Revolution, they were faced with hostile groups that used terrorist tactics against them for many months. Khomeini replied with counter-terrorist means, in the course of which much blood was spilt and many people died, some being tortured to death.

The Khomeini regime was toughened by this revolutionary baptism of fire, and it gained experience of terrorist warfare. Realising its capabilities and effects, it was decided to continue to operate this form of warfare covertly. Khomeini and his colleagues had taken a liking to terrorism and were reluctant to abandon it. Executions, torture and imprisonment were carried to excess to eliminate internal opposition, while abroad the leaders of opposition groups and 'enemies of the state' were assassination targets.

From the Bekaa Valley, Hezbollah launched a number of airliner hijacking exploits in the 1980s and early 1990s. Some were mounted by the extremist Dawa group, first against Libya, which it accused of kidnapping and then killing its senior Shia cleric, and then against Kuwait, demanding the release of 17 imprisoned Dawa members who became known as the 'Kuwaiti-17'.

International terrorists were hired to form hijacking teams. In June 1985 one such team, led by Fawaz Younis, seized a TWA airliner just after it had left Athens. The plane was flown to Beirut, where a dramatic 17-day saga unfolded, watched in fascination by millions of TV viewers throughout the world. The hijacked plane flew to and fro between Beirut and Algiers. Eventually the hostages were released in Beirut and the hijackers slipped away.

A similar TV drama occurred in April 1988, when a Kuwaiti airliner was hijacked by a Hezbollah team and flown to Mashhad in Iran. There a 'relief' team led by Imad Moughniyeh, an international terrorist, took over. The 15-day saga that followed was recorded 'live' for international TV screens. The plane eventually ended up in Algiers, where once again the terrorists slipped away. Both hijackings were claimed as Islamic fundamentalist terrorist victories.

The seizure of the US embassy in Tehran in November 1979 by Revolutionary Students, and the subsequent holding of American hostages for 444 days had demonstrated the vulnerability and helplessness of powerful Western nations such as the United States, which had been labelled the 'Great Satan' by Khomeini.

In Lebanon, from 1984 until 1992, Hezbollah snatched and held a number of American, French and British hostages, and also many Middle Eastern ones, some for long periods, savouring the embarrassment inflicted on Western nations. A few hostages were killed, such as William Buckley and Colonel Higgins, both alleged to be CIA operatives. Some died in captivity, and probably three or four escaped. The remainder survived and were eventually released. Hezbollah gained considerable publicity – the 'lifeblood of terrorism'.

Despite the London Accord of December 1986, under which Western nations agreed not to bargain with terrorists for the release of hostages, many countries made covert arrangements that sometimes involved huge sums of ransom money and political concessions. In some cases terrorists held in Western prisons were exchanged for hostages held by Hezbollah groups.

Hezbollah also trained suicide terrorists and activated them against Western and Israeli troops in Lebanon, boasting that it had 48 suicide bombers ready to attack Israeli targets. Several suicide attacks were made. One in August 1983 against the American embassy in Beirut killed 63 people. In October of that year twin suicide attacks were made in Lebanon, one against a fortified US position, which killed 241 US Marines, and the other against a French post, killing 58 French soldiers. Suicide bombers became prestige cult figures. They caused many casualties and much dread. Israel responded with air strikes on terrorist camps. The CIA also entered this covert struggle, not always effectively. In March 1984 it organised an explosion at the house of a prominent Hezbollah leader. Over 200 people were killed – but the target was not at home that day.

When the Lebanese Civil War (1975–90) drew to a close, Hezbollah's presence in the Bekaa Valley became more restricted. It turned much of its attention to attacking Israelis in southern Lebanon. Israel continued to make air strikes on its bases; and in July 1989, in a helicopter raid into Lebanon, kidnapped Sheikh Abdul Karim Obeid, a senior Hezbollah leader. Later, in May 1991, another Israeli helicopter raid killed Sheikh Abbas Moussawi, secretary general of Hezbollah.

In the 1990s the Tehran government began to sponsor the Palestinian Hamas (Islamic Resistance Movement), which was dedicated to the destruction of Israel and disruption of the Palestinian–Israeli peace agreement. Iran turned an amateurish organisation into a deadly active one that attacked Israeli settlers and Israeli targets in the occupied territories. Hamas's 'Qassam Brigades' fought violent battles against Arafat's 'Fatah Hawks'.

In November 1992 the Iranian government formally entered into an alliance with Hamas, promising to provide political and financial backing. Hamas guerrillas began to train in Iran. In December Israel deported over 400 Hamas activists and supporters to 'no man's land' in southern Lebanon, the Syrian-backed Lebanese government having refused to allow them entry. There they remained encamped for over a year, publicising their cause to the world and thus obtaining more 'lifeblood'.

By 1994 Hamas activists were operating inside Israel. A policeman died at their hands – the 'Toledano incident' – after which Israeli security forces destroyed 15 Hamas cells and arrested 120 Hamas activists. Hamas had been killing Palestinian informers and collaborators for some time; but on the other hand Israeli undercover agents were accused of taking similar action against Hamas and other Palestinian organisations – it was a very dirty war. In October 1994 a Hamas suicide bomber boarded a bus in Tel Aviv during the rush hour. The subsequent explosion killed 22 people and injured nearly 50. Other suicide bombing incidents inside Israel followed.

For some time the Tehran government had been funding and otherwise supporting illegal groups in Egypt, striving to turn that country into an Islamic fundamentalist state by violence. In November 1981 one such group assassinated President Sadat because he had visited Israel. Sadat's successor, President Mubarak, fought back using military means, mass arrests, show trials and executions, and is still fighting hard. Adjacent Sudan, a country involved in its own civil war with dissident forces in the south, also faces Islamic fundamentalist opposition, supported by Iran.

The Tehran government has also been giving support, expertise and money to the Algerian Islamic Salvation Front (FIS) and the Armed Islamic Group (GIA) in their violent struggle against the military government and their 'assassination of foreigners' campaign. The Algerian government cancelled elections when it was thought that the Islamic fundamentalists were about to win, which presented Western democratic moralists with a problem.

During the past 16 years Iran has spread its terrorist tentacles into several Western countries, often those with Muslim minorities, providing money and other support to active antigovernment organisations. It has also liaised with national terrorist groups, including the IRA, and continues to employ international terrorists to undertake hijacking, bomb explosions and assassination operations, whilst blithely denying every allegation cast against it. Hostile Iranian political leaders in exile remain assassination targets.

Internally, for some time after seizing power, the Khomeini regime had a hard ride, as its opponents too realised the value of naked terrorism. In June 1981 the powerful Mujahedeen Khalk, in alliance with other groups, declared war on the Khomeini regime. A terrorist struggle ensued, and is still in progress. Casualties have been heavy. In the month it all began an explosion at a meeting of the IRP demolished the building in which it was held, killing 74 people, including the IRP leader, 12 government ministers and 28 Majlis deputies: the top layer of the IRP. In August 1981 an explosion at a cabinet meeting killed the president, the prime minister and several others. The assassination of major personalities was frequent. President Rafsanjani survived three attempts on his life.

The expression 'Islamic fundamentalist' had come to mean in general parlance a radical Islamic militant activist, committed either to preserving an Islamic state such as Iran, or to turning a Muslim country into an Islamic state by any means, including armed insurrection and terrorism. The concurrent burden of Iran's war against Iraq (1980–88), which it lost, affected neither its Islamic vision nor its use of terrorism.

Islamic fundamentalism came to the world's attention with Ayatollah Khomeini. Iran became a role model and helper, but not necessarily an originator, as discontent was already smouldering in some Muslim countries due to Westernisation, and dictatorial and corrupt leaderships that had pushed age-old Islamic authority coldly aside. The death of Khomeini in July 1989 changed little in Iran. His heirs and successors have both his Islamic vision and his taste for terrorism. Westerners, with their philosophy of popular democracy, toleration and compromise, have failed to understand that Islamic fundamentalism seeks none of these characteristics: it does not want recognition for its cause, nor dialogue, compromise, equality with the West, a truce or a condominium: it only wants total victory.

The civil war within the Muslim world may continue for another generation or so; but eventually it will either burn itself out in defeat or be smothered by the pervasive influence of the electronic superhighway that is encompassing the earth. Islamic fundamentalism may even dissolve much sooner, due to that other giant leap in modern communications technology – satellite television, offering as it does many alternatives to the stilted official Islamic channels. Tehran has over a quarter of a million satellite dishes, and Algeria over 100 000. They are now forbidden in Iran, but the miniaturisation of satellite dishes is making detection difficult, to the acute discomfort of the mullahs. When in exile, Khomeini sent taped casettes of his inflammatory sermons into Iran to be played in the 80 000 mosques. Now, unconsciously or otherwise, the West is using its advanced state-of-the-art technology against his Islamic vision. In this book brief comments are made on other countries affected by Islamic fundamentalism, including some European Countries, Morocco, the Philippines and Tunisia – the common link being the Iranian Connection.

The final chapter ponders on the mythology and reality of 'International Terrorism Inc., so beloved by the media and novelists. Does it exist, and if so, does it have a recruitment problem? Do its activists have a 'sell by date', and how do they managed to remain underground and at large? Has growing expertise, combined with the ability to instil the glory of suicide missions into Islamic fundamentalist terrorists, turned them into an exclusive club, making former international terrorist personalities commonplace and expendable? Is there a 'hiring and firing' agency? Carlos the Jackal was sold to France by Sudan as he was surplus to requirements. Who may next be put up for auction – Abu Nidal?

EDGAR O'BALLANCE

Acknowledgements

The information contained in this book was gathered over a number of years, during which I attended numerous press conferences in many parts of the world on terrorist incidents, studied sheaves of official handouts, asked questions, and at times discussed terrorism with ministers, ex-ministers and their senior security officers. I also talked to numerous 'activists' who were anxious either to tell me how they 'did it for posterity', to blame some one else, to criticise or praise their leadership, or to plant false information.

All opinions, views and deductions are my own.

I have read with interest and attention the following periodicals (translated extracts in some cases), and where information or material has been used from a particular published source, accreditation is given within the text.

UK	TV and radio: BBC, ITV, Channel 4. Periodicals: *Sunday Telegraph, The Sunday Times, The Times, Daily Telegraph, Newsweek, Time Magazine – Middle East, Middle East International, Middle East Economic Digest.* News agency: Reuters.
USA	Television: CBS, CNN. Periodicals: *New York Times, Washington Post, USA Today, Middle East Watch.*
France	Periodicals: *Le Figaro, La Parisien, Le Quotidien.* News agency: Agence France-Presse.
Israel	*Jerusalem Post. Maariv.*
Iran	TV and radio: VVIR, Radio Tehran, Free Voice of Iran. Periodicals: *Jumhuri Islami, Kayhan, Tehran Times.* News Agencies: Islamic Republican News Agency, PARS.
Lebanon	Radio: Radio Lebanon, Voice of Lebanon. Periodical: *al-Nahar.*
Russia (USSR)	News agencies: Tass, Interfax.
Argentina	*Claron.*

List of Abbreviations

AIS	Army of Islamic Salvation (Algeria)
CENTO	Central Treaty Organisation
CIA	Central Intelligence Agency (US)
DST	Direction de Surveillance du Territoire
EEC	European Economic Community
EHRO	Egyptian Human Rights Organisation
EU	European Union
FBI	Federal Bureau of Investigation (US)
FIS	Islamic Salvation Front (Algeria)
FLN	National Liberation Front (Algeria)
FORG	Free Officers of the Revolutionary Guard (Iran)
GCHQ	Government Communications Headquarters
GIA	Armed Islamic Group (Algeria)
GIGN	Groupe d'Intervention, Gendarmerie Nationale (France)
HCS	High Committee of State (Algeria)
IATA	International Air Transport Association
ICO	Islamic Conference Organisation
IDF	Israeli Defence Force
IISS	International Institute for Strategic Studies (London)
IMF	International Monetary Fund
IRA	Irish Republican Army
IRNA	Islamic Republican News Agency (Iran)
IRP	Islamic Republican Party (Iran)
KDPI	Kurdistan Democratic Party of Iran
KGB	Soviet Committee of State Security
MI5	British Military Intelligence – internal
MI6	British Military Intelligence – overseas
MKO	Mujahedeen Khalk Organisation (Iran)
MNF	Multinational force (in Lebanon)
MPRP	Muslim People's Republican Party (Iran)
NATO	North Atlantic Treaty Organisation
NIF	National Islamic Front (Sudan)
NIRM	National Iranian Resistance Movement

NLA	National Liberation Army (Iranian exiles)
NRC	National Resistance Council (Iran)
OPEC	Organisation of Petroleum Exporting Countries
PFLP	Popular Front for the Liberation of Palestine
PFLP-GC	Popular Front for the Liberation of Palestine – General Command
PKK	Kurdish Workers Party (Turkey)
PLO	Palestine Liberation Organisation
PUK	Patriotic Union of Kurdistan (Iraq)
RCF	Revolutionary Council of Fatah (Palestine)
RJO	Revolutionary Justice Organisation (Lebanon)
ROSM	Revolutionary Organisation of Socialist Muslims (Iran)
SAS	Special Air Service (Britain)
SCIRI	Supreme Council of the Islamic Revolution in Iraq
SFF	Socialist Front Forces (Algeria)
SIS	Secret service (MI-6) (Britain)
SPLA	Sudan Peoples' Liberation Army
SSNP	Syrian Socialist Nationalist Party
TWA	Trans World Airline
UN	United Nations
UNIFIL	UN Interim Force in Lebanon
UNTSO	UN Truce Supervision Organisation
US	United States
VVIR	Voice and Vision of the Islamic Republic (Iran)

Chronology

1979

1 February	Ayatollah Khomeini lands in Tehran
9–12 February	Battles on the streets of Tehran
11 February	Declaration of neutrality
1 April	Islamic Republic of Iran declared
6 May	Pasdaran (Islamic Revolutionary Guards Corps) formed
4 November	American hostages seized in the US embassy in Tehran
11 December	Revolutionary Students' International meeting in Tehran (held until 21 January 1981)

1980

February	Bani-Sadr elected president of Iran
24 April	US Operation Eagle Claw
30 April	Siege of the Iranian embassy in London (ended 5 May)
9 July	July Plot, Iran
28 July	Death of Mohammed Reza Shah in Egypt
4 September	Iraq–Iran War began

1981

6 April	Assassination of President Sadat of Egypt
28 June	Explosion at IRC meeting in Tehran
30 August	Explosion in Tehran kills president and prime minister
4 September	French ambassador killed in Beirut
15 December	Explosion at Iraqi Embassy in Beirut

1982

24 February	Kuwaiti airliner hijacked
3 June	Israeli ambassador shot in London
6 June	Israel invades Lebanon

| 14 June | Iranian 'volunteers' sent to Lebanon |
| 21–31 August | PLO withdraw from Beirut (after 73-day siege) |

1983

18 April	Explosion at US embassy in Beirut
23 October	Twin suicide-bombing against US and French troops
4 November	Suicide driver hits Israeli HQ in Lebanon
12 December	Dawa car bombs explode in Kuwait

1984

7 February	Assassination of General Oveissi in France (The Butcher of Tehran)
8 March	Bir el-Abed incident
20 September	Suicide-bomb explosion at US base in Beirut
4 December	Dawa hijacks airliner to Iran

1985

25 May	Dawa suicide driver rams emir's motorcade in Kuwait
28 May	Tehran meeting sanctions 'suicide bombings'
14 June	TWA hijacking (terminated on the 30th)
11 July	Cafe bomb explosions in Kuwait
18 September	US Operation Golden Rod

1986

| 15 April | US warplanes raid Libya |
| 11 December | London Accord |

1987

| 14 December | Hamas formed |

1988

| 5 April | Hijacking of Kuwaiti airliner (terminated on the 20th) |
| 20 August | Ceasefire in Iran–Iraq War |

1989

14 February	Iranian fatwa against Salman Rushdie
3 June	Death of Ayatollah Khomeini
24 June	Rafsanjani elected President of Iran
13 July	Assassination of Iranian Kurdish leaders in Vienna
28 July	Israelis capture Sheikh Obeid in helicopter raid
30 September	Taif Accord

1990

July	Sheikh Omar Abdul Rahman enters the United States as a tourist
5 November	Rabbi Meir Kahane killed in New York

1991

22 May	Syrian–Lebanese Treaty
6 August	Assassination of Sharpour Bakhtiar in Paris

1992

16 February	Israelis assassinate Sheikh Moussawi in a helicopter raid
28 August	Explosion at Algiers airport
18 September	Assassination of Iranian Kurdish leaders in Berlin
November	Rioting in some Iranian provinces
12 December	The Toledano Incident in Israel
8 December	Mass deportation of Hamas members to Lebanese border (remained until 9 September 1994)

1993

26 February	Explosion at the World Trade Center, New York
17 March	Explosion at the Israeli embassy in Buenos Aires
14 June	Trial of Islamic fundamentalist suspects begins in New York

19 August	Sudan put on the US List of States supporting Terrorism
4 October	Hamas suicide bombing begins in Israel
November	International terrorist conference in Tehran (IRA attended)

1994

January	Attacks on Christians in Iran
February	Disturbances in eastern province of Iran
27 February	Hebron massacre
22 April	Fatah–Hamas peace accord
3 June	Plot to bomb Israeli embassy in Thailand
2 June	Death of British intelligence personnel in air crash
18 July	Explosion at Israeli embassy in Buenos Aires
19 July	Air crash in Panama, Israeli/Jewish personnel on board
26 July	Explosion at Israeli embassy in London
27 July	Explosion at Balfour House in London
24 December	Hijacking at Algiers airport

1995

10 January	Rome Peace Assembly suggestions rejected by Algerian government
22 January	Natanya (Beit Lid) massacre in Israel
31 January	Explosion in centre of Algiers

1 Hezbollah Looks West

Almost casually, on Tuesday 26 July 1994 an attractive, expensively dressed middle-aged woman of Middle Eastern appearance drove a grey Audi 100 car along London's Kensington High Street, a prestige shopping centre and haunt of Middle Eastern diplomatic and wealthy families. At 12.10 p.m. she turned into Kensington Palace Gardens, a private tree-lined road that contains a Royal Palace and a dozen or so embassies and ambassadorial residences, often referred to locally and by London taxi drivers as 'Embassy Row'. The security guard at the gated entrance to the road briefly spoke to her, and seemingly satisfied raised the barrier to let her car through. His responsibility was to record vehicle registration numbers, check individuals' proof of identity and ascertain the purpose of their visit.

Once through the barrier the car turned sharp left into number 1 Kensington Palace Gardens, a private block of apartments, and parked in a vacant space in front of the building, which was cheek-by-jowl with number 2, the Israeli embassy. As the woman was walking from the car an Israeli security man on duty at the embassy, alarmed by the presence of an 'unknown' car, went to the security guard at the road barrier. The latter had already been joined by a member of the Diplomatic Protection Group of the Metropolitan Police, which covered Embassy Row and the Kensington Palace area. The woman had said she was merely visiting number 1 and would only be a few moments. She was carrying a Harrod's shopping bag, the prestige symbol of the world-famous London store, a common enough sight in Kensington High Street. This seemed to satisfy the security guard, despite the Israeli's protest that 'She is a Palestinian'.

As the woman was walking towards the entrance to the apartments and the policeman was making a vehicle check by telephone, a bomb in the car, later said to have consisted of 30 pounds of semtex, exploded, injuring 14 people, fortunately none seriously, and badly damaging parts of the Israeli embassy. In the confusion the woman disappeared. That is

1

what was reported to have happened in two vital minutes, although slight variations have since been aired. The security guard, the policeman and the Israeli were among the injured. The explosion was said to have been heard seven miles away. It certainly shook the immediate neighbourhood and many windows were shattered in Kensington High Street.

Just a few hours earlier – across the Atlantic, on the White House lawn in Washington – King Hussein of Jordan had been shaking hands with Itzhak Rabin, prime minister of Israel. Under the benevolent and paternal gaze of President Bill Clinton, the handshake had signalled the end of the 46-year war between their countries.

The bombing at the Israeli embassy in London was yet another terrorist operation in the long and violent campaign against the state of Israel. Recriminations began immediately. Israel insisted it had warned the British authorities that something like this was about to happen, blaming the Islamic fundamentalist group Hezbollah, a Lebanese Shia umbrella organisation, and complaining that Israel's warnings had not been heeded. Since Islamic fundamentalist terrorists had struck at an Israeli target in Argentina a few days earlier, Mossad executives had visited the security authorities in London and warned them that the UK was a hotbed of Islamic fundamentalist plotting and planning, and that major terrorist acts against Israeli or Jewish targets were imminent. The British did not fully agree with the Israeli assessment, and therefore took no extra precautions over and above what was considered to be normal security practice and procedure.

There was more to the Israeli reaction than simple pique. British–Israeli intelligence liaison had not yet recovered from a clash of interests way back in July 1988, when the British had arrested Ismail Sowan, who had been found in possession of Palestinian Liberation Organisation (PLO) arms in Hull, north-eastern England. Sowan, a double agent working for the Israelis and others, had been given the task of infiltrating the PLO's activities in Britain and had stumbled on a small cache of PLO weapons. British intelligence had no knowledge of this covert Israeli operation, and when it came to light was upset and reacted aggressively. Later, forged British passports were found in an Israeli embassy envelope in a telephone booth in West Germany.

The five-man Israeli Mossad team was expelled from Britain and relations between the two intelligence services were ruptured. In January 1989 the head of Mossad (identified by the European media as Nahum Adnom, whose name had been kept secret in Israel for security reasons) prematurely resigned his post. Covert Israeli operations in Britain were said to be among the misjudgments levelled against him.

Perhaps Mossad had not been completely open with the British, but then all national intelligence services guard their sources jealously, no matter how cordial relations might be with friendly countries. Besides, the British security chiefs had been deeply involved in their own war against Irish Republican Army (IRA) terrorists. For example, on 16 June a bag containing bomb components and semtex explosive had been found on a railway train, causing them to suspect that the more probable immediate danger was from IRA terrorist activity in southern England. The train had been travelling towards Brighton on the south coast, where the annual Conservative Party conference was due to be held in October. Back in 1984 the IRA had planted a 'sleeping' bomb at the Grand Hotel in Brighton, which exploded when the annual Conservative Party conference was in session, wrecking part of the building, killing five people and injuring many more. The prime minister, Margaret Thatcher, only narrowly escaped death or injury. The IRA had intended to kill members of the British cabinet. One source (Evans, *The Times*), stated that MI5 spent half its annual £150 million budget on countering IRA terrorism.

Although deep resentment was felt by Israel following the bombing of its embassy, its comments about Britain's lack of reaction to its warnings were restrained, and leaders and personalities on both sides spoke in platitudes of 'their confidence in each other', and of 'their good cooperation'. British security measures were immediately stepped up, and personnel were switched away from IRA security duties to afford armed protection to some 100 potential Jewish targets in England, where the Jewish minority numbered about 300 000.

Members of the SO-13 Department of the Metropolitan Police were diverted to, among other things, examining miles of footage from dozens of external security video cameras mounted on shops, offices, hotels and houses near the Israeli embassy, and in Kensington High Street, to try to discover the identity and escape route of the perpetrator. It was rumoured that the monitor in the security control room inside the embassy had not been switched on at the vital moment, about which Israel remained silent. Perhaps all with security responsibility had been neglectful in some detail. The Israeli ambassador, Moshe Raviv – who had been away from London at the time of the bombing – returned, and the following day, surveying the damage and debris in his office, declared 'All staff have arrived, everyone is at their desks'.

THE BALFOUR HOUSE EXPLOSION

At 12.50 a.m. on Wednesday 27 July, the day after the embassy bombing, a bomb planted in a car parked outside the offices of the Israeli Joint Appeal (in Balfour House, North Finchley, North London) exploded, causing considerable damage to the building and slightly injuring six passers-by. Balfour House was one of the 100 potential Jewish targets for which the British had promised to provide extra security. On the 26th an armed policeman had been posted outside the building, only to be withdrawn at 6 p.m., after which police patrol cars made hourly visits. At 9.30 p.m. the building's own security staff left and their surveillance cameras were turned off. Israel publicly complained that the police had not even banned the parking of cars in the street outside Balfour House. The car involved was a red Triumph with false number plates, a clone of a car legally owned by someone else, so that if stopped and checked by police the driver would be presumed to be the legal owner.

In answer to questions at a press conference at Scotland Yard, the Metropolitan Police HQ, it was explained in relation to the 100 potential targets that surveillance was in three categories, and that only a few actually received on-the-spot 24-hour armed guards, the remainder being either covered by patrolling police vehicles or by periodic visits by officers from local police stations. This amused neither Israel nor the Jewish population in Britain.

BRITISH EMBARRASSMENT

Unusually, the previous month Stella Rimington, director general of the security forces, explained something of their work in the annual Dimbleby Lecture in London. She described spy thrillers and lurid speculation about secret service work as totally misleading of what actually took place. She said 'I blame George Smiley [a fictional character in the novels of John le Carré] for some of the confusion, in his role as Karla-watcher and mole-hunter'. She said that it was with 'some hesitation I set out to shed some daylight', and that 'I have a sneaking feeling that the fiction may turn out to be more fun than the reality'. She went on to boast that 'members of Islamic extremist terrorist groups ... have been identified and their plans disrupted'. She had spoken too soon.

Britain (the first country to make a definitive public statement on the subject) has three different security and intelligence services. They are the Security Service, more commonly known by its long-time title MI5 (Military Intelligence, Branch-5); the Secret Intelligence Service (SIS), better known as MI6 (Military Intelligence, Branch-6), and the Government Communications Headquarters (GCHQ); all separate services with different functions. The normal role of the SIS and GCHQ is to collect the foreign intelligence needed to protect and support British interests, while MI5 is a defensive service, being a national security agency.

Putting on a brave face the British prime minister, John Major, in a speech in London the day after the second bombing, promised an 'unceasing hunt for the bombers', saying 'We must seek out its perpetrators and bring them to justice'. He added that the 'international community must unite for this purpose', and named Iran, Iraq and Libya as likely culprits. Within a few hours a photofit of the embassy bomber was produced and widely circulated. In both instances the cars used had been bought a few weeks previously, and their registration plates forged.

BRITISH INTELLIGENCE OPENS UP

Previously, on 2 June, the British intelligence services had suffered a severe top-level loss when a group of very senior officers, travelling by helicopter from northern Ireland to a conference in Scotland, had run into bad weather. The helicopter had crashed and all aboard had been killed. The dead included six MI5 agents, ten Royal Ulster Constabulary Special Branch officers and nine senior military ones. The four crew members had also died. This accident was described officially as one of the greatest setbacks in the British fight against terrorism. At a commemorative service the dead were described as 'Fallen heroes who fought the Silent War'.

When the modern British secret service was formed in 1909 it really was secret – its very existence was never mentioned officially and its funding was hidden away in other allocations. As may be expected, it developed and expanded during the two world wars, but only the barest of details were given in official histories, prompting fiction writers to use their imagination, which many did luridly, profitably and often inaccurately. Spy stories were immensely popular with the public, especially during the period of the Cold War. Successive British governments remained tight-lipped on the subject, refusing to discuss the matter, neither confirming nor denying what was said or written. Officially, the British secret service did not exist.

In the 1980s a hard-up, retired, long-serving member of MI5, Peter Wright, then living in Australia, sought to publish his memoirs (*Spycatcher*). The British government went to court in several countries to try to prevent publication. This was probably the worst thing it could have done, as it generated huge public interest in a mysterious fascinating subject that was wildly popular. The endless court appearances and arguments rebounded badly on both the government and the secret service. In time, however, the ending of the Cold War caused the government to decide that its secret service should be recognised, formalised by an Act of Parliament, and made accountable for its activities, as was the case in the United States. Slowly and reluctantly the British secret service allowed the world to peep into it.

In February 1992 Stella Rimington became the first woman head of the British Secret Service. Unprecedentedly her appointment was made public and the media were allowed to photograph but not interview her. Her Dimbleby Lecture was her first public speaking appearance, but again no questions were permitted. In 1992, after a series of IRA successes, MI5 became responsible for directing and coordinating intelligence gathering against the IRA in mainland Britain, in which the police forces had a large degree of autonomy.

In an attempt to give British intelligence gathering an acceptable face among a largely sceptical British public, which was demanding ever more accountability and was avid for inside information, Stella Rimington gave the 'James Smart' annual lecture in London in November 1994 (after the IRA ceasefire on 1 September). She claimed that MI5's coordinating role had produced 'significant dividends in countering terrorism, not all of them visible to the general public'. She ruled out further involvement with police investigation into drug trafficking and organised crime, unless such plots 'involved national security', as she was reluctant to have MI5 personnel involved in court proceedings. 'Our organisations complement one another', she said. The real backroom boy of the British Security Services was revealed as David Bickford, a senior official in the Foreign Office (*The Times*).

Despite the establishment of the Intelligence and Security Committee, a sort of watchdog that oversees the work of the intelligence and security services, they remain very secret. Civil liberty activists concerned about possible misuse, abuse or politically motivated activities, complain that the committee is only able to 'ask' for information, which may be withheld unless the head of the service decides it is 'safe to disclose it'.

On 17 January 1995 the British security services were ordered by the Treasury to trim their budgets by between 10 per cent and 15 per cent, the first financial cuts they had suffered for some years. The cuts were assumed to have been brought about by the ending of the Cold War, aided perhaps by an optimistic view of the IRA ceasefire.

More information about the services were revealed. For example, James Adams of *The Times* said that MI5 had a staff of 2200, 'more than half of them women', while GCHQ, which employed 6000 personnel and had an annual budget of over £500 million, was to be monitored by the parliamentary

Intelligence and Security Committee. Sir John Adye was named as the director of GCHQ, which is based in a sprawling campus in Cheltenham, some 80 miles west of London, its satellite dishes visible to all, with outstations in Cyprus and Hong Kong.

Suddenly, on 20 January 1995 two Palestinians, a man and a woman, named as Jawad Botmeh and Nadia Zerka, were arrested and charged with the London bombings.

THE ISRAELI ATTITUDE

Meanwhile Israel's external secret service, Mossad (Shin Bet being its internal one), had started its own enquiries, reinforced by personnel from Israel with instructions to hunt down the terrorists responsible for the London bombings. They soon declared they knew the identity of the woman terrorist, but did not reveal her name, saying simply that she was a widow, and that her husband and son had been members of the Abu Nidal group – the Revolutionary Command of Fatah (RCF) – before being killed by Israelis in a shoot-out in 1990. After their death she had become a dedicated terrorist, but was not in the RCF. According to Israel she was a member of the Lebanese-based Hezbollah, acting under orders from 'Department 15' of the Iranian Intelligence and Security Ministry in Tehran, which had been planning a series of major terrorist attacks overseas.

In Washington, Prime Minister Rabin and King Hussein declared that the London bombings had been designed to destroy the peace agreement they had just signed. Rabin named Hezbollah and Hamas (a Palestinian extremist resistance group) as being responsible for the war of terrorism that was being waged against his country. He castigated the Iranian government, accusing it of being the 'driving force of international terrorism'. (Hamas operated in the Israeli 'occupied territories', while Hezbollah operated farther afield.)

THE IRANIAN SCENARIO

In London the acting head of mission at the embassy of the Islamic Republic of Iran wrote a letter to *The Times*, denying

Rabin's allegations and declaring that 'Iran wants no part in international terrorism'. He went on to say that his 'Embassy disassociates itself from any group wishing to perpetrate terror'.

Nonetheless the governments of Britain and the United States openly blamed Iran, Libya and Iraq for the London bombings, emphasising that on this occasion the main blame fell on Iran. Was this justified, especially as Iran repeatedly denied all allegations that it was involved in terrorism? Would a sovereign state, a member of the United Nations, really indulge in terrorism to further its own strategic ends, seemingly out of sheer spite and vindictiveness? Or was the United States, out of helpless frustration, having been the butt of Iranian terrorism, just looking for a major bogeyman to replace the former Communist USSR to justify its belligerent attitude and wounded pride?

The British public had been aware of the Iranian affairs for some years, the popular press having followed the activities of the young shah – then thought of an an enlightened leader and friendly to the West – and his succession of glamorous wives. Increasingly, however, his dictatorial style was noted and sympathy for him faded, so that when he was pushed aside by the Muslim extremist leader, Ayatollah Khomeini, in February 1979 his fall was not particularly mourned. But neither was Khomeini welcomed, especially as reports of mass executions and other forms of extremism began to emanate from Tehran.

London acts as a magnet to many repressed and discontented peoples of the Middle East, and its fairly liberal tradition of political asylum began to attract Iranian dissidents, some of whom demonstrated on its streets for opposing causes, occasionally clashing with each other.

A dramatic incident of note in London was the Iranian Embassy Siege, which began on 30 April 1980 when six Ahwaz Liberation Front terrorists seized the building and demanded the release of Arab Iranians held in Iranian prisons. Ahwaz (Arabistan), Iran's oil-rich western province, had mainly an Arab population, which was discontented with the harshness of Khomeini's centralisation policy. British SAS troops stormed the embassy on 5 May, killing five of the terrorists and releasing the hostages. In September 1980 Iraqi troops marched into western Iran and Ahwaz province became a battlefield for some eight years. The Iranian Embassy Siege had been all in vain.

Evidence that Iranian 'hit squads' were roaming the streets of London in search of victims soon became obvious. Their activities were not always successful, and some were self-destructive. On 17 May 1981, a member of an Iranian hit squad that was charged with eliminating the sole surviving terrorist of the Iranian Embassy Siege was killed and his companion injured when the bomb they were assembling exploded in their hotel room in London. In December a car bomb exploded prematurely near Marble Arch while the car was on its way to an Iranian target, killing two of the hit squad and injuring another.

Other terrorist incidents occurred periodically in London, directed against the Iranian regime's enemies. For example in November 1985 a person at the Iranian embassy was injured by a parcel bomb. In August 1986 an explosion in a video hire shop – run by an Iranian dissident who was distributing anti-Khomeini and pro-shah videos and literature – killed one person and injured eleven. In July 1987 the Iranian representative of the National Iranian Resistance Movement (NIRM) was injured when a bomb planted in his car blew up in north London. In October 1987 an Iranian hit squad burst into the apartment of two notorious dissidents and shot them both dead. And so on.

In the meantime, elsewhere in the world Iranian government-backed terrorists carried out a wide variety of activities that included the hijacking of airliners and the kidnapping of Westerners, all of which gained universal publicity as the Iranian regime used terrorism as an arm of foreign policy.

SALMAN RUSHDIE

On 14 February 1989 Ayatollah Khomeini issued a fatwa, an Islamic command, on Salman Rushdie, the British author of *Islamic Verses*. Rushdie was sentenced to death for blasphemy, a price was put on his head, attempts were made on his life and he had to go into hiding under state protection. In March the British government severed diplomatic relations with Iran. On 3 August a terrorist blew himself up with his own bomb in a hotel room in London. His obituary was sent to media offices in Beirut, saying that 'Muslims are mourning their first Martyr, Gharib, who died while preparing to attack the apostate, Salman Rushdie', adding that 'future martyrs would hit the target'. Radio Tehran confirmed this, claiming that the 'martyr' was Gharib Mazreh, a member of the Lebanese-based Hezbollah.

HEZBOLLAH

It was estimated by Israel that the Lebanese-based Hezbollah coalition, operating under a variety of code names, probably numbered about 1000 people. It was thought to have an extensive intelligence network amongst exiled Iranian groups in London, and to be making 'protection' demands on the more wealthy. Mossad had found it difficult to penetrate Hezbollah, which had many 'sleepers' (members waiting to be activated), and insisted that Hezbollah was both funded and directed by Iranian agents working under diplomatic cover. Because London was a high-profile Western capital and a main centre of media communication, any terrorist exploits were immediately given top international billing.

HIZB UT-TAHIR

A major meeting was held on 7 August 1994 in Wembley Stadium, London, while feelings about the anti-Israeli bombings in London were still running high in Britain. It was organised by the Islamic fundamentalist group Hizb ut-Tahir (Liberation Organisation), founded in 1953, which was striving to establish a Khalifah (a single Islamic state) in the Middle East. The British authorities considered that Hizb ut-Tahir's objective was unattainable and utopian, so it was not classed as part of the violent fringe of extremist Islamic movements in Britain. Although the Israeli and French governments and several British organisations and personalities urged the Home Office to ban the group, it refused to do so, in spite of the fact that ten members of Hizb ut-Tahir had been convicted of plotting to assassinate King Hussein of

Jordan; and that in February 1991 Omar Bakri Mohammed, leader of its British branch, had been arrested in London for calling for the assassination of the British prime minister. He was later released without charge.

At Wembley, despite speakers calling for the destruction of Israel and issuing thinly veiled 'calls to arms', the meeting, attended by some 8000 people, many from abroad, passed off peacefully under the watchful lenses of several international intelligence video cameras. British intelligence liked to keep suspect activities out in the open for as long as possible for ease of surveillance.

The main complaint by those who had opposed the meeting was that speakers would further inflame resident members of foreign dissident organisations, some against each other and some against national covert organisations, thus turning the city into a battleground. Indeed some were seeking to achieve their aims by dubious or terrorist means, while sheltering within the minority community they were trying to subvert. Examples of this were the Iranian Mujahedeen Khalk, which was pitched against Iran's Islamic government; the Kurdish Workers' Party (PKK) against the Turkish government; the Algerian Islamic Salvation Front (FIS) against the Algerian government; and Islamic fundamentalist dissidents from Saudi Arabia, Tunisia and Bahrain, to mention but a few. The Wembley meeting was considered by objectors as facilitating, not to say encouraging, dissidence and terrorism, it being felt that the spirit of liberal sanctuary and free speech was being abused by those who sought to install closed dictatorial regimes in their own countries, and to terrorise their exiled compatriots into obedience.

Already abuse of liberalism in France and Germany was turning those two countries into skirmishing grounds for rival foreign dissident groups, and both governments were tightening up regulations to curb or eliminate imported violence. Vacillating uncertainly, the British government hesitated to proscribe some undesirable groups, especially as it was openly condemning some countries for not observing the Helsinki human rights charter. More realistically perhaps, the Home Office did not want to risk a terrorist backlash as it had more on its hands than it could handle with IRA activities, and so it contented itself with doing what it could to soften the situation by quietly deporting undesirable elements whenever possible.

Most of the politicians and so-called 'security experts' who were interviewed on TV and radio, or expressed themselves in print (and they were legion), to make themselves 'critic-proof' prefaced their comments with the platitude that 'There is no absolute defence against terrorism', before going on to expound their opinions and criticise the authorities for mis-judgements, neglect and omissions.

THE PANAMA AIR EXPLOSION

The London bombings drew attention to certain other terror-ist activities related to them, indicating that Hezbollah was cer-tainly looking westwards. In Panama on 19 July 1994 a bomb exploded on a Panamanian commuter airliner on an internal flight over a mountainous area, causing the plane to crash and killing all 21 people on board. Twelve of the victims were Jewish, four of whom were Israeli. Responsibility was claimed by 'Ansarollah' (Partisans of God), a code name for a Hezbollah faction. A statement was distributed in Sidon, southern Lebanon, part of which read 'Suicide martyr squads have been formed to confront and combat Zionism every-where. The Argentine and Panama operations are evidence of this continuing confrontation'. Both the Iranian government and Hezbollah denied any involvement.

THE ARGENTINE EXPLOSION

The Argentine operation referred to in the statement had oc-curred the previous day (18 July) in Buenos Aires during the morning rush hour, when a massive bomb exploded in a building occupied by the Argentine–Jewish Mutual Aid Association. Ninety-six people were killed and over 200 were injured, although it took several days to ascertain the true figures. Situated in a mainly Jewish area of Argentina's capital city, the seven-storey building was wrecked, as was a nine-storey block of apartments across the road. Argentina's Jewish popu-lation then stood at about 300 000, the largest in South

America. At first it was thought that a massive car bomb in the street had caused the explosion, but after investigators had searched through the rubble they came to believe that the bomb had been planted in a van that had been towed into the basement under cover of the construction work that was in progress in the building.

Argentina immediately closed its borders in an effort to detain any escaping culprits. One Iranian was arrested, but later released. Intelligence representatives from Israel and other countries travelled to Buenos Aires to help with the investigations. The finger of suspicion was pointed at Hezbollah, it being thought that this explosion was in revenge for the Hebron massacre of February 1994, when an Israeli settler fired into a mosque, killing 29 Palestinian worshippers and injuring several others.

For several weeks the Argentinian government had been alert to the danger that some sort of terrorist outrage could be in the offing against a Jewish target, as an Iranian, Monousheh Moatamer, described at first as a defecting diplomat, had fled with his family from Buenos Aires to seek refuge in Venezuela, where he had given certain information to the police. Five days before the explosion the Venezuelan government had expelled four Iranian diplomats for kidnapping Moatamer and five members of his family and holding them hostage in a Caracas hotel. When the Iranian Ambassador to Venezuela protested, he too was expelled.

After the explosion in Buenos Aires, the Argentinian judge who had been appointed to investigate this terrorist incident flew to Caracas to interview Moatamer, and seemed to obtain a considerable amount of information from him. Supposed extracts from the judge's report and an Argentinian intelligence report were printed in a local periodical (*Clarin*), which claimed there was a chain of links between Iranian diplomats in Caracas and underground Hezbollah cells throughout the South American region; and that Iranian diplomats provided terrorists with 'logistical support, arms and explosives, using the diplomatic pouch for such purposes'. Explosives had been delivered to Hezbollah terrorists through Islamic Shia communities in southern Brazil, and it was said that this was common knowledge to Western intelligence agencies.

These reports indicated that the authority behind the assassination of Iranian dissidents abroad was Hojatolislam Ali Fallahyan, the minister in charge of the Iranian intelligence and security service, 'VEVAK', and that Iran had tried to distance itself from direct acts of terrorism by employing the Lebanese-based Hezbollah. VEVAK controlled Islamic Jihad, led by Imad Moughniyeh, a terrorist mastermind and organiser of international terrorist activity since the 1970s, who was now in charge of Hezbollah's 'foreign operations department'. Moughniyeh was suspected of planning the recent bombings in London and Panama. All this tended to confirm what Israel was saying.

President Menem's office in Buenos Aires stated later that Moatamer had given the Argentinian judge advance warning of Hezbollah's intention to bomb targets in London, and that this had been passed on to the British, but did not mention to whom exactly. British intelligence continued to insist that it had received no precise prior warning from any external intelligence source. There may have an element of truth in this, as national intelligence agencies seldom talked to one another. International intelligence liaison and exchange of information, although often aired and commended in a platitudal manner by statesmen, usually turns out to be largely illusionary.

In early August the Argentinian judge ordered the arrest of four Iranians, allegedly diplomats at the Iranian embassy in Buenos Aires, for suspected implication in the bomb explosion, although it was thought they might have already left the country. Iran said the four men had not been in Argentina at that time, denied that Moatamer had ever been an Iranian diplomat, and accused the United States and Israel of planting the bomb in order to force Syria to take part in the Middle East peace conference.

The Iranian ambassador in Buenos Aires was threatened with expulsion for non-cooperation with the judge's enquiry, but to thwart this he was recalled to Iran 'for consultations' on 16 August. Argentina reciprocated in kind.

President Menem said although the explosion had been carried out by foreign organisations, there had been some Argentinian involvement. Three Argentinians were arrested and charged with forging the papers for the van used in the explosion and removing its engine, presumably to make room for the bomb. The Argentinian Foreign Office admitted that so far no proof had been found against any particular 'individual, group, state or combination of all three'. Moughniyeh was a shrewd operator, smooth, efficient and professional. Prime Minister Rabin could only add 'It is clear the trail of this bombing leads to Muslim extremist'. Hard evidence was missing.

On 24 August the Argentinian authorities stated there was insufficient evidence to charge the four Iranian diplomats. Immediately Iran demanded an apology for the accusation. The US secretary of state said that 'Iran is the Patron of Hezbollah' (*NYT*).

Perhaps the Argentinian authorities should have been more security conscious, and from past experience they should have been aware of the vulnerability of Israeli targets in the country, as on 17 March 1992 an explosion at the Israeli embassy in Buenos Aires had killed 28 people and injured 252. This was believed to have been a revenge attack by Hezbollah for the death of Sheikh Abbas Moussawi, Hezbollah's secretary general, who had been assassinated by Israel on 16 February that year in southern Lebanon. Argentinian officials said the terrorist explosion could not have occurred without the logistical help of Iranian diplomats. The US State Department concurred, saying 'We don't have proof, but we have a very strong suspicion of Iranian complicity' (*Clarin*).

THE EAST IS NOT OVERLOOKED

Hezbollah looked to the East as well as to the West for potential Israeli targets. On 3 June 1994 the Thai police announced the discovery of a plot to blow up the Israeli embassy in Bangkok. Three Iranians were detained in relation to this conspiracy, and were charged with the murder of a Thai employee of a lorry hire firm and falsifying vehicle documents. A fourth Iranian was sought. A vehicle bomb was to have been the means of destruction. The Iranian foreign minister denied all knowledge of the plot, protested to the Thai government about the arrest of 'innocent Iranians', and urged the Thais to be more careful about 'attempting to damage Iran's prestige overseas'.

2 Gama Islamiya

Islamic fundamentalist terrorism hit the United States of America for the first time on 26 February 1993, when an explosion wrecked the prestigious twin-tower, 110-storey World Trade Centre, New York's tallest building. A 1200 lb, homemade, 'low-tech' bomb, composed of ordinary, commercially available materials and planted in a vehicle in an underground car park, tore a huge hole in the ceiling, sending rubble on to the subway station below, killing six people and injuring 1042. It was thought that the intention of the terrorists had been to demolish one of the twin towers. Having no previous experience of terrorism of this magnitude, the people of the United States were stunned. The 20-year-old building had been constructed before New York fire and safety regulations for skyscrapers had been tightened up, and some casualties were caused by the lack of fire-proof doors to stop the fire and smoke from spreading.

The New York authorities were taken completely by surprise, although Police Commissioner Ray Kelley revealed that the United States was already on a low-grade security alert against possible Iraqi-inspired terrorist activity. Lack of evidence of sophisticated devices such as semtex explosive seemed to rule out international terrorism, although initially the finger of suspicion pointed at Saddam Hussein, who might have been making a 'terrorist statement' to anti-Israel Muslim groups on the second anniversary of the Gulf War; or even to Serbian groups as the United States was in confrontation with Serbs in the Balkan peninsula.

Some 60 telephone calls claiming responsibility were received by the police, but for several days the Federal Bureau of Investigation (FBI) had no idea who the culprits might be. Some doubted the implication of Muslim groups, as 26 February was the first day of Ramadan, the month in which all good Muslims should fast during daylight hours, and which should be a time of peace. On 1 March the World Trade Centre building was partially reopened.

Immediately after the explosion New York suddenly became security conscious, and widespread checks were made on vehicles in car parks and on the streets as it was feared that similar explosions might occur. Washington followed suit and guards at government buildings were placed on special alert. In some places, including the White House, mirrors were used to inspect the undersides of vehicles entering the area, as well as the use of sniffer dogs, trained to detect explosives. A Pentagon spokesman said that security had been stepped up, but declined to specify measures or locations.

About 50 000 people worked in the World Trade Centre complex and probably a further 50 000 visited it daily. New York commodities and other financial markets based in the building had to move to temporary accommodation until sections of the complex were declared structurally safe. Many New York financial concerns were monetarily hard hit, for example one Japanese company complained that it was losing $20 million a day while its wrecked office was closed.

While the planning and execution of the bomb plot appeared to have been meticulous, conversely the plotters were detected largely by their own naivety or carelessness. Led by James Fox, head of the FBI in New York, investigators, sifting through the evidence discovered that the bomb – a crude one, constructed of fuel oil and fertiliser – had been in a van, whose engine had been removed to accommodate it.

One of the conspirators, Mohammed Salameh, a Palestinian taxi driver with a Jordanian passport, had gone to the Ryder Truck Rental Company, just across the Hudson River in New Jersey City, two days before the explosion and hired a yellow Ford van. He had paid the $400 deposit in cash, given his real name and address, and presented his own driving licence. He was accompanied by his friend and co-conspirator, Nidal Ayyed, a Kuwaiti-born Palestinian who shared Salameh's apartment and worked as a chemical engineer. Salameh returned to the rental office within two hours of the explosion, claiming that the van had been stolen and demanding the return of his $400 deposit. This was refused, Salameh being told that police substantiation was required.

Salameh returned three days later with police documentation that confirmed the van had probably been stolen; but he was still not given his deposit. By this time the FBI, having identified the van by the manufacturer's number on a fragment of its rear axle, was on to the Ryder Truck Rental Company, apparently arriving just after Salameh had left. An FBI agent, claiming to be from the rental company, made a telephone call to Salameh and said that if he called in his deposit would be refunded. Salameh fell into the trap, and was arrested by waiting agents when he returned to collect his deposit. The rental documents were said to smeared in nitrates. (An FBI agent later soliloquised to me that he wished all major crime could be solved so easily.)

However Salameh's naivety, greed for a comparatively small sum of money, amateurish behaviour and lack of caution puzzled investigators, who felt he must be a minor, low-mentality, expendable cog in the conspiracy. Salameh and his friend Ayyed (who was arrested on 10 March) were linked to an Islamic fundamentalist group led by Sheikh Omar Abdul Rahman, a blind Egyptian cleric who was alleged to be the leader of Gama Islamiya (usually translated as Islamic League and sometimes written as Jama'a al-Islamiya). On 5 March Rahman issued a condemnation of the bombing, but this did not take him out of the frame of suspicion.

SHEIKH OMAR ABDUL RAHMAN

Sheikh Omar Abdul Rahman, then aged about 54, was certainly an active Islamic fundamentalist religious leader with a record of anti-government subversive activity in his native Egypt. He first entered the United States on a tourist visa in July 1990 and later obtained residential status as a minister of religion, which was rescinded in March 1992 on the grounds that he had concealed his criminal record in Egypt. US Immigration tried to deport the sheikh, who was wanted in Egypt on charges of fomenting a riot in 1989, but failed when it was discovered that the US–Egypt extradition treaty did not cover political offences. Eventually the extent of his involvement in terrorism was revealed, and on 17 March the immigration authorities tried again to deport him, this time on the grounds that he had been convicted of forging a cheque in Egypt, and that he was a polygamist. The blind sheikh's rousing sermons, which bordered on the subversive, attracted a large congregation to his mosque, including a number of Islamic fundamentalist activists.

The sheikh had first come to the notice of the FBI for suspected involvement in the murder of Rabbi Meir Kahane – the radical Israeli leader of the extreme Kach organisation – at a press conference in a Manhattan hotel in New York on 5 November 1990. Two years later Sayyed Nosair, an Islamic fundamentalist, was charged with this murder but was convicted of the lesser charges of weapons offences and attempting to murder a US postal worker as he fled from the scene. When Nosair's home had been searched, manuals on bomb making, listening and explosive devices and a quantity of AK-47 ammunition had been discovered. Sayyed Nosair, formerly a regular attender at the sheikh's mosque, was handed down a prison sentence of 23 years.

Another regular attender at the mosque, which it was suspected was kept afloat with money from Iran, had been Sultan Ibrahim el-Ghali, who had been jailed for smuggling weapons out of the United States, including 150 lbs of C-4 explosive caps and hundreds of other blasting caps, for use against Israel.

Although the sheikh continued to send tapes of his inflammatory sermons on revolutionary terrorism to mosques in Egypt, he kept a low profile in New York. There seemed to be official reluctance to bring him in for questioning, which was especially baffling as links to the explosion were being traced to him. His followers spoke out on his behalf and denied that he had had any involvement in the bombing. National interest seemed to creep into the scenario, it being feared that if he was arrested and pilloried there would be an unfavourable reaction from the some four million Muslims in the United States, a number that was increasing due to immigration, and this might in turn provoke counter-Israeli activists. For a while the sheikh was left alone, although dark suspicion hovered over him.

Meanwhile, on 30 February 1993 the *New York Times* had received a typewritten letter from the previously unknown 'Liberation Army Fifth Battalion'. It claimed responsibility for the World Trade Centre explosion and warned of further attacks if the United States did not end its military, economic and political aid to Israel, insisting that all diplomatic relations with Israel must be severed and that the United States must not interfere in any Middle East country's internal affairs. The letter went on to claim that the so-called Liberation Army had more than '150 suicidal soldiers'. At this early stage the FBI were still not absolutely certain that Sheikh Omar Abdul Rahman and his Gama Islamiya were responsible.

On 4 March Ibrahim el-Gabrowny was arrested and charged with obstruction while his apartment was being searched. Hearing that he too was wanted by the FBI for questioning, one Balai al-Kaisi surrendered to the police on the 25th. Another suspect, Mahmoud Abu Halima, described by the FBI as a dominant force in Gama Islamiya, had slipped out of the country on the 6th, but was extradited from Egypt and was in US custody by the 25th, to be charged with 'aiding and abetting'. By the end of March the FBI had five main suspects under arrest but still hesitated to move against the sheikh. By this time the FBI was convinced that the sheikh was the godfather of Gama Islamiya, whose members had caused the explosion at the World Trade Centre.

Then followed a pause, and although Sheikh Omar Abdul Rahman was clearly in the frame, still no move was made to arrest him. It was thought that the delay was due to pressure from the attorney general's office, which seemed hopeful of being able to deport him quietly and thus rid the country of a very dangerous catalyst. On 5 April, in an interview in the *New York Times*, President Mubarak of Egypt claimed that the bombing could have been prevented if US intelligence officials had heeded Egypt's warnings about Islamic fundamentalists in the United States, but the State Department later denied that any warning had been received. As mentioned earlier, national intelligence agencies are notorious for their reluctance to talk to other national intelligence agencies. On the 16th Judge Kevin T. Duffey, presiding over the investigation, put a 'gag on lawyers and law agents', which was described as being 'unprecedented in its sincerity' (*Middle East International*)

AN ISLAMIC FUNDAMENTALIST PLOT

Suddenly, by 14 June 1993 in New York City FBI agents had arrested six members of the Gama Islamiya group. The FBI claimed it had cracked a massive Islamic fundamentalist plot to assassinate Boutros Boutros Ghali, the UN secretary general, plant a car bomb in the underground carpark of the UN building, blow up the Holland and Lincoln road tunnels into the city, and bomb the FBI headquarters in New York. Had this been effected it would have caused terrific devastation, killed or injured thousands of people and brought chaos to the whole city. In short, it would have produced an apocalyptic scenario.

Plotting had begun in May 1993, when Emand Salem, an ex-Egyptian military officer and explosives expert, approached Ahmad Mohammed Ajaji, a New York taxi driver and member of Sheikh Abdul Rahman's Gama Islamiya. Salem said he had access to timing devices and a knowledge of bomb making. The burgeoning plot soon came to embrace eight Islamic fundamentalists. This time the FBI was in at the beginning to watch the scheme unfold, tapping telephones and filming individuals and meetings. Again it seems the plotters were naive and amateurish. They spoke openly on the telephone and appeared to take few if any of the precautions a professional terrorist would consider elementary necessities. By speaking openly the plotters were unconsciously providing the FBI with 'an electronic trail' to the guilty.

The FBI were in no hurry to make any arrests as they hoped to incriminate as many of the plotters as possible, but they stepped in suddenly when it became clear that two of those involved were about to leave for Sudan. James Fox of the FBI said, 'As we entered the bomb factory, the five subjects were actually mixing the witches brew'. Sheikh Omar Abdul Rahman was implicated in this foiled plan. The revelation that another Islamic fundamentalist plot had been hatched on their soil and aimed at them raised fears among Americans of 'an enemy within'.

TRIALS

Obviously profoundly influenced by the plot, the US attorney general changed her policy and decided to put Sheikh Omar Abdul Rahman and as many of his Gama Islamiya activists as possible on trial, regardless of any consequential reaction from the local Muslim population. In July the FBI arrested the sheikh, who was detained in a prison in Otisville, New Jersey, some 70 miles from New York City.

It was decided there should be two separate trials, the first to try the four Islamic fundamentalists accused of involvement in the World Trade Centre explosion, and the second to try the sheikh and his activists, who would be charged with involvement in both the explosion and the foiled plot. The World Trade Centre explosion had been dubbed the 'Day of Terror' by the New York media.

On 23 July the FBI arrested Matarawi Mohammed Saleh, an Egyptian suspected of involvement in the World Trade Centre bombing, and Ashraf Mohammed, who was accused of harbouring him. At the same time the US State Department offered a $2 million reward for information leading to the arrest of Ramiz Ahmad Yousef, another suspect in the World Trade Centre bombing.

On 26 August, amid tight security the sheikh was flown by helicopter from Otisville to the New York Federal Court. There, together with 14 accomplices, he was charged with being involved in the explosion and the plot. On top of this they were all charged with plotting to bomb the Diamond District, which had a large Jewish community, to kill certain prominent Jews and FBI agents, and to kidnap hostages to exchange for arrested men. This comprehensive, 'conspiracy' block indictment was levelled against the cell as a whole in order to avoid having to prove that the sheikh had committed a specific crime. This showed weakness and uncertainty, but the attorney general's office obviously felt that it was the best way to tackle a case that, being especially emotive to Muslims, would attract world-wide publicity and might also provoke Islamic fundamentalist terrorism within the United States. The US secretary of state confirmed that security had been tightened at all US overseas bases and embassies.

The trial of four of the accused began with jury selection on 14 September. Several thousand potential jurists were questioned as to their religious beliefs and their attitude towards Arabs and Israelis. Eventually eight women and four men were selected, whose identities were protected. The defendants were Mahmoud Abu Halima, the alleged cell leader, Mohammed Salameh, who had rented the van, Nidal Ayyed, who had removed the engine from the van to make space for the bomb, and Ahmad Mohammed Ajaji. All pleaded not guilty and claimed religious persecution. The trial began on 4 October 1993.

When Ajaji's home had been searched, false passports, bomb-making manuals and video tapes showing how to mix explosives and stage a bomb attack against a US embassy had been found (Hoffman, 1994) Ajaji was not implicated in the World Trade Centre conspiracy, but he was accused of being involved in a separate plan to assassinate President Mubarak, who had been due to make a state visit to New York in April 1993. When the visit was postponed the plotters had begun to suspect each other of being informers. It seems that the FBI had been on to this one from the start.

HEZBOLLAH AND DRUGS

On 1 July 1993 four Hasidic Jews were shot on Brooklyn Bridge, and on the 4 July three Islamic fundamentalists were arrested by the FBI, which claimed it had had them under surveillance for some time. The ringleader was Rashid Baz, a Lebanese, in whose apartment weapons and other incriminating evidence had been found and who faced several charges of murder. It was said that the Israeli Mossad was involved in this surveillance. None of those arrested had a criminal record, although they were thought to belong to the Lebanese-based Hezbollah and to be involved in an international drug ring.

THE MUSLIM BROTHERHOOD

Egyptian activism dates from just after the First World War and the break-up of the Ottoman Empire, when several Muslim organisations appeared in Arab Middle Eastern countries. Appalled by the spread of secular Westernisation, they did their best to preserve the old Islamic principles and way of life. Some became militant, even violent, and clashed – usually unsuccessfully – with their Western-sponsored national governments.

Probably the most important was the Muslim Brotherhood (the Irkwan), which was founded in Egypt in the 1920s by

Hassan al-Banna. It became pan-Arab in character – its branches penetrating into several Middle Eastern states – and campaigned against imperialism, secularism and corruption. The Muslim Brotherhood became a major force in Egyptian politics in the 1940s and 1950s, waging a campaign of violence against King Farouk and his ministers that included several assassinations. Banna was himself assassinated in 1949. President Anwar Sadat boasted that as a young man he had been involved with the Muslim Brotherhood, an offshoot of which was later to assassinate him.

President Gamal Abdel Nasser, who came to power in Egypt in November 1954, admired the Muslim Brotherhood's principles but soon came into conflict with this organisation. When the Brotherhood tried to kill him, he turned on it, executed several leaders, imprisoned others and generally suppressed it with a heavy hand. Anwar Sadat, who succeeded Nasser in 1970, sought reconciliation with the Muslim Brotherhood. He released its leaders from prison and allowed it to publish periodicals and have freedom of speech, but he stopped short of permitting it to become a political party. By this time the Muslim Brotherhood had spawned many splinter groups, mainly on university campuses. The groups bore a variety of code names and acted autonomously.

ASSASSINATION OF PRESIDENT SADAT

One of the most virile of the Muslim Brotherhood splinter groups was Takfir wal-Higra (usually translated as 'Atonement and Flight', a title with Koranic significance), led by Shukri Mustafa, who among other things organised the Cairo Food Riots of 1977. It kidnapped a distinguished Islamic scholar, Dr Husseini al-Dhababi, who supported Sadat. This caused Sadat to clamp down on Takfir wal-Higra, making mass arrests and staging mass trials. Mustafa and others were executed. Islamic unrest continued to fester in Egypt, bursting into activity in November 1977, when President Sadat visited Israel with a peace initiative, and again in 1980, when Sadat gave hospitality to the ousted Shah of Iran. In 1981 Egypt severed diplomatic relations with Iran, blaming its government for supporting Islamic fundamentalist terrorism.

On 6 October 1981, during a ceremonial military parade in Cairo commemorating the 1973 Egyptian–Israeli War, four terrorists in military uniforms suddenly left one of the vehicles taking part in a drive past, approached the reviewing stand and shot dead President Sadat. One assassin was killed by guards, the other three were wounded and captured. They claimed to be members of the 'al-Jihad' branch of Takfir wal-Higra, which was based at the university in Assyut, some 250 miles south of Cairo. The army moved against the Islamic fundamentalists in Assyut, and in the fighting about 118 people were killed and over 220 injured. Some 4000 were detained.

In November 1981 some of the accused were put on trial, which was broadcast live on TV, a decision the authorities came to regret. The accused shouted Islamic slogans, threats and comments while the trial was in progress and were heard nationwide, making them Islamic folk heroes among sections of the population. Some verdicts were delivered in March 1982, when five were found guilty and sentenced to death. They were executed on 15 April. Seventeen others were sentenced to long terms of imprisonment. Only two were acquitted, one being the 'blind' cleric, Sheikh Omar Abdul Rahman, the spiritual guide of Takfir wal-Higra who turned up a few years later in New York. An Egyptian military court also tried 36 military officers, but no publicity was given as the authorities did not wish to expose the armed forces to public scrutiny. Twenty-two officers were convicted and 14 acquitted.

President Hosni Mubarak, Sadat's successor, clamped down heavily on all active Islamic fundamentalist groups, whose members either fled abroad or went deeper underground. Iran and Sudan give sanctuary to many. The Iranian government, which probably had not been involved in the Sadat assassination, now began to support Egyptian Islamic fundamentalist groups.

THE EGYPTIAN CONNECTION

In Egypt, President Mubarak's government was fighting a virtual civil war against Islamic fundamentalists, who wanted to bring it down and turn the country into an Islamic fundamentalist state. In March 1992 several fundamentalist groups launched a campaign of terrorist violence against government security forces, and this was followed by another against foreign tourists, warning them to stay away from Egypt. Tourism was a lucrative foreign currency earner for Egypt, a country with an extremely fragile economy and a rapidly increasing population that had to be fed.

The Egyptian government hit back hard, and in December 1992 it began to seek out terrorists in their lairs in Cairo and throughout the country, shooting first and making mass arrests, which were followed by mass trials and executions. Allegations were made of ill-treatment and torture of those in detention, and this was chronicled by Amnesty International.

For example Mahmoud Abu Halima, who was involved in the World Trade Centre bombing and was extradited from Egypt to the United States, while in Egyptian detention 'confessed' to his involvement and gave details of his accomplices and other incriminating matters, saying that the actual plot had been hatched in Peshawar (Pakistan), and that funds had been provided by the Muslim Brotherhood. In New York Halima claimed he had made the confession under torture, and that none of it was true. The Egyptian Human Rights Organisation alleged that detainees were systematically tortured and this was confirmed to some extent by the New York-based *Middle East Watch.*

One of the main terrorist groups was Gama Islamiya, which Egyptian intelligence was convinced was headed by Sheikh Omar Abdul Rahman, who motivated the group by sending tapes of his inflammatory sermons to be played in mosques in many parts of Egypt, and who directed its activities from his sanctuary in New York. The Egyptian government wanted very much to get its hands on him, and again applied for his extradition on 6 July 1993.

On the 'Day of Terror' in New York (26 February 1993), a bomb had exploded in a street cafe in Tahrir Square in central Cairo, killing four people and injuring over 20, including some foreign tourists. Responsibility had been claimed by Gama Islamiya. This had been the first such incident in the capital for some years, and about 100 suspects had been subsequently rounded up.

The hard and vicious struggle between the security forces and several Islamic fundamentalist groups continued throughout 1993. The attacks on foreign tourists increased, masterminded, the authorities claimed, by Ahmad Zaki. The minister of tourism stated that during 1992 the country's tourist industry had lost over $700 million, with only three million tourists arriving instead of the anticipated four million plus. While raiding terrorist strongholds in Cairo and Aswan in March 1993, the security forces killed nearly 40 people, including Ahmad Zaki. Probably well over 6000 suspects were in long-term detention without trial, many since the end of the previous year, and some since the assassination of President Sadat.

In April 1993 the interior minister was removed from office for agreeing to allow the Ulema, the religious body of top Muslim clerics, to negotiate between the security forces and Islamic fundamentalist terrorists fighting hard to topple President Mubarak's government. He was replaced by a hardliner. That month military courts sentenced seven terrorists to death and others to long terms of imprisonment, while emotional antigovernment slogans were chanted in court. Attacks continued on both tourists and senior officers in the security forces.

On 15 May a bomb exploded in central Cairo, killing 21 people and injuring many more. Over 800 suspects were arrested. The authorities considered that in this case the newly formed Talai al-Fatah (variously translated as the 'Vanguard of Islam' or the 'New Jihad'), an offshoot of the al-Jihad group, was responsible. It had become a virile and active organisation. Although Gama Islamiya continued to claim responsibility for terrorist acts, as did several other mysterious bodies, in practice it seemed to be overtaken in terrorist zeal by its new rival. This was put down to the fact that Sheikh Omar Abdul Rahman, back in New York, was keeping a low profile, and when arrested in July was unable to exert his malign, long-distance influence.

The Egyptian government had no doubt that Islamic fundamentalist terrorism in its country was supported by and organised in Afghanistan, Iran, Iraq, Pakistan and Sudan, so in mid May telephone links with these countries were indefinitely severed to isolate terrorist groups from their patrons. Egypt yet again requested the extradition of the sheikh but was too late, as by this time the US authorities had decided to deal with him themselves.

In June, two Islamic fundamentalist terrorists were executed, and the new interior minister (General Hussein Mohammed al-Alfi) announced that a plot to assassinate ten senior political and public personalities had been foiled. The plot had been hatched abroad, with terrorists moving between Afghanistan, Iran, Pakistan and the United States. During the following month 13 more terrorists were executed, provoking attacks on senior officers in the security forces. The trial of 32 fundamentalist militants opened in Cairo.

On 7 August a senior police commander was killed to avenge the executions. Responsibility was claimed by Gama Islamiya. On the 15th the trial of a further 53 Islamic fundamentalists opened, three of whom were in the armed forces and five of whom were tried *in absentia*. It was also revealed (Agence France-Presse) that 19 prominent radical terrorists had been secretly imprisoned since May for plotting to kill President Mubarak. Amnesty International's reports on the conduct of the Egyptian security forces made horrific reading. On the 18th an attempt was made to kill the new interior minister (al-Alfi) in Cairo by Talai al-Fatah, which attacked his motorcade. Five people were killed in the shoot-out, including two of the escorts, but the minister was unhurt.

In October 1993 President Mubarak began a third six-year term, returning uncontested to continue in office. His new government did not include any opposition groups, and like its predecessor it was committed to dealing with Islamic fundamentalist terrorism by military means. This rigid, uncompromising attitude displeased the US administration – committed as it was to liberal democracy – which, to keep it afloat, was providing Egypt with annual funding that was second in volume only to that provided to Israel. The funding consisted of $815 million in economic aid, $300 million in military aid and $200 million in concessionary loans for food imports. Egypt could not feed itself.

On 1 November al-Jihad called for the assassination of eight judges who had recently passed death sentences on Islamic militant terrorists. President Burhnuddin Rabbani of Afghanistan visited Egypt and agreed to ban anti-Egyptian militants from his soil, but it was a promise he was unable to keep as he himself was locked in a battle for possession of Kabul with Afghanistan's Islamic Fundamentalist prime minister,

Gulbuddin Hekmatyar. On the 25th an attempt was made on the life of the Egyptian prime minister. Responsibility was claimed by al-Jihad, but Egyptian intelligence was of the opinion that the culprits belonged to Talai al-Fatah. Over 100 suspects were arrested. Days later two more terrorists were executed. Terrorist attacks against foreign tourists had continued throughout the year, with dire consequences for the wilting Egyptian tourist industry.

During December another nine militants were executed, six of whom were members of Talai al-Fatah, bringing to 29 the total number executed in 1993. Government security forces continued to fight hard against the Islamic fundamentalists, who fought back and showed no signs of lessening their vicious attacks. Neither side was in the mood for reconciliation; both were seeking total victory.

NEW YORK TRIALS

The World Trade Centre trial in New York, which had begun in June 1993, finally ended on 4 March 1994, when after deliberating for five days the jury found four of the defendants guilty on all counts. The trial had lasted five months, 207 prosecution witnesses had given evidence, four defence witnesses had been called and more than 1000 'exhibits' had been produced. Much of the evidence was circumstantial. On 24 May three defendants – Mohammed Salameh, Nidal Ayyed and Mahmoud Abu Halima – were each sentenced to 240 years imprisonment and fined $250 000. The fourth, Ahmad Mohammed Ajaji, convicted of plotting to kill President Mubarak, was also imprisoned.

Balai al-Kaisi still awaited trial, and two others remained at large: Ramiz Ahmad Yousef, described by the prosecution as 'the evil genius behind the conspiracy', and Abdul Yasin. Sheikh Omar Abdul Rahman and 15 others were arraigned for the second conspiracy trial.

After the first trial in New York the US administration and its security agencies pondered over this new, powerful, destabilising Islamic fundamentalist force that had reached out to touch the United States, South America and Britain.

Previously this type of threat had been thought of as an overseas problem peculiar to some Islamic states, but certainly a dangerous and deadly one as it had caused insurrection in Egypt, the Maghreb and Lebanon. Now its tentacles seemed to be reaching out across the world to embrace non-Muslim states. The United States had always thought that this problem was primarily the responsibility of Europe, many European countries being former colonial powers, but now it was not so sure. Questions were asked about how to cope with this new challenge, criticism was rampant, but few solid ideas emerged.

Rumours abounded about the evidence that was to be presented at the trial of Sheikh Omar Abdul Rahman and his co-conspirators, which multiplied when 'legal leaks' hinted that some of the witnesses who had agreed to co-operate with the prosecution had changed their minds, or had had their minds changed for them. It was also rumoured that the sheikh had had a long, cosy relationship with the CIA, dating back to the 1980s when the CIA was providing arms to Afghan resistance fighters struggling against the Soviet occupation forces in Afghanistan. The sheikh was well known in Afghanistan in Islamic fundamentalist circles, had many good contacts there, and seems to have been of use to the CIA. It was rumoured the CIA 'owed him one', and in return had arranged his US visa and hindered the deportation processes against him.

In December 1994 it was reported the sheikh was seriously ill with tuberculosis, which led some to think he would never be brought to trial; others thought it was a diplomatic illness. The sheikh was the key figure in the case, and without him in the dock as the godfather the prosecution could collapse, or only obtain poor results. Forcing the issue of the trial was likened by the New York media to trying out a new 'high-wire act'. There was also much deliberation over the wording of charges, and which Acts they should be brought under.

The second trial eventually began in January 1995, the sheikh and eleven associates being arraigned on the charge of 'Conspiracy to wage a war of urban terrorism, aimed at the overthrow of the Government of the United States of America'.

THE MASTERMIND IS CAPTURED

Good news came to the prosecution in February, when Ramiz Ahmad Yousef, who had been tried *in absentia* at the first New York trial and described as the 'evil genius behind the conspiracy', was found in Pakistan, arrested and extradited to the United States. His capture was ascribed to well-coordinated international intelligence agency work, headed by the CIA. Certainly it was one of the CIA's successes.

That Yousef was an active terrorist mastermind is illustrated by his activities in the Far East. Slipping out of New York shortly after the World Trade Centre explosion, he arrived in Manila in the Philippines, where he planned to kill the pope, due to visit in January 1995, and to place bombs on Western airliners. Supporting evidence was later discovered in an apartment he had been renting, including Roman Catholic clerical robes. He was accused by the Manila police of planting several small explosive devices in the city in December 1994, some of which were discovered and defused, but one in his apartment accidentally exploded, causing neighbours to call the police. However Yousef had fled before they arrived (Nick Rufford, *The Sunday Times*).

Yousef had had a 'safe house' some 60 miles outside Manila where he had been training about 20 Muslim terrorists, several of whom were arrested. It was said he had been trying to perfect a plastic bomb that would evade airport X-ray detection. On 9 December he boarded a Philippine Airlines aircraft bound for Tokyo but disembarked at an intermediate stop, leaving behind some plastic bombs. One exploded in mid-air, killing one passenger and injuring six others, but the plane made a successful emergency landing at Okinawa. It was thought that while in Manila Yousef had liaised with the Abu Sayyaf group of Muslim fundamentalists, who were operating in the southern area of Mindanao, and this group was originally blamed for Yousef's exploits.

BAD NEWS

Bad news came in March, when Emand Salem, the prosecution's main witness, admitted on oath in the witness box that he had been telling a string of lies about his background and the events leading up to the trial, which discredited his value as a witness. It was also revealed that Salem was an undercover FBI agent, paid (allegedly about one million dollars) to penetrate the blind cleric's intimate circle, which did little for the FBI's credit ratings. While admitting that Salem was a 'teller of half truths and lies', the prosecution sought to maintain that the evidence he had gathered for the FBI, mainly audio and video material, was valid and should be accepted.

In view of these revelations, some were beginning to speculate about whether the trial would either come to an unsatisfactory end or be abandoned; in which case Sheikh Omar Abdul Rahman would once again be let off the hook, as he had been in Egypt in 1982.

3 A Revolutionary Furnace

Some knowledge of the early months and years of the Islamic fundamentist regime in Iran may help the reader to understand what has conditioned and motivated the Iranian government to use terrorism to further its Islamic aims; to strike at enemies in countries with liberal political regimes, free speech and free movement; and to help subversive elements embarrass and destabilise regimes it regards as unfriendly.

From the beginning of its existence the Islamic Republic of Iran was threatened by violent internal terrorism, and in order to survive it fought back by employing even greater terrorism, mass detention, torture, secret trials, executions and selective assassinations. Having both felt its effects and used it ruthlessly against its enemies at home and abroad, the Islamic Republican government understands the effectiveness of terrorism. Searing experiences have given it a taste for both overt and covert terrorism, and it has become a hardened and skilful manipulator of this form of warfare.

On 1 February 1979 Ayatollah Ruhollah Khomeini arrived by air at Mehrabad Airport, Tehran, to a tumultuous and rapturous reception, estimated by attendant international media representatives as involving up to three million people. Nearby roads were so packed that Khomeini had to complete his journey into Tehran by helicopter. He was returning from exile in France, where for months he had been taping revolutionary sermons and sending the cassettes to the mosques of Iran to be played to captive congregations every Friday. His aim had been to rouse his countrymen into rebellion. Khomeini had returned to head the Islamic fundamentalist revolution, establish his authority and sweep aside the shahist regime. Not everyone was pleased to see him, and Ayatollah Shariat-Madari, who was much senior to him in the Islamic hierarchy and an old protagonist, remarked, 'Fancy, he has come to liberate us, travelling First Class in a French Airliner' (Heikal, 1982).

The weeks following Khomeini's arrival in Tehran can aptly be thought of as a time of 'revolutionary furnace', as during that period Khomeini's regime had to fight off armed opposition groups to ensure its survival, which it did by out-terrorising its opponents. Iran had been awash with armed opposition groups protesting against the autocratic and despotic shahist regime, and in a rare moment in history practically all, many with varying aims and motivations, eventually came together to topple the regime and support Ayatollah Khomeini unquestioningly.

Mohammed Reza Shah had already left Tehran on 16 January, officially for a vacation and medical treatment. He had not departed willingly, but had been pushed out by US General Robert Huyser, deputy commander of the United States Armed Forces in Europe and supervisor of the US Military Assistance Advisory Groups in the Middle East. Huyser had been sent by President Carter, as his special envoy, to Tehran early in January to urge the Iranian high command to support Prime Minister Shahpour Bakhtiar, thus ensuring there would not be a military coup. Bakhtiar had been appointed barely hours before the shah departed. Carter had wanted the shah to go, but did not want him to be replaced by a military junta. Nor did he want the revolutionary firebrand Khomeini to come to power, hoping that Bakhtiar, with Iranian military support and covert US assistance, would be able to establish a Western-type democratic government in the country, while at the same time keeping the Islamic cleric at bay.

For a long time Iran had been stricken with strife and unrest, and during 1977 and 1978 the internal situation had steadily deteriorated until it verged on anarchy, as protests, demonstrations, strikes and acts of terrorism mounted in frequency and intensity. Mohammed Reza Shah had become the focus of hatred, stirred up by the some 120 000 mullahs who preached against him in the 80 000 mosques as they writhed under his secular, unsympathetic rule. Lacking cooperation from the mullahs, whose influence extended throughout the country, law and order was breaking down, rendering the authorities unable to cope with the oppositional activities.

By January 1979 central authority had been so weakened in some towns and parts of the country that self-appointed 'Revolutionary Committees' (Komitehs) sprang into existence to fill the political and administrative void. Most were Islamic orientated, but not all. Some were dominated by communists, Marxists, socialists or extremists of one sort or another, or by ethnic groups. For example the Mujahedeen Khalk was extremely right wing and the Fedayeen Khalk was extremely left wing. Iran was a country of minorities, including Arabs, Azerbaijanis, Baluchis, Kurds, Zoroastrians, Armenian and Chaldean Christians, Bahais and Jews.

Even before setting foot in Iran, from his exile in France Khomeini had announced the formation of a 'Revolutionary Islamic Council', intended at the right moment to 'replace the illegal shahist government'. On 5 February 1979 Khomeini appointed Mehdi Bazarghan as his prime minister, and so in an atmosphere of fear, confusion and uncertainty the two opposing governments struggled abrasively with each other for power.

One by one elements of the armed forces opted for Khomeini's cause; and street fighting erupted in Tehran between them – aided by other 'revolutionaries' – and the Imperial Guard, other loyal units and the pro-shah Rastikas Party militia. Apart from revolutionaries with political agendas, other groups, factions and gangs with varying demands, grievances, thirst for vengeance or simply seeking criminal opportunity joined in the confused melee. Military desertion was rife. Some politically motivated deserters fought against their own officers and units, others joined gangs, but most disappeared to their homes.

On the 9th armouries were broken into and arms were distributed to various factions. From the 9th to the 11th several very bloody, violent battles were fought on the streets of Tehran and elsewhere as the Bakhtiar government, with an ever-decreasing number of loyal forces, vainly sought to defend the remnants of the crumbing shahist structure. Bakhtiar had failed in his belated attempt to establish a moderate National Unity Front of Iran.

MILITARY DECLARATION OF NEUTRALITY AND ITS AFTERMATH

On 11th February 1979 senior shahist generals told Bakhtiar that they were ordering their troops back to barracks, and would stand aside from the revolutionary struggle 'to avoid dismembering the unity of the nation'. This so-called Declaration of Neutrality was signed by 24 senior generals, of whom eight were executed within days. Military withdrawal from the counterrevolutionary struggle allowed the pro-shahist elements to be quickly overwhelmed. Khomeini's revolution, fought out on the the streets of Tehran, triumphed as shahist resistance ebbed away. Bakhtiar resigned and went underground, leaving the field clear for Bazarghan.

A bloodbath began as groups of victors turned on their victims to wreak vengeance. A welter of killing, kidnapping, arrest, torture and execution ensued. In Tehran the Israeli diplomatic mission was ransacked, the Egyptian and American embassies were attacked, the Majlis (Assembly) was stormed and many buildings were set on fire, some by politically motivated arsonists, others by mindless mobs of vandals. Arbitrary arrests were made, including that of several foreigners, and people 'disappeared', not all due to revolutionary causes as many private scores were being settled. Khomeini ordered the release of non-Iranians. Victors swarmed into Bakhtiar's office, but he had already decamped.

Khomeini ordered all shahist restraints on political activity to be removed, and at once about a hundred different parties, organisations and groups came out into the open to declare themselves and their aims. Having obtained weapons, many used violence, not only against their rivals but also against the new Islamic authority, venting their disappointment and disillusionment. They were labelled 'terrorist gangs'. Once the revolution had been accomplished and its popular aim – to remove the shah – achieved, the wafer-thin facade of national unity dissolved.

In some major cities impromptu groups of 'Islamic Guards', identified by badges, took control of Courts and public services, pushing the local police aside. In towns and villages Revolutionary Committees began to interpret Khomeini's edicts as they individually thought fit, as they struggled against each other for power and territory. Khomeini therefore ordered the formation of a Central Revolutionary Committee, headed by Hojatolislam Mohammed Reza Mahdavi-Kani, to control and coordinate their activities

Khomeini's 25-man Islamic Revolutionary Council (IRC) was to be the supreme religious and civilian authority. It was

established in Qom, where Khomeini resided for some
months until he felt that Tehran was safe to return to. Initially
the names of the members were kept secret, ostensibly for
their own safety in view of the rampant hostility and terrorism.

ISLAMIC TERROR

Khomeini established a number of Islamic Revolutionary
Courts, under Ayatollah Sadiq Khalkhali, which in secret tried
and executed over 600 people within a span of about five
weeks, and imprisoned many more. Victims included many
who had held political office under the shah, senior military
officers and administrators, and others who had been prominent supporters of the shah's power base. It should be noted
that a proportion of those executed so arbitrarily were alleged
to have committed blasphemy, or otherwise offended against
the Islamic code, such as organising prostitution or being
homosexual.

SAVAK, the shah's much-hated and feared secret intelligence and security organisation, was officially dissolved by
Bazarghan on 5 February 1979. It had been established in
1957 with the help of the CIA and later the Israeli Mossad. In
1976 it was reported to have had 40 000 full-time members
and over 50 000 informants (CIA report). It had, for example,
been able to operate freely in the United States amongst
Iranian citizens. Internal security cases in Iran had been
tried by secret military courts, which invariably accepted
SAVAK evidence without question. This evidence it was frequently alleged, had been obtained by torture (Amnesty
International). Many senior SAVAK officers were executed,
and during some of their trials details of their nefarious
crimes, methods and activities were made public.

Although Khomeini was quickly to dissolve SAVAK, this did
not mean he intended to manage without a secret service of
his own. On 2 August 1979 it was announced that the Iranian
National Information and Security Organisation had been
formed to operate both inside and outside Iran. Hojatolislam
Mohammed Mofateh is usually credited with forming this new
Islamic secret service, which eventually became the Ministry
of Information and Security. On 19 December Mofateh was

shot dead in Tehran by two men, who made their escape on a motorcycle. Responsibility was claimed by Forqan, a small Islamic extremist group that opposed the assumption of a political role by the mullahs.

The shah's record was further blackened by Sadiq Gotbzadeh, director of Iran's radio and television services, who stated on 17 February that since 1972, under the shah, over 300 people had been executed in Iran. He also berated the Western media for criticising the verdicts of the Islamic Revolutionary Courts, and for conveniently ignoring '13 years of massacre' in Iran, during which time more than '60 000 Iranian Muslims had been killed and 100 000 injured' in the struggle to establish an Islamic republic. He inferred that most of these casualties had resulted from Iranian armed forces shooting at demonstrators on the streets. The shah and certain members of his family were sentenced to death *in absentia*.

Even Khomeini must have realised that Ayatollah Khalkhali was going too far in his executionary zeal (his Islamic Revolutionary Courts were being likened in the Western media to the 'French Revolutionary Terror' of 1793), because on 16 March he issued an edict suspending all their proceedings until a new judicial system was established. New regulations came into force on 5 April, specifying powers and limitations. The Islamic Revolutionary Courts were to try only counterrevolutionary offences, not criminal ones. However the executions continued and it is probable that some 60 000 political prisoners remained in detention, mostly without trial.

In May Khomeini instructed prosecutors that they should only ask for the death penalty in cases of torture or murder. He did authorise public executions, but in October he ordered their suspension, an instruction that seemed to be ignored or neglected, which is somewhat at odds with the consideration that Khomeini's slightest word was an instant command. One source (the Iranian Association of Political Prisoners) reported that since March 130 prisoners had been executed, and that some 1500 were awaiting trial. It also said that some of the trials lasted barely 15 minutes; that a condemned person was sometimes executed within four hours of the verdict being delivered; and that 'methods of torture had not changed since the Shah's day'. Even so it did seem that the fire in the revolutionary furnace was subsiding somewhat.

THE ARMED FORCES

The shah's armed forces, which were about 240 000-strong and splendidly equipped with modern weaponry, were a dangerous barrier to revolutionary progress so special efforts were made to neutralise them. To the surprise of many revolutionaries, some of whom wanted to disband the armed forces completely, Khomeini would not allow this. Most of the top layer of the military command, from the rank of colonel upwards, was sheared off. Many of the most senior generals fell victim to the Islamic Revolutionary Courts (21 were executed in February, for example), while most of the others were either dismissed or allowed to resign. Those with no political connections were left alone. I remained quite openly in touch by telephone with one forcibly retired general, whom I had come to know quite well. He lived unmolested in his comfortable home in north Tehran throughout these revolutionary times and during the Iran–Iraq War, and continued to receive his army pension.

Up to two thirds of the military personnel were conscripts, mostly unwilling, who deserted in droves after the February street battles, leaving behind a comparatively small regular cadre consisting mainly of officers, technicians and specialists. These were all willing professionals, and after the Declaration of Neutrality they were only too glad to return to barracks and keep a low profile. Khomeini indicated that this was how he wanted it to be.

ISLAMIC REPUBLICAN PARTY

In March 1979 Khomeini formed his own political organisation, the Islamic Republican Party (IRP), headed by Ayatollah Mohammed Husseini Beheshti, Hashemi Ali Akbar Rafsanjani, Ali Hussein Khamenei and other carefully selected 'safe Islamic Shia hands' to 'Guard the Revolution, and foil counter plots'. Originally based on 15-man cells, the IRP developed a 30-member central committee, and through the medium of mullahs in their mosques launched a nationwide appeal for support. The IRP encouraged Islamic associations – such as those formed in factories, universities and schools – to affiliate with it. A referendum on a draft Islamic constitution was held on the 30–31 March.

THE ISLAMIC REPUBLIC OF IRAN

On 1 April 1979 Ayatollah Khomeini proclaimed the Islamic Republic of Iran, which was instantly recognised by the Soviet Union and Egypt. Ayatollah Hussein Ali Montazeri became president of the Constituent Council of Experts, which was charged with formulating a constitution that accorded with the book Khomeini wrote when in exile – *Wilyat e-Faqir* (Rule of the Theologians). In addition a Council of Guardians was formed. The philosophy was that only those with Islamic qualifications were fit to govern. There was nothing to bar Islamic dignities from entering government, politics, business or any of the professions. Khomeini wanted to ensure that the main organs of state were in safe Islamic hands.

THE PASDARAN

On 6 May 1979 Khomeini formally established the Pasdaran, or more properly the Pasdaran-e Inqilal-e Islami (Islamic Revolutionary Guards Corps), to be commanded by Ayatollah Hassan Lahouti. Previously known as the Mujahedeen of the Islamic Revolution, it had been formed in March to combine the functions of an Islamic army and a police force, based in the mosques. Its founders had been Ibrahim Yazdi, soon to be deputy prime minister in charge of revolutionary affairs, and Sadiq Gotbzadeh, director of radio and television, both of whom were IRP members. Khomeini had simply changed its title and defined its duties, which were to guard Islamic personalities, watch military barracks and police stations, monitor the activities of left-wing organisations, break up hostile public demonstrations and cope with insurgency.

The Pasdaran developed into an armed political—military—religious militia, formed into small companies. It was purged of all left-wing elements and was soon reputed to have 10 000 permanent members and some 100 000 reservists who were responsible only to the Islamic Revolutionary Council. Flamboyantly, Khomeini lauded his Pasdaran, saying its job was 'to support liberation movements and spread Iran's Islamic Revolution throughout the world'.

Elections were held in August for a 73-member Constituent Council to formulate the new Islamic constitution. Ayatollah Hussein Ali Montazeri became its president. In addition an 11-man Council of Experts was formed.

HEZBOLLAH

Another armed militia was Hezbollah (Party of God), a street gang that had distinguished itself in the February fighting and became the secret military arm of the Islamic Republican Party. Working together much of the time, the Pasdaran and Hezbollah took on the internal enemies of the new Islamic Republic of Iran. Originating in the southern part of Tehran, an area populated by the poor and oppressed, Hezbollah had welcomed the arrival of Khomeini and was anxious to do battle on his behalf against his opponents and detractors. Unruly and undisciplined, aggressive groups of its members rode motorcycles through the streets of Tehran, displaying Islamic fundamentalist insignia and shouting slogans in support of Khomeini.

Recognising their potential, they were given a sort of cohesion by Hojatolislam Hadi Ghaffari, who knocked them into shape and linked them to the IRP. Initially the members of the IRP were reluctant to be openly associated with such a disreputable body, which accounts for the original secrecy about this link. Later, when it was better organised and disciplined, several senior clerics liked to say that they were founder members of Hezbollah. By mid-1981 Hezbollah had become the respectable and acceptable face of the IRP vanguard. The official radio and TV, the Voice and Vision of the Islamic Republic (VVIR), often interrupted its programmes to call for Hezbollah's assistance when IRP personnel or property were in trouble, directing it to the scene of danger. Grudging necessity had changed the attitude of the IRP from furtive need to open reliance on Hezbollah.

AYATOLLAH KHOMEINI

Khomeini's original intention was that the Shia clergy would assume a supervisory or arbitrational role, leaving the business of government and administration of the country to suitably pious laymen. Hence his choice of Bazarghan as head of the initial provisional government, and later his support of Bani-Sadr as the first president of the Islamic Republic of Iran. To foreign visitors Khomeini appeared unworldly and naive, a man who clearly did not understand the West or its economics. For example he 'believed that [the West] could not manage for long without the 4-million barrels of oil a day that Iran produced' (Heikal, 1982).

Frequent demonstrations were held across the country in support of Khomeini. These often attracted counterdemonstrations by his opponents – mainly left-wing, liberal and nationalist groups. This seemed to worry him slightly, so he ordered his supporters to come out in force on 17 July in mass demonstrations to prove that the opportunists were lying when they claimed the people had ceased to support his revolution. Several million people did turn out to show their solidarity with him, but so did a few of his opponents. Khomeini must have suddenly felt the need for reassurance, probably suspecting that his popularity ratings were not all his cronies said they were.

Heartened by this massive boost to his ego, on 16 August in a broadcast on Radio Tehran Khomeini called on 'all oppressed Muslim peoples to overthrow the corrupt and tyrannical governments in the Islamic world, and on Islam to rise against the great powers and to annihilate their agents, in particular in Southern Lebanon where the Lebanese and the Palestinians are victims of the Iraelis'. Boastfully he added, 'If we wish we can, within a few hours, exterminate the US agents in Iran and in the United States' satellite countries'. Although melodramatic and illusionary, this revealed his empirical line of thought, barely disguised in Islamic jargon, which was ridiculed by the West as wishful thinking, especially as the Iranian armed forces seemed to have been neutered.

To understand Khomeini's life-long singleness of purpose, as well as his dedication to overthrowing the Pahlavi dynasty and turning his country into an Islamic fundamentalist state, it is helpful to delve briefly into his background and conditioning influences. Born Ruhollah al-Musavi in September 1902 in the village of Khomein, Khomeini is a 'seyyed', that is, one who claims direct descent from the Prophet Mohammed. The Musavis were one of the largest seyyed groups in old Persia. Orphaned shortly after birth (his father, a mullah from a landowning family, was killed by agents of a rival landowner), Khomeini was brought up by an elder brother, also a mullah, and given an Islamic education. He advanced through the Islamic heirarchy to reach the early eminence of Ayatollah by the 1950s.

The details of Khomeini's early life, like those of many men who rise to high position, are rather opaque as his biographers have tended to differ in detail. Some accounts relate that Khomeini always regarded the Pahlavis as upstarts, mainly because of their cold attitude towards the Islamic Shia heirarchy, and that this motivated him to be politically active against them. The Pahlavi dynasty had snatched power in Persia in 1925, when Reza Khan, commander of a small Cossack Brigade and father of Mohammed Reza Shah, forced the abdication of Ahmad Shah Qajar and ascended the Peacock Throne. In 1935 Reza Shah decreed that the name of his country should be changed from Persia to Iran.

In his youth Khomeini supported an anti-shah terrorist group called the 'Fedai'in' (Sacrifice of Islam), and was widely believed to have been actively involved in assassinations, one victim being Ahmad Kasravi, a notable historian who advocated a new form of religion, based on Iranian nationalism. Two prime ministers also fell victim to Fedai'in assassins (*Hazhir Teimourian, Times*).

For his involvement in anti-shah demonstrations and riots, Khomeini was exiled and settled in the Shia holy city of Nejaf in Iraq. From there he issued a steady stream of propaganda leaflets and news sheets, distributed by underground means to mullahs in Iran to incite their congregations to overthrow the shah and establish an Islamic state in Iran. Following protests from the government in Tehran, Khomeini was expelled from Iraq in October 1978. He moved to Paris to continue his propaganda campaign against the shah, seemingly with the tacit approval of the French government.

Other accounts of Khomeini's life differ somewhat, charting a politically blameless Islamic youth and mid-life career. So much so that when Reza Shah returned to Tehran in 1953 from his political sojourn in Rome, with CIA support, he chose Khomeini, then a brilliant rising Islamic star, to be his advisor on Islamic matters and mullah of the shah's mosque. Khomeini became an 'establishment man', reputedly in contact with the CIA, which was bolstering the shah. This cosy relationship changed when his youngest son Ali was killed, together with others, in mysterious circumstances. Khomeini immediately accused SAVAK of the crime and demanded an enquiry, which was held by the minister of the interior, then Abbas Hoveida. The enquiry absolved SAVAK of all blame, commenting that Ali's death had occurred in a fracas between rival Peking- and Moscow-orientated communist groups, with which he had been involved.

Infuriated, Khomeini approached the Supreme Shia Council, then chaired by Ayatollah Shariat-Madari, also a rising Shia star, and asked it to issue a fatwa demanding that the shah dissolve SAVAK. Shariat-Madari refused. When the shah heard what Khomeini had done he was incensed, their cosy relationship fell apart and Khomeini was ordered to leave Tehran and live in Qom, from where in 1962, he 'escaped' to Iraq. This failed attempt by Khomeini to enforce Shia religious supremacy caused him to embark on 'his mission of vengeance'. When the Islamic Revolution began Abbas Hoveida was one of the very first to be executed, reputedly without even the bare formality of a 'Khalkhali trial'. The vicious streak in Khomeini's character was apparent from an early stage. (Heikal 1982).

Ayatollah Shariat-Madari was a powerful Shia cleric with a strong Azerbaijani base. He claimed the loyalty of all Turkic-speaking Iranian Shias, then estimated to number over 17 million. He avoided politics and stood on the sidelines watching Khomeini's progress, perhaps somewhat cynically. Khomeini's chances of survival were uncertain in the early stages of the revolution. Never forgetting the fatwa rejection, Khomeini mounted a campaign against Shariat-Madari and forced him to retire to Qom, virtually under house arrest. Shariat-Madari's silence over Azerbaijani demands for independence were taken by Khomeini, a rigid centralist, to mean unspoken support for them.

Iran is the only country with a Shia majority – albeit a narrow one – and a Shia government. (Bahrain has a Shia majority, but a Sunni leadership.) Islam, which claims almost one billion adherents, has two main streams, both with their roots in early Islamic history but divided over disputes about leadership. The larger of the two is usually known as 'Sunni', or orthodox, from the word 'Sunna', roughly meaning 'usage or custom'. The other is 'Shia', or 'Shi' ites', meaning 'party or following' from 'Shiat Ali, the Followers of Ali', who believe the correct line of descent is through the Prophet's daughter, Fatima, and that only such caliphs and imams can be divinely inspired, something that is not accepted by Sunnis. Shias, unlike Sunnis, have a graded heirarchy of mullahs, sheikhs, hojatolislams, ayatollahs and grand ayatollahs. At the pinnacle is the 'marja taqlid', supreme leader of the claimed 100 000 plus Shias, who incidentally has his seat in Iraq.

Persia was Sunni for some 900 years, but in 1502 it was forcibly converted to the Shia persuasion, which it has retained ever since. Estimates tend to vary slightly, but it is generally thought that Sunnis form some 85 per cent of Islam and Shias about 15 per cent or less.

The violent deaths of Ali and his son Hussein in the dynastic Battle of Karbala in 680 AD gave the Shia sect a taste for martyrdom, flagellation and mysticism. In memory of Ali and Hussein, Shias annually commemorate the '10th of Muharram', when men work themselves into a frenzy and beat their own bodies with hard-tipped flails that draw blood.

This trait influenced Khomeini's early upbringing and contributed towards the formulation of his dogma for the Islamic Republic of Iran. It certainly influenced Hezbollah – which later produced suicide bombers in Lebanon – and the thousands of teenage members of Baseej e-Mustazafin, a part-time militia run by mullahs from their mosques. In the Iran–Iraq War members of this militia advanced in 'human waves' against Iraqi guns, despite being mown down in their thousands on the battlefield. Such traits have given a sharp edge to Iranian terrorism.

As a generalisation, in Western parlance the term Islamic fundamentalism has come to mean militant, politicised policies and individuals whose main aim is to establish and maintain an Islamic state, ruled according to the precepts of the Koran and Islamic custom. There are variations of this loose definition. The word fundamentalist has become accepted in the West as meaning a Muslim extremist, and embraces both Shias and Sunnis. In contrast moderates tend to hold the general view that Islam is a personal matter between an individual and his God, and has little to do with governing a modern state in a modern age. Moderates are usually content with a secular form of government that takes minorities into account, but as the governments of Muslim countries have to consider the weight of religious opinion, it may be more accurate to describe such moderate governments as semi-secular.

POWER CENTRES

A confusion of authority seemed to develop in Iran, as separate power centres appeared. Although Khomeini was a centralist and cracked down on all signs of separatism, he seemed reluctant to exercise tight, central, 'hands on' control, preferring to remain aloof and remote from the dust of the arena. It is debatable whether this was a deliberate policy, whether he tired of day-to-day events, or whether he wanted able, ambitious men to be out in the open, kept busy with administration and expending their energy on competing with each other for ministries or top jobs under his surveillance, rather than being pushed to the sidelines to plot against him in frustrated secrecy.

The foremost power centre was the Islamic Revolutionary Council, presided over by Ayatollah Khomeini himself, still based in Qom. Others were the provisional government, headed by Mehdi Bazarghan, who continually complained he was being overridden by the IRC, and the Islamic Revolutionary Courts. The Revolutionary Committees, some headed by senior mullahs and others by opposition and left-wing leaders, held local power in towns and villages across the country. The Pasdaran, another centre of power, gave sparse selective acknowledgement to the IRC. Finally there was what was known as 'Khomeini's Office', or the 'Committee of Aides', a group of people close to Khomeini, headed by his son, Ahmad Khomeini, that developed into a sort of lobbying authority and power-broking cabal. Khomeini seemed to be ensuring that no single one of these power centres gained too much authority and prestige.

BANI-SADR GOVERNMENT

On 5 November 1979 Bazarghan handed the resignation of his entire government to Ayatollah Khomeini, who accepted it and ordered the IRC to govern the country until the forthcoming elections were over. On the 17th the names of several members of the still secret IRC were revealed. Some were given ministerial appointments and were instructed to form a provisional government. This was dominated by Abdol Hassan Bani-Sadr, who took over foreign affairs, finance and economic affairs. Bazarghan obviously had had no prior knowledge of the Islamic Revolutionary Students' seizure of the American embassy, and had lacked the power either to free or to protect the captives. Bazarghan was not an 'insider'.

An attempted military coup against the Khomeini regime was revealed in January 1980, and it was reported that those responsible had already been executed. The minister of national guidance stated that 23 Western journalists had been expelled in 1979 for 'distorted reporting', and on 14 January 1980 he ordered the immediate expulsion of about 100 American journalists and the closure of all US news agencies.

AMERICAN EMBASSY HOSTAGES

Needless to say, relations between the United States and Iran were at rock bottom. Since the British had withdrawn from 'east of Suez' in the early 1970s, the United States had built up the shah to act as their 'policeman' in the Gulf area. Now that the shah had been ousted the US administration was in a quandary. The Cold War was still in progress, and Iran had pulled out of the Central Treaty Organisation (CENTO) – a bulwark of nations cobbled together in support of NATO to form a 'southern barrier' against Soviet communism in southern Asia – leaving a vulnerable gap in the line of defence. The Americans were divided over how to handle this new and unexpected situation – 'unexpected' as the fall of the shah had been a major miscalculation on the part of the CIA.

Some Americans felt it would be best to cut the United States' losses and abandon Iran completely, and instead try to persuade other nations to ostracise Ayatollah Khomeini, whose arrogant and grandiose utterances displeased the governments of many Middle Eastern and Southern Asian nations. But this would leave the Iranian field clear for the Soviets to exploit. Others thought that the best should be made of the very bad situation and the excesses of the Islamic Revolution forgotten, in an effort to remain friends with Iran. By doing so it was hoped that the United States could persuade Iran to remain neutral, and so thwart the Soviets. While pondering on this dilemma the US administration was confronted with another one.

The now-exiled shah, who had reached Mexico, was asking permission to be admitted to a hospital in New York for medical attention, which would virtually mean affording him sanctuary at a time when the Tehran government was demanding his extradition. Cyrus Vance, the US secretary of state, persuaded President Carter, against the advice of State Department officials, to grant this request and show the world that the United States did not abandon old allies. Accordingly, on 22 October 1979 the shah was flown from Mexico to a New York hospital.

Suddenly, on 4 November 1979 a group of 'Islamic Revolutionary Students', organised and led by Ayatollah Mohammed Moussavi Khoiniha, occupied the American embassy in Tehran, holding all inside hostage and demanding in exchange for their safe release that the shah be handed over to Iran. The hostages were accused of working for US espionage agencies. The Islamic Revolutionary Students claimed that their action had been approved by Ayatollah Khomeini himself, which instead aroused suspicion that he may actually have had no prior notice of this exploit. It has since been confirmed that the operation was well planned and well prepared, but it remains debatable whether Khomeini was aware of it in advance. It is probable that Khomeini approved the basic plan but left the details to Ayatollah Khoiniha, remaining unaware of the exact timing but going along with it once under way. On the 6th the Islamic Revolutionary Students stated they would not deal with the provisional Bazarghan government, but only with the Islamic Revolutionary Council, headed by Khomeini himself.

There were 60 US citizens in the embassy and 36 non-Americans, mainly Indian and Pakistani employees. The non-Americans were soon released. On the 6th two other US citizens were seized in Tehran and taken to the embassy to join the hostages, who were being detained in exceedingly uncomfortable conditions. On the 17th Khomeini ordered that 'white women and black men' be released on the grounds that 'Islam respected women, and that blacks were oppressed' in the United States. The remaining hostages were in for a very long period of captivity.

One authority told me that when the siege at the embassy began, Ayatollah Shariat-Madari told his chief aide, 'Make no mistake, it is Khomeini who is the butcher. Mullah Kalq Ali (who was organising the executions) is only the butcher's mate' (*Heikal: 1982*).

On the 5th, six US citizens (four diplomats and two of their wives) sought and received sanctuary in the Canadian embassy in Tehran, Eventually, furnished with false Canadian diplomatic passports, they were able to slip out of Tehran on 26–27 January 1980. This was revealed by the Canadian periodical *La Presse* on the 29th, after they had arrived safely in Canada. The Canadian ambassador and the diplomatic staff were withdrawn hurriedly.

Also on the 5th, the British embassy in Tehran was briefly occupied by Islamic demonstrators. They demanded the extradition of Shahpour Bakhtiar, believing that he had been given sanctuary in Britain after fleeing Iran. When it was explained that by this time Bakhtiar was in France, the British embassy was cleared of demonstrators by the Pasdaran, which had made no move at all to help the American hostages.

As the hostage situation developed, Khomeini came more to the fore, and on the 18th stated that all the hostages would be tried as spies by Islamic Revolutionary Courts unless the shah was returned to Iran. Open support was given to the Islamic Revolutionary Students by Khomeini's Office, the Council of Experts, most leading Islamic personalities, and many opposition groups. However a brake was put on any thoughts of further exploitation of this form of terrorism when, on the 19th, the IRC announced that in future the taking of hostages (together with strikes in factories) would be regarded as counterrevolutionary activities, against which the Council would take action.

All attempts by foreign emissaries to obtain the release of the Americans were unsuccessful. Relations between the United States and Iran deteriorated even further, and at one point Khomeini, fearing that US military invasion was imminent and exhibiting his unworldliness, dramatically called upon Iran to 'produce 20 million young men quickly to be given military training to confront' them. Tit-for-tat decisions were made. The United States banned oil imports from Iran and froze all Iranian assets under its control, while Iran refused to pay foreign debts, and so on. Agha Shahi, foreign affairs adviser to President Zia of Pakistan, visited Tehran and told Khomeini that Zia expressed 'full solidarity of the people and Government of Pakistan with the Islamic Revolution'. As Pakistan was a member of CENTO, this was a further blow to the United States' international prestige.

UNITED NATIONS

On 4 December 1979 the UN Security Council unanimously adopted a resolution urgently calling on Iran to release the hostages being held in Tehran, to grant them protection and to allow them to leave the country. This was ignored by Iran. On the 17th a UN General Assembly consensus resolution adopted an international convention on the taking of hostages, defining the crime, urging all states to do all they could to bring about the release of the hostages, and calling for punishment of the offenders. But such resolutions were not binding and little was done by the international community, some governments secretly enjoying the United States embarrassment.

ISLAMIC WAY OF LIFE

By mid-1980 the Islamic state was forcing its stamp on the people of Iran. Alcohol was completely forbidden, as were drugs. 'Un-Islamic music' was banned, and women were forced to wear either a hejab (a form of headscarf) and modest, loose-fitting clothing, or the all-enveloping chadour. Moral and religious censors, many self-appointed, abounded and proclaimed their disapproval of 'immoral' Western-type posters, advertisements and photographs in periodicals. Western dress, customs and affectations were frowned upon. Khomeini condemned those who 'go to work to chew gum', and forbade the practice in government offices.

OPERATION EAGLE CLAW

In frustration, on 24 April 1980 the United States launched 'Operation Eagle Claw', which was designed to 'snatch like an eagle' the embassy hostages. However the operation was poorly conceived, poorly executed and failed disastrously. Each US military service was determined to 'get a piece of the action'. The rescue force was flown in helicopters to 'Desert One', a temporary staging point in the desert some 200 miles east of Tehran. Whilst the helicopters were moving to be refuelled two of them collided, causing several to be destroyed by fire and killing eight US servicemen. The mission had to be aborted. Charred bodies and a wealth of maps, plans, orders and data were salvaged by the Iranians, and together with US body-bags these were taken to Tehran to be exhibited outside the US embassy.

The unworldly Khomeini stated that 'Allah had intervened with a sandstorm'. President Carter accepted full responsibility for this humiliating disaster, which did not help his reelection chances. The official excuse was 'equipment failure'. After this aborted rescue attempt the American hostages were largely dispersed and confined away from the US embassy.

Khomeini also bore down on the universities, criticising them for being over Westernised ('Westoxicated' was the word he coined to describe them). He said 'At one end a "believer" goes in, and a "non-believer" emerges'. He also complained that both universities and government offices were 'still full of Satans, who want to drag our young people into corruption'.

To rectify this 'gross state of deterioration', Khomeini announced that he had ordered what would be the world's largest Islamic university to be built in Tehran, which would emphasise the teaching of foreign languages so that mullahs could spread Islam throughout the world.

STONING TO DEATH

On the 3rd July 1980 a unique judgement was made by the Islamic Revolutionary Court in the southern city of Kerman, when it decreed that two men and two women found guilty of sexual offences should be publicly stoned to death – the old tradition of 'sangsar'. The condemned persons were visited by a mullah, ritually washed, and shrouded in a white garment with a ceremonial hood. Mullahs inspected the stones to be thrown, which were required to be between one and six inches in size. Witnesses stated that the victims, who were buried up to their chests, took 15 minutes to die.

Apart from Saudi Arabia, where sangsar is still used as a means of execution, there seem to have been no other recorded cases in any other Middle Eastern country within living memory. It appears that this overenthusiastic Islamic Revolutionary Court was trying to revert to fundamentalist basics and to set a trend, but it did not catch on. An argument was put forward that sangsar was a Semitic punishment, mentioned frequently in the Bible, and not really an Islamic one. Commenting on this issue, Ayatollah Khalkhali said 'Stoning certainly teaches people a lesson' (*The Times*). Death by firing squad was becoming the customary method of execution, news of which was almost a daily occurrence.

THE JULY PLOT

On 9 July 1980 Hojatolislam Mohammed Reyshahri, head of the Islamic Revolutionary Court of the Armed Forces, announced that a major coup conspiracy had been detected, that many arrests had been made and more were expected. President Bani-Sadr gave orders to close the airports, seaports and land borders for 48 hours to prevent suspects from fleeing the country, a fact that was afterwards denied as Bani-Sadr had not formally asked Khomeini's permission. It was alleged to be a military – civilian plot, in conjunction with exiles in

France, to overthrow the Islamic government, declare martial law, and institute a secular democratic government under Shahpour Bakhtiar.

The mastermind was said to be General Ahmad Ali Mohaqaqi, a former head of the National Gendarmerie, who was responsible for 'synchronisation and coordination'. He was assisted by General Saeed Mehdiyoun, who had briefly commanded the Iranian Air Force just after the revolution. It was claimed the conspirators had set up a secret organisation, code named 'Neghab' (mask), four or five months previously, and that this had been discovered and infiltrated. The basis of the plot was to use airborne bombs and rockets to kill Khomeini in his home in north Tehran (he had returned from Qom), and then to bomb the runways of Tehran airport and air base to prevent government planes from taking counter offensive action (*Kayhan*).

The coup was to be mounted from the tactical air base at Hamadan (about 120 miles from the Iraqi border), which was near the Nozeh garrison, where the conspirators, many former military officers, and a unit of Kurdish Special Forces were waiting to fly to Tehran (some 200 miles distant) to take control of key government buildings. Military garrisons across the country were on alert for code words to instruct them when to rise. General Mehdiyoun would have been in overall military command of a National Military Council of Iran, and General Mohaqaqi would have headed the attacking force of 17 aircraft.

Things went badly wrong. According to General Mohaqaqi, who made a full confession, the bus that was to take the leaders from Tehran to Hamadan on the night of the 9th did not arrive, and when they attempted to get there in private cars they were chased by Pasdaran in vehicles and arrested. Those in the garrisons waited in vain for the code words, although it was said there were some shootouts and casualties.

On 20 July the first five conspirators, including General Mohaqaqi, were executed by firing squad in Evin Prison less than 12 hours after their trial had ended. Magnanimity was not on offer, but a good measure of torture probably was. The head of the Air Force, General Amir Bagheri, a presumed conspirator, beat the rap by escaping into Iraq in one of the few remaining Iranian Phantom fighter aircraft. Two officers escaped to Turkey by helicopter. The Iranian authorities demanded the return of both the helicopter and its occupants, but Iran's relations with Turkey were not of the best, mainly over Kurdish border insurgent activities, and while the helicopter was returned the two plotters were accorded asylum. Bani-Sadr later said he had known about the plot for a month, and had had the Nozeh garrison under surveillance (PARS News Agency).

The July Plot had obviously given the Islamic revolutionary regime a very great fright, as Hojatolislam Javid Bahonar (a senior member of the IRC, soon to die violently himself) told the Majlis, quoting from seized conspiratorial plans, that had the coup succeeded there would have been mass executions of the leaders of the Islamic revolution in the squares and main streets of Tehran. The counterrevolutionaries felt they owed the revolutionaries a bloodbath. Deputies in the Majlis remained silent and thoughtful. Bahonar said the plotters had planned to release the American hostages and hinted at CIA involvement. There was no mention in the seized documents of restoring the shah to the Peacock Throne.

The July Plot gave the Islamic regime confidence in its new National Information and Security Organisation, its secret service, which had previously been suspect as it had been built on the ashes of SAVAK and reputedly still employed agents who had served the shah. Its success in the detection, surveillance and arrest of the July plotters showed that it could be a valuable and competent state instrument in the fight against insurrection, and accordingly funds and official support were given more generously to this shadowy organisation.

MEDIA FREEDOM

During the frantic, euphoric months after the Islamic fundamentalist revolution, free rein was given to expression of all shades of political and religious discussion – the media, publishers and poster printers all being officially unhindered. In short there was no official censorship. However this freedom was curtailed by groups who wanted to make their own prejudices clear and force their views on to others. They used violence and intimidation, smashed printing presses, set fire to media premises, and killed or threatened personnel. Hezbollah was one such group. In defence, publishers recruited security personnel.

As the IRP gained power within the Majlis, selective censorship began to creep in, and one by one offending newspapers were officially closed down – over 20 in the first twelve months of the republic. Many publishers of pamphlets and posters met a similar fate, driving staff and ideas underground as they had been in the shah's day. Foreign agencies and journalists were able to operate for the time being, but under increasing restraint and hostility.

WAR WITH IRAQ

On 4 September 1980 war broke out between Iran and Iraq, and on the 10th Iraqi troops entered the Iranian border town of Qasr Sherin. Initially it was Iraq that made all the territorial gains. The temptation to strike at a weakened Iran, and redress the unfavourable clauses in the Algiers Treaty of 1975, had been too much for Iraqi President Saddam Hussein.

Ayatollah Khomeini presided over a divided nation, his regime being maintained precariously in power by secret trials, executions, wholesale imprisonment, the Pasdaran and mullah-led Revolutionary Committees. Khomeini's immense personal prestige, power and influence held the Islamic regime together. The July Plot had concentrated Islamic fundamentalist minds. Had it succeeded and Khomeini been killed, the regime would most probably have fallen apart and civil war would have ensued.

Invasion by an historical enemy caused a tide of nationalism to develop in Iran, providing a cementing incentive to unite and resist. Nevertheless several factions remained doggedly opposed to the Islamic government and refused to cooperate with its war aims, including the Mujahedeen Khalk, the Fedayeen Khalk, the Kurdistan Democratic Party of Iran (KDPI) and a few other small embittered, nationalist, ethnic and socialist factions.

With Iraqi troops marching into Ahwaz, Iran's oil-rich western province, the 'Iranian Committee for the Restoration of the Shah' was established in Europe, producing a so-called

Free Iranian Government, which Bakhtiar was hoping to lead and establish soon in Ahwaz, with Iraqi support.

RELEASE OF THE AMERICAN HOSTAGES

The next event of major importance in Iran occurred on 21 January 1981, when after 444 days in captivity the American hostages in Tehran were freed. Their release had been deliberately delayed, for reasons of 'prestige and pride', until President Carter had bowed out and President Reagan had taken office. There had been continual, inconclusive arguments within the Islamic leadership over whether to release or retain the hostages, or put them on a show trial as 'war criminals'. There had also been bouts of infighting between the Islamic Revolutionary Students themselves over this issue. The hostages had outlived their political usefulness to the Iranians, who were glad to see them go as they were becoming an internal catalyst instead of a prized trophy. The Iranian negotiator, Behzad Nabavi, obtained the best deal he could get from the United States, which mainly amounted to the release of US military spares, already paid for by the shah, and other items that had been embargoed in November 1979.

This long drawn out hostage siege, and Americans' reaction to it, deeply impressed on the Iranian leadership the high regard the West placed on the value of human life and liberty. Iran had also shown that a small country was able to defy even the greatest super power on earth, whose military might and gigantic nuclear arsenal were of little avail in such situations. It was a lesson well noted for future reference. Hostage taking was now firmly in the Iranian armoury, to humble, frustrate and embarrass mighty foes. The oft-repeated Clausewitzian dictum that war is an extension of politics by other means, had been extended by the Islamic fundamentalist regime in Iran to include terrorism, assassination and hostage taking.

4 Hezbollah in Lebanon

Although Iran was locked into a ferocious and deadly war with neighbouring Iraq – which was by no means resolved, and in which Iran had lost a considerable amount of territory – Ayatollah Khomeini's thoughts and ambitions stretched farther afield. He was watching the ongoing Israeli–Palestinian confrontation in Lebanon with shrewd interest. His openly declared aim was to 'march to Jerusalem', and being a Shia through and through, he perhaps intended that when he got there the Islamic holy places in that city would come under his Shia administration, and that the present Sunni guardians would have to take a back seat. Khomeini's attitude in this respect was somewhat unusual, as generally speaking there was little friction between Shia and Sunni sects as such, and they usually existed on a 'live and let live' basis having other pressing secular problems to contend with.

On 14 June 1982 it was announced in Tehran that about 500 Iranian volunteers had been flown to Lebanon to fight side-by-side with Palestinians against Israeli troops in Lebanon. The media labelled them 'Revolutionary Guards', that is, Pasdaran, but in fact they were mostly members of the Iranian Hezbollah, the military arm of the the Islamic Republican Party, which under the leadership of Hojatolislam Hadi Ghaffari had expanded to a reputed strength of about 20 000, being mainly engaged in battle with the anti-Khomeini Mujahedeen Khalk inside Iran.

The remit of this Iranian detachment, which was under the control of Sheikh Mahmud Hussein Fadlallah, was not particularly to fight Israelis in battle, but to 'colonise' the whole of the Lebanese Shia population. He established a firm base in the upper Bekaa Valley, itself full of competing dissident sects and groups, sheltering there under nominal Syrian occupation authority. With Islamic revolutionary zeal Fadlallah began to activate the Shias inhabiting the southern part of Lebanon, adjacent to Israel. He also began to coordinate and launch acts of terrorism, firstly against Khomeini's enemies, and secondly against Israel.

For some time the Iranian VEVAK had been employing free-lance international terrorists to carry out its exploits in the belief that this would enable Iran to distance itself from terror-ism in the eyes of the world and give official denials of involve-ment a smack of credibility. The Iranian Ambassador to Lebanon, Mahtashemi Pur, was responsible for coordinating his government's covert activities in that country, and the US CIA came to label his embassy the 'spy centre for Iran'. Three almost separate groups of Iranian-orchestrated Shias ap-peared; one in Beirut, controlled directly by Pur; one in the Bekaa Valley, led by Fadlallah; and the other in southern Lebanon, based with Amal.

Iranian Islamic fundamentalists had been active in terrorist operations in Lebanon for some time. For example, when the French ambassador was shot dead in Beirut on 4 September 1981, responsibility was claimed by the Lebanese Red Brigades, a Shia group supported by Iranian money. The motive in that instance was revenge against France for afford-ing Bani-Sadr political asylum. Other terrorist incidents in Lebanon occurred, in which an Iranian hand was becoming apparent. The most serious was an explosion on 15 December 1981, at the Iraqi embassy in Beirut, in which the ambassador and 62 people were killed and almost 100 injured. Iraq accused Iranian and Syrian agents of responsibility, and vowed revenge.

Syria was inherently hostile to Iraq, the two countries being governed by rival branches of the split Baath Party, which had a semisecular, pan-Arab platform. Syria was one of the few Arab countries to side openly with Iran in its war against Iraq. Syria also sheltered and sponsored terrorists, providing them with training facilities, and in this sphere liaised closely with the Soviet KGB. This was revealed later, when secret East European files were unearthed. With KGB assistance, inter-national terrorists sheltering in Iran, Iraq, Libya, Syria and South Yemen were able to penetrate into Western Europe, often through the (then) divided city of Berlin. The govern-ments of these countries were able to assist the spread of inter-national terrorism westwards to embarrass states hostile to them, while blandly denying any involvement.

It had long been the custom of many governments to harbour political exiles from unfriendly countries, and this extended to separatist or insurgent guerrilla movements. In the past Britain and France in particular prided themselves on their liberal attitude towards political asylum seekers. The Middle Eastern states mentioned above had long sheltered and aided their enemy's 'dissident terrorist' groups. As terrorist groups have a tendency to divide, mercenary splinters, strapped for cash and devoid of a specific political commitment, began to develop, and such cadres became useful pawns in national secret agendas and as insurance counters against hostile terrorist attacks. Certain small, virile terrorist groups with spectacular track records came to be thought of as 'secret weapons' in a 'twilight world', ready for action as and when the opportunity arose or necessity demanded, their employer-nation being able blandly to deny any part in their deeds.

During 1982 the Iranian Ambassador to Syria (Hojatolislam Ali Akbar Mohtashemi) and the Iranian Ambassador to Lebanon worked with Shiekh Fadlallah to establish the Hezbollah umbrella organisation in the Bekaa Valley.

ABU NIDAL

One international terrorist, Abu Nidal, whose real name was Sabri Khalil Banna, was already on the Iranian payroll. Originally a member of Arafat's Fatah organisation, he had broken with it, and in 1973, was condemned to death by a Fatah court. Taking a section of Fatah with him, Abu Nidal had formed the breakaway 'Revolutionary Council of Fatah' (RCF) (not to be confused with the Fatah Revolutionary Council, which remained the controlling body of that group). Abu Nidal originally received some support from Iraq, but being short of cash, he made full use of his many international contacts and soon gained a reputation as a competent and deadly international terrorist leader. A terrorist by vocation rather than political conviction, Abu Nidal served several paymasters and was regarded by them as a very useful tool. He was very much a wandering lone wolf, and his Revolutionary Council of Fatah remained outside the PLO umbrella.

Abu Nidal organised the shooting of Shlomo Argov, the Israeli Ambassador to London, on 3 June 1982. Believing that the Palestine Liberation Organisation was in some way responsible, on the 4th Israel launched heavy air attacks on PLO positions in Lebanon, including Beirut, to which the Palestinians responded by rocket barrages against northern Israeli settlements.

ISRAEL INVADES SOUTHERN LEBANON

On 6 June 1982 Israel launched a full-scale invasion of Lebanon, advancing as far north as Beirut. Some authorities say that the assassination of Argov was the catalyst that triggered off this major Israeli operation, but as it had to be carefully planned, reservists recalled, and vehicles and weapons mustered and deployed, Argov's death was probably a convenient excuse. On the 9th, in a statement issued in Beirut, one 'al-Asifa' claimed responsibility for shooting Argov, which Israeli intelligence regarded as a code name for Abu Nidal.

When Israel invaded Lebanon for the second time in June 1982 (the first time had been in 1978), the southern Shias welcomed the troops as allies in their fight against the occupying PLO forces, but when the Israelis joined forces with Lebanese Christian militias the Shias turned against them. The Israeli forces continued their advance northwards to Beirut and besieged that city for 73 days, until in August they drove the PLO fighters from the country to fragment in far-flung exile. The Israelis then slowly withdrew southwards to their self-designated 'security zone' in southern Lebanon.

LEBANON

It is an understatement to say that tiny, multireligious Lebanon, consisting of about 6600 square miles with a population of about three million (60 per cent Muslim, 34 per cent Christian and 6 per cent Druse, IISS figures), wedged between Syria and Israel, was in a tumultuous and disastrous state. A civil war had begun in Lebanon in 1975, mainly between Christian and Muslim political parties. Gradually other factions were sucked in, causing the Syrian army to intervene and occupy a large part of northern Lebanon. Quarrelsome factions fought amongst themselves, old wounds were reopened, fresh blood was spilt, and the war-stricken country became a free range for terrorists of all types.

Earlier, when the PLO had been defeated in the short 'civil war' in Jordan (1970–71) and the Palestinians had been ejected from that country, the PLO had settled in the southern part of Lebanon. The weak Lebanese government, itself striving desperately to survive, had been powerless to prevent this from happening. Once established in southern Lebanon the PLO used it as a garrison area, training base and a springboard for raids into Israel and the bombardment of northern Israeli settlements. Israel often retaliated with air strikes on suspected guerrilla camps and bases in Lebanese territory.

The southern part of Lebanon was inhabited by about one million poor and underprivileged Shias known as the Mustaafin (the deprived), who had long lacked political awareness. In 1957 Imam Moussa Sadr, an Iranian and long-time friend and colleague of Khomeini, had been sent to Lebanon to rouse the Shias into political activity. In 1967 he had formed the Higher Shia Communal Council.

During the first part of the Lebanese civil war Imam Moussa Sadr formed a political organisation called Amal (Hope), which developed its own militia. Until that time the Lebanese Shias had been regarded as an insignificant military factor in the country, and those who had joined or had been conscripted into the army or other militias, had been regarded as individuals, rather than representatives of their sect.

In August 1978 Sadr, now the 'spiritual leader' of the Lebanese Shias, visited Libya and was not seen alive again. Colonel Gaddafi of Libya insisted that Sadr had left the country of his own accord at the end of his formal visit. His disappearance roused the formerly rather docile Lebanese Shias into protests and demonstrations. The general opinion for some time was that Sadr was being held captive in Libya and a number of aircraft were hijacked by Shia-based Amal militiamen in an effort to obtain his release. When Ayatollah Khomeini came to power he took a keen interest in the disappearance of Sadr, who was eventually believed to have been murdered on Gaddafi's orders.

Actively encouraged by the Islamic fundamentalist government in Iran, Amal expanded. Its militia, known as 'Resistance Brigades', reached a strength of about 4000 and came into confrontation with the Palestinian militias, which they regarded as armed intruders in their country. In April 1980 Nabih Berri was appointed secretary general of Amal, and Hussein Moussawi (not to be confused with Sheikh Abbas Moussawi) became the leader of its armed militia. In October 1981 Berri led an Amal delegation to Ayatollah Khomeini in Tehran. Khomeini gave them a warm welcome and promised his help and support, which he gave generously. He was rewarded for this, as in March 1982 Amal proclaimed Khomeini the 'Imam of all Muslims throughout the world', which pleased Khomeini and boosted his already considerable ego, but did not find favour in Lebanon among high-profile, established Sunni political groups.

Meanwhile the eighth hijacking aimed at securing the release of Imam Moussa Sadr had occurred on 24 February 1982. A Kuwaiti airliner flying out of Libya had landed at Beirut airport after being seized in flight by Shia gunmen calling themselves the 'Sons of Imam Moussa Sadr'. The following day the hijackers had surrendered to the Lebanese authorities, and all passengers and crew had been released safely. The leader of this hijacking, code named 'Hamze', was reputed to have led six previous hijackings, all unsuccessful, and on each occasion had been quietly released by the relevant national authorities, as indeed he was on this occasion. According to documents released by East Germany after reunification, 'Hamze' had links with the Iranian government. His identity remains uncertain, but he was probably one of the first mercenary terrorists hired by the Lebanese Shia Resistance Brigades, by courtesy of Ayatollah Khomeini.

THE BREAKAWAY ISLAMIC AMAL

By the end of 1982 the Amal militia had risen to a strength of about 30 000, to become second only in size to that of the Christian Falangists. Nabih Berri was a politician who now sought to take a major part in the political life of his country as the secular Shia leader. He wanted to use his militia for this purpose, and settled in the southern Shia suburbs of Beirut, the poorer section of the city. He seemed little interested in using terrorism as a weapon, and this brought him into conflict with Khomeini's chief agent in Lebanon, the Iranian ambassador in Beirut.

Nabih Berri also had differences with his military commander, Hussein Moussawi, who was expelled from the Amal Command Council. Moussawi formed his own armed group from Amal defectors, which became known as Islamic Amal. The latter concentrated largely on terrorism and worked closely with Sheikh Fadlallah's Hezbollah. Berri's Amal militia was soon engaged in positional battles with the Lebanese army and Palestinian militias and factions.

LEBANESE HEZBOLLAH

In the Baalbek area in the Bekaa Valley, in Shia-inhabited terrain that was nominally under the control of the Syrian occupation army, Sheikh Fadlallah formed a comprehensive Islamic political–military–intelligence structure, which developed into an umbrella under which a number of small terrorist groups worked and sheltered. Fadlallah had a two-pronged programme. The first was to 'colonise' the Shia population, rouse it into political activity and enforce Khomeini's brand of Islamic fundamentalism. Local committees were formed to muster and control the people. The committees distributed – or withheld for non-compliance – food, medical care, education and other welfare necessities. Money and other forms of aid poured in from Tehran. Lebanese Shias in their villages were certainly 'have nots', and for years they had been neglected. Now photographs of Khomeini were displayed everywhere and demonstrations were frequently organised at which pro-Khomeini slogans were shouted. Fadlallah's plan was to push out all non-Shia sects and factions, which were crowding the Bekaa Valley, and the growing Shia unity enabled him to elbow them aside. A radio station poured out pro-Khomeini propaganda, and Khomeini's taped sermons were replayed in mosques.

Fadlallah's other prong was to develop Hezbollah into an efficient terrorist organisation, in which Imad Moughniyeh, a Lebanese Shia in Iranian service, became a most important executive. The small group led by Moughniyeh, who was in charge of Hezbollah operations, became known as Jihad al-Islami (or al-Jihad al-Islami). By vocation Moughniyeh was an international terrorist, master planner and operator.

On 21 November 1982 Hezbollah led an armed rebellion against the local authorities in the Baalbek area, shouting slogans in favour of Khomeini and remaining in occupation of part of the town. The Lebanese government blamed Iran for instigating this 'revolt', and its foreign minister protested to the Iranian ambassador in Beirut, threatening to break off diplomatic relations with his country if the Iranian contingent in the Bekaa Valley was not withdrawn. The newly elected president of Iran, Ali Akbar Khamenei, stated he had no intention of recalling them.

THE MULTINATIONAL FORCE

After August 1982 an international peacekeeping force began to be deployed in Lebanon. The force eventually consisted of US, British, French and Italian troops, and these soon came under hostile pressure from the various militias. In February and March 1983 numerous terrorist attacks were made against them, and throughout these months and after there were spasmodic spates of car-bomb incidents.

As the Iran–Iraq war progressed the armed militias in Lebanon, some of which were very small, supported by one or other of the warring countries began to fight against each other, as well as against their other enemies and the enemies of their sponsor countries. This further complicated and confused the chaotic Lebanese scene.

SUICIDE BOMBINGS

Behind the scenes Hussein Moussawi and Imad Moughniyeh were selecting, recruiting and conditioning candidates to operate as 'suicide drivers', in other words to drive to their deaths in vehicles loaded with explosives, something that appealed emotionally to Shias steeped in a tradition of martyrdom. Sheikh Abbas Moussawi, secretary general of Hezbollah, claimed, rather dubiously, that he had invented suicide-bomb tactics, and in February 1983 boasted that he had 48 suicide drivers ready to attack Israeli targets in Lebanon. In fact it was a team effort, with mullahs exhorting, and terrorist leaders planning and training.

One of the first of Imad Moughniyeh's major suicide-bomb attacks occurred at about 1 p.m. on 18 April 1983, when a van containing some 440 pounds of explosives was driven across the forecourt of the American Embassy in Beirut and into the side of the building. The subsequent explosion killed 63 people, injured over 120 and completely destroyed the consular section. Among the dead was the driver of the van, the CIA director for the Near East and South Asia, and six CIA employees.

Responsibility was claimed by Jihad al-Islami, which stated in a communique that the explosion had been 'part of the Iranian Revolution's campaign against the imperial presence throughout the world'. This attack, and the terrific loss of American life, was an abrupt shock to the multinational force. The major Shia objective was now to drive these forces from Lebanon, as they supported the weak Lebanese government and were a barrier to Khomeini's colonisation ambitions.

Immediately all the multinational detachments in Lebanon, and indeed all the Israeli ones too, began to take what precautions they could against this new and deadly terrorist weapon. Where possible, high earth walls were constructed around camps and concrete bollards formed narrow winding chicanes to slow down approaching vehicles. Marksmen were posted ready to shoot any driver who failed to stop at an outer checkpoint. Usually an armoured vehicle was used to block off the entrances to camps, and was removed only briefly to allow inspected vehicles to enter or leave. Buildings were plastered with sandbags as protection against blast and flying debris.

US military personnel in particular were targeted, as Ayatollah Khomeini regarded the United States as the 'Great Satan'. Two US Marines were seized on 29 September when they wandered into the southern sector of Beirut, controlled by Amal, but their release was obtained by Nabih Berri, who had political considerations in mind. On 14 October two other US Marines were shot dead; on the 17th five were wounded by sniper fire; and on the 19th a car-bomb explosion wounded five more. The Amal organisation was generally blamed, but Nabih Berri denied responsibility.

Car bombing remained an ugly feature of the terrorists' scheme in Beirut, and elsewhere in Lebanon. It was a form of warfare that gave the bomber a good margin of safety and escape, as he or she could park the vehicle, walk away and leave it, the bomb being exploded either by a timing device or by remote control. The Americans refused at this stage to train Lebanese government counterterrorist teams in case the expertise and techniques were used against them and their establishments. However President Reagan did approve certain covert operations against terrorists who struck at US targets or interests.

On 23 October 1983 two suicide bombers coordinated their attacks, hitting US and French bases in Beirut simultaneously at 6.20 in the morning causing great loss of life and considerable damage. One suicide bomber, his truck loaded with over 500 pound of explosives, crashed through the perimeter fence of the US Marine base and into the lobby of a four-storey building, where it exploded and completely demolished the building. The final death toll was 241 marines. The unidentified driver, who had previously been blessed by his mullah (reputed to be Sheikh Fadlallah himself), went willingly to his death. The UN Marines' orders had been that weapons should not remain loaded within the base, but it was said that had loaded weapons been instantly available the suicide driver could have been shot dead before his vehicle got close to the building, and so the explosion could have been avoided, or its impact much reduced. This order was changed, and from then on weapons remained loaded, and ready, within the US bases in Lebanon.

The second suicide driver drove his vehicle, also loaded with explosives, straight at a building that housed a French military detachment. The vehicle exploded on impact, killing 58 French troops. This driver too had been blessed by his mullah, and had gone willingly to his death, knowing he would be the first to die. Responsibility for both explosions was claimed by Jihad al-Islami, but general suspicion still centred on Amal, then in open confrontation with Lebanese government troops. Later on the 27th, Hussein Moussawi denied that Islamic Amal had been involved in either attack, pointing out that Amal members had participated in the rescue operations, and that some of the injured had been taken to hospital in Amal ambulances.

However he added in his communique that he approved of the actions, and hoped 'to participate in them in the future'.

On 24 October George Shultz, the US secretary of state, said he thought that the Soviet Union, Iran and Syria were behind these twin suicide bombings. He told a US Congressional enquiry that US troops would remain in Lebanon, despite terrorist dangers, 'because it is a region of vital strategic and importance for the free world ... and because it is an area of competition between the USA and the Soviet Union, and because we have a deep and abiding commitment to Israel'. Words he was soon perhaps to regret.

Shultz tried to persuade the Lebanese government to close down the Iranian embassy in Beirut, where he alleged terrorist planning was taking place, but due to Syrian pressure this was resisted. The Syrian and Iranian governments were jogging along fairly well together at this stage, and both were cooperating in terrorist acts against Western countries in an attempt to destabilise them.

On the 26th President Reagan claimed (*New York Times*) he had sufficient evidence to show that Syrians were involved in Iranian terrorism, and that Syria had 'facilitated their entry' and provided the munitions. Tension between the United States and Syria escalated. Syria, daily expecting a major US military landing in Lebanon, called up its reservists and placed its armed forces on special alert. The United States froze the funds allocated to Syria on 12 October because of 'Syria's hostile attitude'

Later, on the 1 November, the US authorities admitted that a warning of a suicide-bomb attack on the US Marine base had been given on 20 October in the *National Intelligence Digest*, a summary distributed daily to senior US government officials and senior military commanders with specific links with the US troops in Lebanon. Syria was placed on the US 'List of Countries Supporting Terrorism', which entailed an arms embargo and other deprivations.

SUICIDE ATTACK ON THE ISRAELIS

On 4 November 1983 Ahmad Qassir, aged 15, after being blessed by his mullah, bade goodbye to his mother in his home village of Deir Qanon e-Nahir. He told her he would explain all to his father and brothers one day, then stepped into the driving seat of his truck, which was laden with explosives. Qassir travelled to Tyre, where he headed towards a building in an Israeli base. Although the vehicle was brought to a halt some five yards from the building when look-out marksmen shot Ahmad Qassir dead, the truck exploded and killed 61 people – 28 Israeli soldiers and 33 others, either Palestinians or Lebanese awaiting interrogation. The explosion destroyed part of the building and set off a chain reaction of ammunition explosions, which hampered rescue work for some hours.

Responsibility was claimed by Jihad al-Islami (by telephone to a media bureau), who stated 'We are prepared to send 2000 of our fighters to die in southern Lebanon in order to expel the Zionist enemy from our country'. Israel's response was a series of air strikes against suspected terrorist training camps in Nabchit in the Bekaa Valley, the reputed HQ of Islamic Amal and Hezbollah. In the first such air strike since August 1982, Israel claimed to have killed at least 30 people.

French aircraft, flying from an offshore aircraft carrier, joined in this military retribution. They raided camps near the town of Ras el-Ain near Baalbek, which was said to be occupied by Islamic Amal. The French claimed to have extensively damaged buildings and killed almost 40 people. Two days later journalists were invited to visit Ras el-Ain but they saw no sign of damage to buildings, nor fresh graves. This was later confirmed by US intelligence photographs. This tactless US confirmation of an exaggerated report upset Franco-American relations. It also showed that terrorists were not the only ones to overstate their claims. For practically every terrorist incident that occurred in Lebanon, and they could average up to a hundred a month, a multiplicity of claims were made, and at times it was difficult to determine who was actually responsible for which crime, in the mad rush to obtain propaganda glory and status. However certain hallmarks tended to indicate which groups were responsible.

During the first months of their operations the names of suicide drivers who died completing their missions were not released by the terrorists, for fear of multinational-force and Israeli retribution against their families and villages, and this was so in the Tyre explosion. It was not until January 1985, by which time the Israeli armed forces had withdrawn farther south and the multinational force had departed, that posters suddenly appeared in the Bekaa Valley and elsewhere in Lebanon, proclaiming that 'Ahmad Qassir is a Martyr of Islam' and depicting his face emerging from the ruins of the shattered Israeli HQ building in Tyre. This brought great honour to his family, and also special benefits such as pensions, housing and education. However the multiple claims tended to cheapen the currency of martyrdom.

Not all suicide drivers became martyrs, as some attacks were not pressed home completely. Some changed their minds at the last minute, 'mechanical breakdown' being an excuse often peddled by failures to their superiors. Imad Moughniyeh was said to have blamed the failures on the mullahs for providing insufficient Shia indoctrination. (Drugs formed part of the operational motivation, a fact often denied by terrorist groups.) On one occasion, on 24 December 1983, a suicide driver drove his vehicle towards a French position near the town of Nasra. At the last minute the driver jumped from his cab, the vehicle rolled downhill and exploded against a concrete outer protecting wall, killing eight French soldiers and injuring 17 others.

KHOMEINI'S CONGRATULATIONS

In January 1984 Hussein Sheikholism, Iran's deputy foreign minister, visited Sheikh Mahmud Hussein Fadlallah, now the official spiritual guide of Hezbollah in Lebanon, to pass on Khomeini's congratulations for the success of his suicide missions. More Iranian money was allocated, enabling Hezbollah to expand its welfare programmes and include pensions for the families of 'martyrs'. Posters of Khomeini still adorned many parts of the Bekaa Valley in 'Khomeini country', although this was not so in other parts of Lebanon.

THE BIR EL-ABED INCIDENT

By this time the CIA had identified Sheikh Fadlallah as the prime motivator of terrorism against the US forces in

Lebanon. Accordingly the CIA planned to 'take out' Fadlallah and his family. On 8 March 1984 a massive car bomb exploded outside Fadlallah's house in Bir el-Abed, killing 80 people and injuring over 200. The CIA had either not done its intelligence research thoroughly or had overlooked one important point – Fadlallah was not at home at the time.

As minister of justice in the current Lebanese government, Nabih Berri had to handle the matter. He ordered an enquiry. The CIA's excuse was that its agents had operated in a 'freelance' manner. However, the United States got its way in one respect, as the Iranian embassy in Beirut, the 'nest of spies', was at last closed down by the Lebanese government. Although this handicapped Iran somewhat, it certainly did not stop its terrorist intervention in Lebanon.

The day after the CIA's failed bid on Fadlallah's life, a suicide driver, a girl, later named as 16-year-old Sanna Mheidi, drove her car into an Israeli military convoy near the town of Khiam and died in the explosion. This incident gave rise to conflicting claims. The Jihad al-Islami claimed that nine Israeli soldiers had died and eleven people had been injured. This was denied by the Israelis, who stated that only the girl had died. Originally the claims made by the groups organising the suicide drivers – that is, the Islamic Amal of Hussein Moussawi and the Jihad al-Islami of Sheikh Fadlallah – were reasonably accurate, denoting a touch of professionalism, which perhaps stemmed from Imad Moughniyeh. As the incidents increased in number the communiques claiming responsibility became less reliable – some tended towards exaggeration while others were downright fictitious.

THE MULTINATIONAL FORCE WITHDRAWS

The withdrawal of the multinational forces began in February 1984. Hezbollah had won, and President Reagan had lost this round against fundamentalist terrorism in Lebanon. US diplomats and the remaining military staff moved out of Muslim-dominated Western Beirut into the eastern, mainly Christian-held sector for safety. However this proved elusive. On 20 September 1984 a suicide driver drove his explosive-laden truck through a chicane to reach the six-storey building in which the Americans were housed, even though guards were firing at him as he approached. The explosion killed 23 Americans and injured 21. Responsibility was claimed by Jihad al-Islami, who said it had been an act of revenge for the attempt on Fadlallah's life.

During 1985, the 'year of the suicide driver', as Israeli troops compressed themselves further southwards into their self-declared 'security zone', terrorist exploits against them increased. The groups manipulating suicide drivers began to produce photographs and videos showing them being blessed by mullahs, saying goodbye to friends and families, and making dramatic final statements of dedication to their mission. These were distributed widely by propaganda sections to the international media, once the exploit had been completed, and had star billing on Iranian TV.

That year also saw the emergence of the Syrian Socialist Nationalist Party (SSNP), which was based in the Lebanese crossroad town of Chtaura on the edge of Syrian occupied territory. The SSNP began to dabble in terrorism, issuing many false claims. Syria and Iran had begun to compete for influence in parts of Lebanon, and the former cooperation between their sponsored terrorist groups began to wane. The Syrian-government-supported SSNP never really gained credibility, and the Tehran government continued to call the terrorist tune in Lebanon.

DAWA

One other virile terrorist organisation to hit the headlines in the early 1980s was 'Dawa' (Hizb al-Daawa al-Islami – the Islamic Call), which had been founded as an underground Shia organisation in the 1960s in the Shia city of Nejaf in Iraq. Dawa mounted demonstrations against the Baathist government, and also carried out sabotage operations and assassinations. Many Dawa members were imprisoned, and some were executed. When living in exile in Nejaf from 1962 to 1978, Ayatollah Khomeini made contact with Dawa and encouraged its activities. Farsighted, he was hoping that one day he might be able to harness Dawa to his long-term plans for colonial expansion.

When the Iran–Iraq war began (September 1980), Khomeini was instrumental in forming what became known as the Supreme Council of the Islamic Revolution for Iraq (SCIRI), led by his old Shia friend Ayatollah Bakr Hakim, who had replaced the missing Imam Moussa Sadr. SCIRI consisted of a collection of anti-Baathist Iraqi Shia dissident groups, which included Dawa. In mid-1982, when Iran formed the Hezbollah umbrella organisation in the Bekaa Valley, elements of Dawa joined it, but seemed to concentrate upon Kuwaiti targets as Kuwait had come out openly on Iraq's side against Iran.

On 12 December 1983 Dawa launched six vehicle-bomb attacks in Kuwait City. An explosive-laden truck was driven through the gates of the US embassy, where it exploded and killed five people. The driver, who not been on a suicide mission as all six bombs were to have been exploded by remote control, was blown to pieces. His severed thumb, whose print was matched in Iraqi security force records, later enabled him to be identified as a Dawa member. The other man in the truck, who had been injured, was arrested. Of the five other car-bomb explosions, one was against the French embassy and the others against various buildings. In all 48 people were injured.

Within days ten terrorists, all Dawa members, were arrested in Kuwait, and their interrogation resulted in more Dawa arrests. Eventually 17 Dawa terrorists were tried and convicted in Kuwait. Some were sentenced to death, but none were executed. The Kuwaiti authorities feared repercussions, and therefore exercised caution. These men became known as the 'Kuwaiti-17' and their release was continually demanded by Dawa.

During the trial of the Kuwaiti-17 the twin sons of a Kuwaiti diplomat were kidnapped in Beirut, but were eventually released on condition that the name 'Dawa' was not mentioned at all during the trial proceedings.

Dawa was an independently minded group, accustomed to a free-ranging terrorist remit, and differences of opinion arose between it and Hussein Moussawi of Islamic Amal, and Sheikh Abbas Moussawi, leader of the Lebanese Hezbollah, that led to complaints to Khomeini about Dawa's indiscipline and attitude and requests for its expulsion. Khomeini ordered that

Dawa should remain part of Hezbollah, but should concentrate upon Kuwaiti targets.

Dawa continued its attacks against Kuwaiti targets, this time coordinated by Hezbollah, and under threat of its funding being withdrawn if it defaulted. On 1 March 1985 Dawa killed an Iraqi diplomat and his young son in Kuwait City. In May a suicide driver rammed the motorcade of Sheikh Jaber al-Ahmad al-Sabah, the ruler of Kuwait, killing three people and injuring twelve. The sheikh himself was slightly wounded. Responsibility for both incidents was nominally claimed by Islamic Jihad, which demanded the release of the Kuwaiti-17. The sheikh resisted all threats and was applauded by Western states for his determined stand against terrorism.

In July two bombs exploded at beach cafes in Kuwait, killing eleven people and injuring 89. Responsibility this time was claimed by the 'Arab Revolutionary Brigades Organisation', Hezbollah having taken to using various code names for some operations in order to confuse international intelligence agencies. Eventually four Dawa members were brought to trial for this exploit, of whom two were sentenced to be executed.

5 Hijacking Involvement

If there were any doubts about Ayatollah Khomeini's grandiose ambitions, both spiritual and territorial, they should have disappeared by January 1985, when it was revealed (*The Times*) that the exiled National Iranian Resistance Movement (NIRM), led by Shahpour Bakhtiar, had acquired certain documents relating to an important meeting that had been held in Tehran on 28 May 1984 to discuss a project that was said to have been previously approved by Khomeini without amendment or alternation. Chaired by Ayatollah Mohammed Khatani, minister of Islamic guidance, the meeting was attended by certain ministers, senior military commanders, department Heads and Ayatollah Bakr Hakim, leader of the exiled 'Supreme Council of the Islamic Revolution for Iraq', which was sponsored by the Tehran government.

The purpose of the meeting was formally to approve and implement a plan to recruit and train suicide squads to carry out terrorist operations in countries opposed to the Islamic Republic of Iran. This was required as Iran, still engaged in its long-running war with Iraq, had insufficient military muscle to effect the removal of offending governments. The policy was to be one of striking 'blows from within'.

The star of the meeting was Hussein Moussawi, leader of Islamic Amal and code named 'Mir Hashim'. Moussawi was most probably the mastermind behind the plan, although others were anxious for a share of the kudos. Moussawi requested that specialised instructors from the armed forces be seconded to his organisation, and that between 1500 and 2000 men under the age of 30 be recruited. The latter had to be 'completely committed to martyrdom'. He anticipated his 'suicide force' would be ready for action by mid-1985. He also requested cooperation in sending his intelligence agents abroad in the guise of military attaches.

The suicide force was to be built around a nucleus of a few groups of people currently serving in Lebanon. Officially it was to be a secret branch of the Pasdaran (the Islamic Revolutionary Guards Corps), but it would be completely

75

independent and report directly to Khomeini. Moussawi said the primary targets were Saudi Arabia, Kuwait, the United Arab Emirates and Bahrain; then Jordan, France and any other country hostile to Iran, in that order.

HIJACK SPECTACULARS

The Western world, and indeed all countries with international TV reception, had become accustomed to major terrorist exploits being shown on their TV screens almost as they occurred, such was the professional expertise that had been developed to expose the fascinating, raw, naked edge of terrorism. National security forces and intelligence agencies hated this intrusion, which could put their every move under the all-seeing eye of TV cameras and provide terrorists with international publicity for their cause, the so-called essential 'lifeblood of terrorism'. Hijacking had especially attracted public interest as very many more people had begun to travel by air, for example on cheap package tours, and this enabled them to relate to on-going hijacking situations. Major highjacking incidents began to acquire 'entertainment and interest value'.

This public fascination had begun with Palestinian hijackings in 1968 and deepened in September 1970, when in one operation the Popular Front for the Liberation of Palestine (PFLP) seized five international airliners, three of which were eventually flown to Revolution Airfield (Dawson's Airfield) in Jordan, where nearly 300 people were held hostage for several days. The hijackers were demanding the release of three PFLP members held in Switzerland and another three held in West Germany. This operation, organised by Wadieh Hadad, a terrorist mastermind, began on 6 September and lasted until the 13th, when, after the hostages had been taken from the planes (to be eventually rescued by Jordanian troops), the three airliners were dramatically blown up, TV cameras recording the vivid details. Colonel Moamor Gaddafi of Libya was the reputed paymaster of this operation. The six Palestinians in Western European custody, and others who had been arrested, were released, as were a number of detainees in Israel. It was a dramatic terrorist victory, which whetted the public's appetite for more.

The public was not to be disappointed, as more Palestinian terrorist spectaculars followed in the 1970s to fascinate TV viewers. A notable one was led by the well-known assassin 'Carlos' (now in French custody), who on 21 December 1975 kidnapped OPEC ministers attending a meeting in Vienna. Carlos demanded, and received, an aircraft to fly them all out of Austria. So began a saga that took in Algeria, Libya and then Algeria again. En route 'neutral' oil ministers and others were released as ransoms were paid or other advantages obtained. This operation, which lasted until the 23rd, had been organised by Wadieh Hadad, who had hired Carlos to lead the terrorist team. Again Libya was reputed to be the paymaster. It was watched on TV by hundreds of millions of viewers worldwide. Once again the terrorists had won, gaining yet more 'lifeblood' and in this instance considerable sums of money and prestige, to the embarrassment of several national security forces.

IRAN'S INVOLVEMENT IN HIJACKING

Iran was an early participant in hijacking, and indeed was occasionally on the receiving end of such exploits. For example on 27 August 1983 an Air France airliner, on a flight from Vienna to Paris, was hijacked by five members of the Islamic Liberation Movement (an early Hezbollah code name) after a stopover in Geneva. The pilot was forced to fly the plane, with refuelling stops in Sicily and Damascus, to Tehran, where security forces surrounded the aircraft and a 'nominal siege' ensued. The hijackers demanded the release of all Lebanese in French detention, and also that the French government modify its policies towards Lebanon. The hijackers 'surrendered' on the 31st and were granted asylum. This had all the hallmarks of a put-up job by the Iranian-supported Hezbollah in Lebanon, directed from Tehran. France closed down an Iranian cultural centre in Paris and ejected three Iranian diplomats; Iran reciprocated in a like manner.

A similar exploit occurred on 31 July 1984, when an Air France airliner, en route from Frankfurt to Paris, was hijacked by three men claiming to be members of the Liberation of Quds (Jerusalem) organisation. This was believed to be a code name for Abu Nidal, who was then working in conjunction with Hezbollah in Lebanon. The pilot was ordered to fly the plane to Tehran. Upon landeding the hijackers demanded the release of five men being held in France on the charge of attempting in 1982 to murder Shahpour Bakhtiar, the former shahist prime minister, then in exile in France. The French government refused, and a similar charade of 'siege, surrender and asylum' was enacted by the Iranian authorities.

However the Iranian government was often the loser. For example on 6 July 1983 an Iran Air Boeing 747 flying from Dubai to Tehran was hijacked by five members of the Iranian opposition Mujahedeen Khalk, after making a scheduled stop at Shiraz in southern Iran. The pilot was ordered to fly the airliner to Paris. During a refuelling stop at Kuwait, many of the passengers were released. The plane landed at Orly Airport, Paris, on the 7th, whereupon the hijackers demanded the release of Mujahedeen Khalk members being held by the Iranian government. Masoud Rajavi, leader of the Mujahedeen Khalk and exiled in Paris, while loudly denying any prior knowledge of the incident, persuaded the hijackers to release their hostages and surrender to the police.

The Iranian government demanded the extradition of the five hijackers, but the French refused and instead granted them asylum, which infuriated Speaker Rafsanjani, who declared 'Iran will take revenge' (IRNA).

Another Iranian misfortune occurred on 8 September 1984, when an Iranian airliner on a internal flight from Tehran to Bandar Abbas was hijacked by a Mujahedeen Khalk member. The pilot was forced to fly first to Bahrain, then to Cairo and then to Baghdad, where the passengers and crew were released and the hijacker was afforded asylum.

Previously, on 7 August 1984, an Iranian Airbus carrying Iranian pilgrims to Mecca had been hijacked by two members of the Mujahedeen Khalk. The pilot complied with their order to fly to Paris, making refuelling stops at Bahrain and Cairo. The French refused to accept the aircraft, which landed instead at Rome, where the passengers and crew were released. After demanding the freedom of comrades held in Iranian detention, the hijackers surrendered. The Tehran government demanded their extradition, but Italy refused and put them on trial. One was convicted and sentenced to a term of imprisonment, the other was acquitted and afforded sanctuary. The plane was returned to Iran.

Next, on 4 December a Kuwaiti airliner flying from Kuwait to Karachi was hijacked during a stopover at Dubai in the United Arab Emirates. A five-man Dawa team forced the pilot to fly the plane to Tehran, demanding the release of the Kuwaiti-17. In the hijacking process an American United Nations official was killed. Having landed at Tehran, the aircraft was farcically surrounded by a security ring and a period of waiting began, during which the hijackers shot and killed another American UN official and ill-treated some of the American and Kuwaiti passengers. On the 9th Iranian forces 'stormed' the plane, released all the hostages and 'arrested' the hijackers.

It seems this exploit was carried out by Dawa with Khomeini's direct approval and the help of Hezbollah in Lebanon, but the local Tehran authorities seemed to have been caught by surprise. They responded in a conventional manner to impress the watching world, so that no blame would rest on Iran. President Reagan was not fooled, and commented that 'Iran is not being as helpful as it could, or should be' (*New York Times*). Kuwait demanded the extradition of the hijackers, but Iran refused, saying they would be put on trial, although the plane was eventually returned. Nothing more was heard of them, so presumably they safely made their way back to their base in the Bekaa Valley in Lebanon.

These incidents resulted in the formation of a highly trained group of 'anti-hijacking' commandos as an official part of the Pasdaran. Armed guards were provided on Iranian passenger aircraft, especially on internal flights. Several hijackings were thwarted, including an attempted one on 12 August 1984 on a flight from Tehran to Shiraz, when five individuals were 'arrested'. Nothing more was heard of them. Another attempt was made on the 17th between Tehran and Bushir, when again three men were 'arrested' and disappeared from view. A third attempt was thwarted on 4 October 1984 on an airliner flying from Mashhad to Tehran, with a similar outcome; and on 5 August 1985, on a flight from Tehran to Bandar Abbas, one hijacker was shot dead and his accomplice arrested. The Mujahedeen Khalk was largely thought to be responsible for this early spate of aircraft hijackings, but its failures seemed to cause it to abandon this particular tactic. Being taken into Iranian custody for such a crime was a most unpleasant prospect, and seemingly acted as a deterrent.

BEIRUT AIRPORT

Security at airports and in relation to air travel in general was tightened up, but certain countries dragged their heels owing to a shortage of funds or lack of professionalism, and some by deliberate neglect. Airports were soon graded accordingly. Beirut airport had a bad reputation. On 12 June 1985, for example, a Jordanian airliner, hijacked after leaving Amman by six 'Shia gunmen', led by 'Nazir', landed at Beirut airport after deviating by way of Cyprus, Tunis and Palermo. After the passengers had disembarked the plane was blown up on the tarmac and hijackers disappeared into adjacent Amal-held territory. It was also alleged that many aircraft hijackings and aerial incidents originated from Beirut, and that terrorists were able to use it during their international travels.

The US State Department and other Western governments were probably secretly hoping that sufficient provocation might cause Israel to make a raid on Beirut airport to destroy its control installations, and thus put it out of action. But Israel hesitated, even though it had done it once before, on 28 December 1968.

HEZBOLLAH LEADERSHIP

As it gained expertise and confidence the Hezbollah umbrella organisation in the Bekaa Valley, although heavily involved in terrorism in Lebanon, began to think in terms of hijacking to extend its growing fearsome reputation and destabilise its enemies. While it appears that the activists in its constituent groups liaised reasonably well together, with the exception perhaps of Dawa, there was still some confusion at the top level. Sheikh Abbas Moussawi of Hezbollah had become the prominent military leader in the Bekaa Valley and southern Lebanon. Moussawi was a good rabble-rouser by nature, but was not autonomous. Sheikh Mahmoud Hussein Fadlallah,

Hezbollah's spiritual guide, was also keenly interested in terrorism. The Iranian ambassadors in Syria and Lebanon also regarded themselves as part of the Hezbollah leadership.

Any casual utterance by Khomeini, subsequently publicised by his son Ahmad, who was virtually his private secretary, was regarded by all Iranians as a gospel commandment that had to be obeyed. Although his many utterances might be interpreted variously, they could not be ignored, no matter how trivial, irritating or frivolous. Now ageing, and perhaps regarding the Majlis with some suspicion, Khomeini seemed to distance himself from it. Speaker Rafsanjani, who apparently was allowed to run his own agenda, was preparing for the future, while Khomeini was preparing for death and his succession. Khomeini's oft-repeated remark that 'permission is not required to strike at the Satans', encouraged several factions to try freelance activities that sometimes clashed with Hezbollah plans.

The original nature of Amal, still led by Nabih Berri, had changed as Berri was using it to further his political ambitions. By the beginning of 1984 his Amal militia was the largest and probably the most powerful in Lebanon. In February that year it took possession of the airport and control of the streets of Beirut' by force of arms. Berri became minister of justice in the Government of National Reconstruction, and as a consequence tried desperately to divorce himself from both terrorism and his former lieutenant, Hussein Moussawi, who had veered away from him into the orbit of Hezbollah. Berri, a secular leader, also tried to shake free from Hezbollah constraints and the religious ambitions of Ayatollah Khomeini. He sought to play a prominent part in a new, multiracial, multireligious Lebanon, Hussein Moussawi had wider Shia religious–political ambitions, and as leader of the 'suicide force' was already a major executive in Khomeini's secret wars against his 'enemies'.

In May 1985 Berri's Amal militia and its 6th Brigade (a former Lebanese-government Shia brigade that had defected to him) began an attack on the three Palestinian refugee camps around Beirut, which contained armed factions. That month was a particularly bloody one, even by Lebanese standards, as almost 600 people were killed on the streets of Beirut.

THE TWA HIJACKING: 14–30 JUNE 1985

In June 1985 a Shia team, assembled by Hussein Moussawi, hijacked an American Trans-World Airlines (TWA) airliner and so began a saga that spellbound TV viewers throughout the world for the 16 days it was in progress. On the 14th, at about 8 a.m., a TWA Boeing 727 en route from Cairo to Rome with 153 people on board, mainly American, was hijacked by two Hezbollah terrorists armed with pistols and grenades, just after the plane had taken off from a stopover in Athens. Telephone calls were received in media offices in Beirut claiming the two hijackers were members of Islamic Jihad, then thought to be merely an operational code name. Western intelligence seemed to lack positive information about the structure of Hezbollah at that time, but in fairness it should be said that detection was clouded by a welter of confusing local communiques, claims, rumours and propaganda, much of it fictional. For a time it was generally assumed that Hezbollah was a fanatical Islamic religious–political party, while Islamic Amal was its terrorist arm that sometimes used the code name Islamic Jihad.

The team of highjackers was originally composed of three men: its leader, Fawaz Younis, code named 'Nazir' (it is not known whether this was the same man who had hijacked the Jordanian aircraft) and Ahmad Gharbeh and Ali Atwa, who had arrived in Athens early that morning to book on to the targeted flight. However only two seats were available, so Atwa was left behind. As soon as news broke of the hijacking, just minutes after the plane had taken off, Atwa and others with him were arrested in the security dragnet operation that immediately swung into action at the airport.

Nazir forced the TWA pilot to divert the airliner to Beirut airport, where it landed at nine in the morning. The hijackers had expected to be met by Amal militiamen, but none were there. Nabih Berri had not been informed of their arrival, nor that he was expected to collaborate with them. He said later that when he had heard the hijacked aircraft was approaching Beirut he had tried to prevent it from landing.

At that particular moment, although the Amal militia controlled a major part of the perimeter, several other armed factions in Beirut were clinging tenaciously to 'foothold access' to the airport. Despite these disadvantages, the airport continued to function somehow, as it was in the interests of most factions that it should. Hezbollah had no direct access of its own, but could enter through the Shia Amal militia sector adjacent to Beirut's southern suburbs. Amal militia had virtual control of the airport buildings. This terrorist hiccup demonstrated the growing divergence between Berri and the Hezbollah leadership.

On the runway a waiting team of six Hezbollah terrorists, led by Imad Moughniyeh, went aboard the TWA aircraft. After the airport authorities had been forced to refuel the plane and 19 hostages had been released, mainly women and children, the plane took off again at about 10.30 a.m., bound for Algiers. The hijackers, now eight in number, became violent towards the people on board, slapping and punching some of them.

The airliner arrived at Algiers airport about 2.30 p.m. (all times are local), and a further 22 hostages were released, mainly Arab women and children. The terrorists made known their demands, particularly the instant release of 660 Lebanese and Palestinians in Israeli detention – these being the remainder of the some 1200 who had been detained in southern Lebanon during the first months of the Israeli occupation, and subsequently moved to the Altit Detention Camp in Israel – and certain other individuals, in return for the safety of the aircraft and the hostages. Failure to meet these demands or even a delay, would mean that the hostages would be killed one by one.

The terrorists also demanded the instant release of their comrade, Ali Atwa, who had been left behind in Athens (if this demand was not met 'seven Greek' hostages on the plane would be killed), and that the Cypriot authorities release Atef Raya, a Lebanese Shia jailed in Cyprus for his part in the hijacking of a Romanian aircraft in 1983. After refuelling, the TWA 727 airliner left Algiers and headed back to Beirut.

Beirut to Algiers and back again

The hijacked plane arrived back at Beirut airport about 7 p.m. and taxied to a spot near the control tower buildings. This time the Amal militia was waiting for Moughniyeh, as was Nabih

Berri. Moughniyeh wanted Berri to cooperate with them and become their official negotiator, but Berri hesitated. An astute politician, Berri wanted to distance himself from this terrorist exploit. Impatient at this unexpected hesitation, at about 11.30 p.m. one of the terrorists, believed to have been Fawaz Younis, shot and killed a hostage – Robert Stretham, an American serviceman. His body was thrown out of the aircraft into the darkness, the thud of it hitting the tarmac being clearly heard in the silence of the night by watching airport staff and journalists, who by this time had assembled in force to cover yet another 'terrorist spectacular'. Berri sent four of his armed Amal militiamen on board to ensure that no more hostages were killed.

Once refuelled, the TWA 727 took off and returned to Algiers, arriving at about 7 a.m. on the 15th. During the day small batches of hostages were successively released. Ali Atwa arrived in Algiers in the afternoon, having been released from Greek custody, and the Greek hostages were freed. Nothing was heard of Atef Raya. The hijackers again demanded the release of the Lebanese held in Israel, which country placed a news blackout on all Hezbollah's demands. The deadline was set for 9 a.m. on the 16th.

After refuelling, at about 8 a.m. on the 16th the hijacked airliner again left Algiers for Beirut. By now there were 44 hostages on board – the pilot, three crew members and 40 passengers, all American – as well as nine terrorists and four Amal militiamen. They arrived about noon to face the international media, many in grandstand positions, marshalled by Amal militiamen. It was a day of negotiations, with the terrorists refusing to release any more hostages until Israel began to free its prisoners, which it refused to do. On several occasions, clearly for the benefit of the TV cameras, the pilot appeared at his cockpit window with a terrorist behind him holding a pistol to his head.

Confused negotiations

The terrorists inside the airliner seemed determined, but outside there was confusion as Israel was refusing to accede to the terrorists' demands. Nabih Berri, Sheikh Fadlallah and the Iranian Ambassador to Lebanon conferred with each other, and then with a horde of Lebanese government and American officials, and indirectly with Israel. On this occasion Red Cross representatives, who were normally foremost in negotiations, hung back as they had previously had unfortunate misunderstandings with Israel.

The US government's concern for the safety of its nationals was patent and aggressive, and it tried both sabre rattling and diplomacy. Delta Force, its ace antiterrorist unit, was reported to be leaving its base at Fort Bragg in the United States, and the US 6th Fleet in the Mediterranean was said to be steaming towards the Lebanese coast. Americans referred to the hijackers as 'Shia Lebanese gunmen', and pilloried Nabih Berri as leader of Amal, holding him responsible for the safety of the American hostages.

During the night of the 16th Berri insisted that all hostages with Jewish sounding names be removed from the aircraft and hidden away in the southern suburbs under Amal control. Later Berri was accused of having made a secret deal with Israel to this effect, although it was never made public whether there were in fact any Israeli or Jewish hostages. Israel was silent on this point for obvious reasons, as were the terrorists for less obvious ones. It was generally assumed that were none on the plane, as if there had been it was thought the Israeli government would have been more flexible and willing to trade prisoners for hostages. Later, one released hostage revealed that he was Jewish, but had concealed the fact.

An unnamed American business magnate offered to pay a ransom of $3 million for the safe release of all the hostages and the aircraft, but his offer was abruptly refused by Imad Moughniyeh, who replied, 'We don't want money. We want to die'.

Another sick hostage was released on the 17th, a day when the terrorists played the international media for all they were worth, with shouted questions and answers. TV cameras were allowed fairly close to the aircraft, and the pilot again had to make dramatic appearances with a terrorist pistol at his head. Two-way conversations between terrorists on the plane and negotiators in the control tower were 'caught' by the media and relayed live around the world. Food was periodically taken out to the aircraft.

On the night of the 17th all remaining hostages were taken from the aircraft by Amal militiamen, a decision made by

Berri as there was apprehension that a US military rescue bid might be attempted. The following day three more sick hostages were released. This left 40 American hostages still in Amal hands, of whom four, all servicemen, were taken by Islamic Amal to the Bekaa Valley. The remainder were divided into five small groups and hidden away in the southern, Amal-controlled, suburbs of the city. The terrorists remained on the airliner.

A period of tension ensued as Berri tried, for his own political ends, to free as many of the Labanese prisoners in Israel as possible, but Israel pleaded confusion over names and aliases, alleging there was duplication that needed time to sort out. Israel was reluctant to make public the true identities of its prisoners, especially when it was thought that their names were not known to the terrorists. The previous month (May 1985) Israel had reluctantly exchanged 1150 prisoners for three captured Israeli soldiers. Eventually Berri was able to persuade them to agree to release 435 detainees, which after some mumbling seemed acceptable to Hezbollah.

Amal press conference

On the 21st Amal arranged a press conference in the airport lounge, which was soon packed with media representatives. When five hostages were led in there was a rush towards them and a mad media scramble ensued. One hostage, acting as spokesman, read from a prepared statement. He said that all the hostages were being treated reasonably well, and that 'our future is in the hands of all the people involved in this', but would say no more. A hooded gunman warned the United States of further hijacking if the Lebanese prisoners were not freed by Israel.

Investigative journalists sought – by bribery and promises to further the terrorists' propaganda – exclusive interviews with both the terrorists and the hostages in their Amal hideouts. It became an undignified scramble for exclusive news, in which ethics were pushed aside.

Realising that neither sabre rattling nor diplomacy were producing any results, President Reagan had to 'stoop to conquer'. Smothering his pride, Reagan made a personal telephone call to President Assad of Syria to ask for his help.

Assad, who was openly siding with Iran in its ongoing war with Iraq, had been accused by the CIA of supporting terrorism, harbouring several international terrorists in Damascus, and being in league with Hezbollah. Assad seized this opportunity to step on to the international stage in support of the United States. By threatening to withdraw all cooperation with Hezbollah, he persuaded the latter not to harm the four American hostages it had taken to the Bekaa Valley. A White House aide was reputed to have said 'It took us some time to find the right man, but when we did, one word from him was sufficient'. Assad's price included US pressure on Israel to release Syrian prisoners, and perhaps other things that were not mentioned publicly at the time.

Although Berri thought he had accomplished the hardest part of the negotiations, which was to persuade Israel to agree to release some its prisoners, he had one more task to accomplish. The United States was planning a heavy military retribution against Amal and Hezbollah camps, in the form of air strikes and naval gun bombardments. President Reagan was angry, very angry, and the Americans wanted revenge. When the suicide attacks had been made on US troops in Lebanon in 1983, causing great loss of life, the United States had made no aggressive response, and Hezbollah was still striking at US citizens. Reagan knew how to please his people and had sent US warships, with aircraft on board and armed with powerful guns, to lie just off the Lebanese coast, waiting for the last American hostage to be freed. On the 22nd Berri warned the United States not to sabre rattle. It seemed the hijackers were prepared to sit it out in the aircraft for a long time. American patience gave way first.

By the 24th Berri had obtained grudging agreement from Robert McFarlane, national security adviser to the president, that the United States would not commit any acts of reprisal on Lebanese territory; and the same day Israel released 37 prisoners unconnected with the hijacking negotiations. The following day Speaker Rafsanjani, in Tehran, openly condemned the TWA hijacking, asserting that if he had known about it in advance he would have tried to prevent it from happening. This seemed to confirm the assumption that Hezbollah took its orders direct from Ayatollah Khomeini, thus by-passing the Majlis.

Even so there were delays, and it was not until 30 June that Nabih Berri gathered together in a school room near the airport perimeter the 35 hostages who had been scattered among Amal safe houses. There was then a wait while the four US servicemen were brought in from the Bekaa Valley to join them. When they arrived the 39 released hostages, together with Red Cross personnel, who had latterly come more fully into the negotiations, left West Beirut in a convoy of cars for Damascus. Later that same day they were all flown to Frankfurt in West Germany.

Meanwhile Imad Moughniyeh and Fawaz Younis, together with their Hezbollah colleagues and the four Amal militiamen, simply walked away from the aircraft into Amal-held territory in southern Beirut. One sting from the American tail came a little later, on 18 September, in furtherance of President Reagan's 'You can run but you can't hide' policy. In 'Operation Golden Rod' CIA agents snatched Fawaz Younis from a rented yacht in the eastern Mediterranean, near Cyprus, and transferred him to a US warship as a first step towards his standing trial in the United States. His fingerprints had been found on the hijacked aircraft.

The release of the Lebanese and Palestinian detainees in Israel took a little longer, but was effected within a comparatively short time under the auspices of the Red Cross. Israel took care to keep the names of those released from the press, as did most of those involved, for their own reasons. There was, as always, as much hard bargaining over certain individuals as over total numbers. One surprise release was Kojo Okomoto, a member of the Japanese Red Army and sole survivor of the three terrorists who had committed the 'Lod Massacre' in May 1972. In that incident 25 Israelis had been killed and 72 injured when automatic weapons had been fired randomly into the airport departure lounge. Okomoto was a prize prisoner of Israel, and the Israelis must have been loath to part with him. One wonders what Israel's price was, and who paid it. Okomoto, a terrorist hero, disappeared into anonymity and is probably still at large somewhere.

A few weeks later the US State Department expressed its displeasure to the French government for not arresting Imad Moughniyeh after the CIA tipped off the French security services that he was in France. Moughniyeh's fingerprints too were on the hijacked aircraft.

Another terrorist victory

However much spin US and Israeli officialdom put on the TWA incident, they could not disguise the fact that it had been an outstandingly successful terrorist spectacular that had largely obtained its objective and held the attention of many millions of TV viewers throughout the world for three weeks. The terrorists had escaped scot-free, one American had been killed and Israel had been forced to release prisoners (this had been done in four batches, the last transfer being made on 10 September), thus breaking its principle of refusing to exchange prisoners for hostages. The volume of publicity – the lifeblood of terrorism – gained by Hezbollah was beyond price. The United States had again been humiliated, its president having had to ask an avowed enemy for help, which had been given. The much-vaunted US Delta antiterrorist force, at its home base in Fort Bragg in the United States, had been too far from Lebanon to be of any instant use. In any case it would would not have been allowed to operate either in Lebanon or Algeria. Thus a world superpower had been unable to prevail against a tiny group of determined terrorists. In Tehran the unworldly Khomeini must have smiled a self-satisfied smile, convinced that his course was divinely preordained, but Hezbollah leaders in the Bekaa Valley had been only partially sated.

Nabih Berri, who had initially wanted no part in the exploit, had been the key to the terrorists' success, and finding himself trapped in the slipstream of events, had had no option but to go along with it. He had trodden through a minefield of negotiations with skill and care. Credit for saving the lives of the hostages (after the first one had been killed) should go jointly to President Assad and Nabih Berri, themselves regarded as 'terrorists' by the US CIA. There was little doubt that the hijackers had intended to kill more hostages, while Hezbollah most probably had intended to kill the four US servicemen who had been whisked away to the Bekaa Valley.

AN ISLAMIC FUNDAMENTALIST REAPPRAISAL

The TWA hijacking had seemingly brought the United States – still smarting over the 1980–82 US embassy hostage saga and the attacks on its armed contingent in the multinational force in Lebanon by suicide drivers – in exasperation to teeter on the verge of a military invasion of Lebanon, which could have seeped over into Syria. Certainly President Assad had real anxieties in this respect. Senior Shia fundamentalist religious leaders were shocked and appalled by the number of personalities who had involved themselves in the negotiations when the situation had stalled, spoiling their exclusivity. It had brought a cold blast of realism, not only to the members of Hezbollah in the Bekaa Valley, but also to the leadership in Tehran, when it had become obvious that their 'allies' – Assad of Syria and Berri of Lebanon – were not wholeheartedly with them in their determined 'march to Jerusalem', but probably had completely different nationalist agendas.

The senior Shia clerics who controlled events in Iran and the Hezbollah in the Bekaa Valley had all been educated and conditioned at religious colleges. Their curriculum had been almost completely devoid of accurate information about the West, and of international relations. Few had visited a Western country in their youth or travelled outside Muslim territories, and consequently their international 'knowledge' had been gathered from Western TV programmes and their own propaganda machines, causing them to regard Westerners as decadent, morally weak, drug- and crime-ridden, and lacking positive resolve. This attitude was reinforced by the fact that the United States had exacted no military retribution against Iran for the US embassy hostage saga, nor in response to the Hezbollah suicide attacks in Lebanon. Some Shia Iranian leaders had been anticipating a fairly easy ride on their 'March to Jerusalem', as their Great Satan seemed to have no teeth, only bravado and empty threats. There were few pragmatists amongst them on this subject, as most had become victims of Khomeini's, and their own, rhetoric.

From bitter experience both President Assad (a member of the minor, way-out Alawite Shia sect) and Nabih Berri (a Shia) had a good understooding of international relations, secular pressures and ambitions. Both were survivors, and neither wanted to preside over a fundamentalist Shia state and become part of Khomeini's Shia empire. Ayatollahs and other senior clerics in Tehran had now come to realise that both men were using them for their own personal ends, and not for the greater glory of Khomeini. Assad was siding with Iran in the ongoing Iran–Iraq War only because Saddam Hussein was his rival in the Baathist socialist dream world.

Berri had ambitions to preside over a multireligious, multiracial Lebanon, where tolerance would be a key factor in its cohesion, not military conquest or religious might. Berri regarded the resident Palestinians as invaders, and was actively fighting them, but his sights were on Beirut, not Jerusalem. These unsettling thoughts caused the Khomeini leadership to become more cautious lest the United States be provoked by 'one hijack too many'. However Hezbollah fanatics continued to tweak the lion's tail.

THE DAWA HIJACKING: 5–20 APRIL 1988

It was almost three years before the next major Hezbollah hijacking occurred. This was to have been a smoother and more sophisticated rerun of the TWA one in 1985, the object being the release of the Kuwaiti-17. On 5 April 1988 a Kuwaiti Boeing 747 aircraft en route from Bangkok to Kuwait was hijacked over the Arabian Sea by a team of seven unidentified terrorists armed with pistols and grenades. There were 112 people on board, mostly Kuwaitis, including three members of the Kuwaiti royal family and 15 crew. The terrorists ordered the pilot to divert the plane to Mashhad in northern Iran. Weapons were thought to have been smuggled aboard in Bangkok, as after the plane had been given security clearance it had stood for 15 hours on an apron, during which time cleaners had worked on it. Bangkok's reputation for airport security was not rated very highly by the International Air Transport Association (IATA).

The hijacked Kuwaiti airliner arrived at Mashhad airport at about 4 p.m. The airport authorities declared that its arrival had been 'unexpected', and that they had only allowed it to land for humanitarian reasons. The Tehran government was angered by this unwelcome exploit, and to distance itself a farcical demonstration was organised for international consumption. The plane was surrounded by security personnel, no one was allowed near it and little information, or access, was given to journalists.

It seemed to be a case of the right hand not knowing what the left hand was doing, although according to PLO sources the whole exploit had been formulated by the Iranian interior minister, Ali Akbar Mohtashemi, with the full approval and authority of Ayatollah Khomeini. Nonetheless the Tehran government may not have had prior knowledge of this hijacking, but Hezbollah certainly had, proof being that waiting at Mashhad airport was a team of eight terrorists, led by Imad Moughniyeh (the leader of the TWA hijacking), who replaced the original team and immediately took charge of the situation. Both teams behaved very professionally–they either wore hoods or covered their faces with scarves, seldom spoke to each other in the presence of the hostages, and never mentioned each other's names. The first team, which had been travelling on false passports and had probably altered their appearance, also donned hoods and scarves when the hijacking commenced, which was probably the reason why none could be identified.

The first-class section of the aircraft was turned into the terrorists' 'operation room', and passengers were bundled out into the remaining space. They were kept in cramped conditions and their wrists were bound together. Some were periodically slapped and given other rough treatment. Weapons, ammunition and sophisticated communication equipment were loaded on to the plane, which was refuelled.

The Iranian deputy prime minister, Ali Reza Moayeri, was rushed to the scene from Tehran. The following day (the 10th) he 'persuaded' the hijackers to release 24 non-Kuwaiti women hostages. A Kuwaiti delegation arrived, and later that day other non-Kuwaiti hostages were released. Moayeri then tried to persuade the Kuwaiti delegation to agree to release the Kuwaiti-17, in exchange for the safety of the remainder of the hostages, now all Kuwaitis. When he found out that the Kuwaiti delegation had no authority to do this, he cut the negotiations short. Iran's excuse for its inaction was that to storm the plane would endanger the lives of the hostages.

Khomeini's plan

The hijacked Kuwaiti airliner took off from Mashhad at about noon on 8 April 1988, bound for Beirut. The airliner had been diverted to Mashhad to release non-Kuwaiti hostages, refuel, and exchange the hijacking team for another one, with the experienced and capable Imad Moughniyeh in charge. The airliner was to land at Beirut airport in an attempt to attract international publicity (of which little was gained in Mashhad). After an international media photo opportunity, the plan was to separate the Kuwaiti hostages into small groups and have them taken by Hezbollah to secret hideouts in Lebanon.

The airliner arrived over Beirut airport at about 4 p.m. and asked for permission to land, but was refused. This was the first real adverse surprise for the hijackers. The aircraft circled the airport and further requests to land were made, but were again refused. The aircraft circled lower and lower, and the hijackers threatened to crash-land it. Syrian army anti-aircraft gunners fired shots towards the aircraft, while Syrian voices in the control tower threatened to shoot it down if it did not go away.

The situation around Beirut airport had changed considerably since June 1985, something Mohtashemi and Khomeini did not seem to appreciate, which reinforces the point that the Iranian fundamentalist leadership was out of touch with current external events, had conducted no analysis of them and barely understood their significance. The Syrian army, now in control of the airport, was at loggerheads with Hezbollah and Amal, neither of which had even a toehold on the airport perimeter. Furthermore Nabih Berri's Amal militia was now in conflict with both the Syrian army and Hezbollah.

The hijackers were at a loss to know what to do about this unexpected turn of events, and fuel was getting dangerously low. Permission to land in Damascus was refused, but in the nick of time the Cypriot authorities said they would accept the aircraft on humanitarian grounds. One wonders what inducements were offered. The plane arrived in Cyprus at Larnaca airport at about 9.30 p.m. and was directed to the far end of the runway. There it was surrounded by security personnel. Something had gone wrong at the Khomeini–Hezbollah level: this terrorist operation was certainly not going according to plan.

The hijacked plane and its hostages remained on the tarmac at Larnaca for six days. Repeated demands for refuelling were refused. Both the US and the British government were bringing pressure on the Cypriot authorities not to allow the plane to leave under any circumstances. A war of nerves followed, with the hijackers referring back to their 'higher authority', generally understood to be Tehran.

At 9.30 a.m. on the 9th a hostage was shot dead. His body, head hooded, was pushed out of the aircraft on to the concrete runway. Later that day the hijackers released one hostage to 'show good will', but a second hostage was shot dead on the 11th, his body too being pushed out of the plane. The terrorists threatened to kill more hostages unless the aircraft was refuelled.

International TV drama

The ongoing drama drew the international media en masse to the scene in anticipation of a repeat of the TWA hijacking, and also hordes of local people and holidaymakers as the plane was isolated at the end of the runway in full view from a public road that ran adjacent to the perimeter fencing. Security personnel were withdrawn from the proximity of the plane, which stood in splendid isolation, apart from a makeshift booth that had been erected for negotiators to use when talking to the hijackers. Media boredom soon set in, as apart from the occasional comings and going of the negotiators, and food deliveries, little activity was visible at all. In the meantime business at Larnaca airport continued as normal.

On the plane, still with their hands tied together, the hostages were suffering increasing discomfort and knew nothing of what was happening on the outside. The hijackers carefully monitored international radio news bulletins and were in constant radio contact with the airport control tower. They seemed to have a detailed knowledge of the aviation world, calling themselves 'Kuwait-422' (the flight number of their aircraft). They remained cool and calm; there were no histrionics or raised voices when demands were refused. When they killed the first hostage, their spokesman merely said on the radio 'Send a coffin and an ambulance'. A Kuwaiti negotiating team arrived, but as they had no authority to release the Kuwati-17 the negotiations again stalemated.

On the 11th Yasser Arafat (chairman of the PLO, who had been attending a meeting of the Islamic Conference

Organisation in Kuwait) arrived. His local Cyprus representative had already contacted the hijackers and he thought, from their accents, that there were 'four Lebanese, two Bahrainis and two others'.

On the 12th the hijackers resorted to drama in an effort to change the mind of the Emir of Kuwait. Several of them donned shrouds and briefly showed themselves to the media in this macabre garb, but to no avail. The terrorists also named the aircraft the 'Plane of Great Martyrs'. That day they had a sudden fright when a US military C-130 transport aircraft, on a routine flight from Athens, landed at Larnaca airport. The terrorists feared that an antiterrorist rescue squad had arrived, but calmed down when they were assured that this was not so.

Departure for Algiers

Early in the morning of 13 April 1988 the aircraft was refuelled – Arafat claimed the credit for this. It was noted that the terrorist overseeing the operation told the airport staff exactly which lubricants were required for the engines and used the correct technical terms, which denoted expert knowledge. The aircraft took off from Larnaca at about 1 p.m. and arrived in Algiers at about 7 p.m. When agreeing to allow the Kuwaiti airliner to land, the Algerian authorities had stipulated that it should not be stormed while on Algerian soil, although it was said that this information was not passed on to the terrorists. The aircraft stood on the tarmac at Algiers airport for seven days while tense negotiations took place. A doctor was allowed on board, and on the 14th one hostage was released.

The Emir of Kuwait remained adamant about his refusal to release the Kuwaiti-17. On the 17th the terrorists held a brief press conference on the steps of the plane, the media being allowed to approach closely. The spokesman stated that they were determined to hold out until the Kuwaiti-17 were released, but if this failed to happen they would blow up the aircraft with all on board, stating that primed explosives had been already placed in position. A deadline was set for the following day, but this was progressively extended.

By this time three Arab heads of state were conferring with each other: President Bendjedid Chadli of Algeria, the Emir of

Kuwait and King Fahd of Saudi Arabia. They agreed to a plan to allow the terrorists to escape, on condition they did not harm the hostages or damage the plane. It was obvious that the Emir of Kuwait was not going to change his mind. Arafat was in on this plan as he relied heavily on Kuwait for support (Kuwait had a large Palestinian population), but he was not keen on it and appeared to have secret thoughts of getting his hands on the terrorists himself. Nonetheless he had to go along with it.

On the 19th the Algerian foreign minister visited Colonel Gaddafi of Libya, ostensibly to talk about an oil pipeline, but in fact to enlist his cooperation. Gaddafi agreed.

The terrorists escape

The hijacking came to a sudden end at about about 4.30 a.m. on 20 April. At the break of dawn an aircraft door opened and the hostages began to emerge. Their walk to freedom was recorded by TV cameras, the international media having already been alerted. Thirty-six hostages left the aircraft – 31 passengers and five crew members, all Kuwaiti. It was assumed that the Kuwaiti-17 remained in detention, but it is believed that in fact two of them were exchanged for the hostages, although this was firmly denied by all concerned. According to PLO sources, Arafat being one of the negotiators, the Kuwaiti-17 had become the Kuwaiti-15. Later, when Saddam Hussein invaded Kuwait in August 1990, they were seized by him, and as all were members of Dawa, an anti-Saddam Hussein organisation, their fate was probably a most unpleasant one.

While all attention was focused on the emerging hostages, the eight terrorists quietly slipped away through a rear exit on the other side of the plane. In the semi-darkness they were taken to a military airfield, and thence flown to Libya, and freedom. Gaddafi had agreed to return them to Lebanon. The real identities of the hijackers were left to speculation, only that of Imad Moughniyeh, the leader of the second team, being officially confirmed. The CIA and other national intelligence agencies later claimed they had been able to photograph the terrorists as they slipped from the plane, but refused to name any of them. If this was so, there might have been some double-dealing on the part of the Algerians, who would have wanted this information for their own records. Also, as the aircraft was left intact there would have been a treasure trove of fingerprints to examine.

Kuwait openly blamed the Iranian government for the hijacking, alleging that Ayatollah Khomeini was manipulating the Lebanese-based Hezbollah, which was targeting Kuwait because it had been siding with, and aiding, President Saddam Hussein in the ongoing Iran–Iraq War. The Tehran government blithely denied all these allegations.

The critique

Intended to be an improved version of the TWA hijacking in 1985, that of April 1988 was a blundering failure from Khomeini's point of view. It had started well, arriving at Mashhad according to plan, but then had gone wrong because its planners had not understood the current Lebanese situation and the new attitude of the Syrian army, which was in confrontation with both the Amal militia and Hezbollah. Once it had landed in Cyprus, no one had seemed in a hurry to storm the plane. A PLO official cynically told me later that, as no Americans or Western citizens had been on board and in danger, the Western negotiators had been glad to see it depart from Europe for an Arab country.

In Algiers the Arab negotiators had tried to persuade the Emir of Kuwait to release the Kuwaiti-17, but he had surprised them all, including Westerners, by remaining adamant. The hijacking had been brought to a tame end due to the emir's attitude and sheer exhaustion on the part of the terrorists. Some thought that the terrorists' resolve had been further weakened by the approach of the month of Ramadan, when all good Muslims are required to fast during daylight hours.

For Hezbollah it had proved to be a 'no win, no lose' venture. International TV coverage had been disappointing, as media interest had tended to wane when it dragged on for so long. The Kuwaiti-17 (or Kuwaiti-15) remained in prison, but all the terrorists had escaped unhurt. For the Kuwaitis a major disaster had been avoided at the cost of two dead hostages (and the disputable Kuwaiti-2). Hezbollah had lost some of its air of infallibility and prestige. The West lavished praise on the emir for his resolute stand against terrorism. No one was wholly satisfied, but no one was all that disappointed, except perhaps Ayatollah Khomeini, Minister of the Interior Ali Akbar Mohtashemi, Deputy Prime Minister Ali Reza Moayeri and Imad Moughniyeh. The pragmatic Speaker Rafsanjani, and others who felt they should have been consulted, kept their own counsel.

A PASDARAN HIJACK

Back in Iran, cracks were appearing in the formerly strong loyalty of the Pasdaran to the Islamic Revolution. Defection and desertion became rife in the latter part of the Iran–Iraq War, and more so in the postwar period. On 21 June 1990 four dissident Pasdaran members, armed with grenades and a pistol, tricked their way on board an Iran Air Boeing 727 plane on an internal flight from Shiraz to Bandar Abbas, and attempted to hijack it. An official statement later claimed that 'No passengers were hurt, but the anti-hijack security guards killed all four, and the plane landed safely'. The culprits were branded as 'mercenaries of the world-devouring United States'. It was later added that this had been the sixteenth hijacking attempt to be successfully foiled by the anti-hijacking Pasdaran security guards since their formation in 1984.

The cracks in the Pasdaran's loyalty reflected the tussle between Ayatollah Montazeri, Khomeini's former nominated successor, and Rafsanjani, who had been elected president in July 1989 and was trying to reduce the power of the senior clergy in political and secular matters. It was said that the would-be hijackers were Montazeri supporters.

6 The Western Hostage Saga, 1984–92

On 17 January 1982 in Tehran, Ayatollah Khomeini held a special reception in honour of the 'Organisation of Islamic Students Following the Imam's Line', a sort of old comrades association of the survivors of the 400 revolutionary students who had stormed the US embassy on 4 November and held the Americans hostage for 444 days. Having taken part in the episode had become a revolutionary battle honour. The survivors were treated as heroes, and many were in positions of importance in government, administration and commerce. Still young, enthusiastic and active, as individuals they wielded considerable influence. Participation in the US embassy siege was a good thing to have on one's record.

The students had promised to return to their studies when the embassy saga was over, but the universities had been closed. In addition the war with Iraq had begun, so their energies were directed into other channels. For example Mohammed Moussavi Khoiniha, the students' leader throughout the siege, became deputy speaker of the Majlis. Two others became ministers, while Morteza Moussavi, who had led the original raiding party, became a senior executive in the Ministry of Intelligence and Security (sometimes referred to as the Ministry of Information and Security).

A small group of the students became successful publishers, having taken the opportunity to seize all documents found in the US embassy. The embassy staff had been feverishly shredding security documents when they were attacked, but a goldmine of classified documents remained unshredded, as despite ominous warning signs they had been caught by surprise in this respect. Every scrap of shredded paper was carefully collected and painstakingly fitted together. The end result was eventually published in 16 volumes, with a Farsi translation and explanation, providing a devastatingly embarrassing account of US foreign policy during the shah's regime. They became 'best sellers'. Armed with the information contained in these documents, the students also instigated the first real large-scale post-revolutionary purge in Iran, a purge that included several revolutionary figures who were found to have previously collaborated with the 'Great Satan'.

Not all the original 400 students had survived, it being reported that 60 had perished in an internecine struggle between those who wanted to subject the American hostages to a public show trial, and those who, especially after the war with Iraq had begun, wanted to negotiate with the United States for the best bargain that could be obtained in exchange for them. One authority stated that an additional 30 had been killed during the siege itself and 50 wounded in the ongoing war with Iran, adding that 'some female members had married' and were now helping to further their husbands' careers (Taheri, 1987). Iran is silent about how many female students were involved in the US Embassy episode, but there had been several in what was an unusual 'mix' of sexes in the Islamic fundamentalist mood prevailing at the time.

The fundamentalist Iranian leadership remained firmly convinced of the value of hostage taking, especially of Westerners, but as it was striving to become a respectable sovereign state on the international stage, and was anxious to regain diplomatic recognition and develop good trading relationships, it pushed all thoughts of this aside for the time being. After pursuing empire-building and destabilisation activities in Lebanon in 1982, the Tehran government encouraged its minions to concentrate on suicide bombing and aircraft hijacking as means of striking at the Great Satan. It was not until the Western military contingents of the multinational force departed from Lebanon that the issue of kidnapping Westerners, particularly Americans, gained momentum.

The wayward Tehran government, which regarded terrorism and political assassination as essential national weapons, was tempted to call the bluff of the United States and other Western nations that ruled out any possibility of meeting demands in exchange for hostages, declaring they would 'not deal with terrorists'. The Tehran government eventually decided to push this tactic to the absolute limit, but by proxy.

Lebanon was an ideal setting, as hostage taking had long been a common practice amongst Lebanese sects and factions, many of which had their own private militias, be these large, small or tiny. Many also had their own private prisons for this purpose, hostages being regarded as an essential form of insurance that none could afford to be without. Hostages were usually held for prestige, punishment, exchange or vengeance, and some were tortured or executed on a reprisal basis. Conditions in the private prisons varied considerably, but most were primitive and hostages suffered deprivation and hardship, sometimes being chained or bound. When Westerners were held hostage, as came increasingly to be the case during 1985, they were often blindfolded as well, and sometimes taped music was played continually to prevent the victims from recognising sounds such as traffic, church bells, Islamic calls to prayer, machinery or unusual noises that might later help to locate the site.

WESTERN HOSTAGES

Two of the first high-profile American hostages seized in Lebanon by Hezbollah were William Buckley, the CIA station chief at the American embassy in Beirut, who was kidnapped on 18 March 1984, and Jeremy Levin, an American journalist kidnapped on the 19th. On 8 May Benjamin Weir, an American missionary, was seized in West Beirut. Responsibility for all three kidnappings was claimed by Islamic Jihad. International publicity was enormous and continual, much to the initial satisfaction of the string-pulling Tehran government.

Western pressure was put on the governments of Syria and Lebanon to take steps to free the hostages and put a stop to this practice. Syria and Iran were unlikely partners, one having a secular Baathist government and the other an Islamic fundamentalist one.

Syria had been troubled for years by the activities of the Muslim Brotherhood, membership of which it had outlawed in 1963 and later made punishable by death. Subversive Muslim Brotherhood activity had re-erupted in Syria in 1980 and rumbled on, a spate of bombings hitting the northern city of Aleppo in November 1981, the month after the assassination of President Sadat of Egypt by one of its offshoots.

In addition, on 3 February 1982 a Muslim Brotherhood uprising had taken place in Hama (about 120 miles north of

Damascus), which had taken the Syrian security forces about three weeks to crush with a very bloody hand. At least 1000 people (some reports put the figure at more than 2000) had been killed, as well as at least 51 soldiers, and part of the city had been destroyed by artillery fire. Allegations were made of atrocities and executions on both sides. The Muslim Brotherhood had acted after blaming Syrian assassins for the death in Barcelonia (Spain) of Nazar Ahmad al-Sabag, a Muslim Brotherhood leader, the previous November.

Syria was not consulted by Iran about the kidnapping of the Americans in 1984, and its relations with Hezbollah deteriorated further. In nominal control of the Bekaa Valley, Syria feared that a resumption of US bombing might extend into Syrian-held territory. The United States had not seemed over concerned about the spate of kidnapping in Lebanon, which had so far avoided US citizens, but this was likely to change now that American lives were at stake. President Assad protested to the Tehran government, but received only partial satisfaction. Tehran merely agreed to bring a temporary halt to the kidnapping of Americans, but would not agree to release the three already held. Tehran did not want to provoke Syria into mounting a military operation to clear its surrogate groups out of the Bekaa Valley, and thus choke off this valuable Iranian terrorist outlet.

In August 1984, Hojatolislam Mohammed Mohammadi Reyshahri became the Iranian minister of intelligence and security, and it was thought at first that he was opposed to a planned campaign to seize Westerners, which Hezbollah was keen to carry out. Kidnapping in Lebanon continued, largely by rival factions for traditional reasons, but also to raise ransom money, as some, especially the smaller organisations, were always short of funds, although in such circumstances most resorted to criminal means and drug dealing to obtain an income. By no means were all kidnappings reported to the Lebanese police, who tried to keep meticulous records of violent deaths, explosions and missing persons. Nor did all attract the interest of the international media, or even the local media, unless factional leaders or local personalities were victims. Often those involved in kidnapping avoided publicity for their own private reasons. However, whenever a Westerner was kidnapped it invariably made the international headlines.

Eventually Reyshahri changed his mind – or it was changed for him by Khomeini, who was reputed to be in favour of the kidnapping of Westerners – and on 8 January 1985 Father Lawrence Jenco, an American priest and head of the Catholic Relief Services Office bureau, was kidnapped in Beirut. The following day so too was Peter Kilburn, who worked at the American University in Beirut. On the 14th an Islamic Jihad statement confirmed that it was now holding five Americans, who would shortly be put on trial as 'CIA spies, and given the punishment they deserved'. On the 28th a video tape of William Buckley was received by a media bureau in Beirut. In it Buckley confirmed he was being held hostage, together with Levin and Weir, and that all three were being 'well treated'.

On 14 February Jeremy Levin arrived at a Syrian army post in the Bekaa Valley. He claimed to have escaped from his captors, but in a communique Islamic Jihad insisted that he had been freed as 'he was not a spy, and was not opposed to Islam'. Perhaps Levin really had escaped.

In March other Westerners were kidnapped by Islamic Jihad. On the 14th Godfrey Nash, a British scientist, was snatched, and on the 15th Brian Levick, a British business-man, was seized. Both were released on the 31st, on the ground they had been mistaken for Americans. On the 18th Terry Anderson, head of the Associated Press bureau in Beirut, was kidnapped.

Two French diplomats, Marcel Fontaine and Marcel Carton, were seized in Beirut on the 22nd, together with a French woman employed at the embassy. In exchange for their release, Islamic Jihad demanded that the French government cancel a deal to provide Iraq with Mirage combat aircraft in return for a quantity of Saudi oil. The woman was released on the 31st. Relations between the governments of Iran and France were very poor as France was openly backing Iraq in the Gulf War, supplying it with arms and also sheltering Iranian exiled dissidents.

Other Westerners were kidnapped by non-Hezbollah groups for a variety of reasons. One doubtful case was that of a Dutch Jesuit priest kidnapped on 14 March. His murdered body was found on the 30th in the Bekaa Valley, with a note pinned to it announcing that the 'Vengeance Party' had been responsible.

Hezbollah denied any involvement, this time with perhaps some degree of truth.

On 25 March Alec Collett, a British journalist, was kidnapped in West Beirut. Responsibility was claimed by the Revolutionary Organisation of Socialist Muslims (ROSM), a code name used by Abu Nidal, the international terrorist, who was never far from scenes of trouble. His demand was the release of three would-be assassins who were being held in British jails after being convicted in March 1983 of the attempted murder in June 1982 of Shlomo Argov, the Israeli Ambassador to London.

It was said that Abu Nidal had just made a deal with the French government for two of his activists, imprisoned in France in 1978 for a term of 15 years. If they were released when half their sentences had been completed, Nidal would refrain from terrorist activities in France. The two terrorists were released in February 1988, and Nidal seems to have kept his word.

Amal and Druse militias captured most of western Beirut in February 1985, which severely restricted the writ of Lebanese government forces and probably facilitated the spate of kidnapping that took place from March onwards. The majority of victims remained Lebanese, as old feuds were resurrected and old scores paid off. Such victims were either held for short periods and secret exchanges made; were later found dead; or were never heard of again.

It was not until 16 May 1985 that Islamic Jihad released photographs of six Westerners they were claiming to hold – the four Americans (Anderson, Buckley, Jenco and Weir), and the two Frenchmen (Fontaine and Carton). In exchange for their safe return, Islamic Jihad demanded the release of the Kuwaiti-17, failing which the captives would be put on trial as CIA spies.

More hostages were seized. On 22 May Jean-Paul Kauffmann, a journalist, and Michel Seurat, a researcher, both French, were seized; and on the 28th so too was an American, David Jacobsen, director of the American University in Beirut. On 10 June Thomas Sutherland, dean of the American University, was kidnapped. This meant that Islamic Jihad now held at least seven American and four French hostages.

Assassination was not overlooked, and Islamic Jihad claimed to have killed Denis Hills, a British teacher at the American

University, and also two Frenchmen in the Palestinian refugee camp at Bourg el-Barajneh.

During the TWA hijacking in 1985, American negotiators unsuccessfully tried to link the release of the five Americans held by Islamic Jihad with those held on the aircraft, although President Assad promised to do what he could in this respect. After this hijacking there was a series of meetings between Hussein Moussawi, leader of Islamic Amal, and Sheikh Sobhi Tufeili, in charge of Hezbollah operations in Lebanon, who were dismayed at the lack of Syrian and Lebanese cooperation with their activities. There were certain differences between them as all had varying agendas that caused friction. President Assad wanted to improve his relations with the United States, for economic reasons, if no other, while Khomeini, who was pleased with Western hostage taking so far, wanted more of it.

An uneasy compromise seemed to emerge, and on 18 September Benjamin Weir was released as a 'sign of good intentions', but with the warning there would be further kidnappings and the execution of some of those already held unless the demand for the release of the Kuwaiti-17 was met. On 4 October Islamic Jihad announced that William Buckley had been executed because 'he was the Head of the CIA station in Lebanon'. This claim was not believed for a while as no positive evidence was produced, but later it was shown to be true. He had been tortured before he died.

In early November a letter from Islamic Amal to the media in Beirut – for onward transmission to President Reagan, appealing to him to enter into negotiations with their kidnappers – was signed by Anderson, Jacobsen and Jenco.

SOVIET HOSTAGES

Meanwhile, on 30 September 1985 four members of the Soviet embassy in Beirut were seized by the 'Islamic Organisation', an occasional Hezbollah code name. Hezbollah denied all responsibility, as it invariably did, posing simply as a political party, working only for Lebanese Shia status and welfare. The presumed objective was to persuade the Soviets to step in to end interfactional fighting between rival militias in the

northern Lebanese port of Tripoli, in which Shia factions were
coming off second best.

The Soviet and Iranian governments were on poor terms as
Iran had cracked down hard on the Tudeh (Communist)
Party, executing some leaders and imprisoning others.
Relations were not improved by a visit to Moscow by
Habibollah Pegman, an American embassy siege veteran.
Pegman told Kremlin leaders they must accept Islam, and
should purge both their Marxists and their Marxist jargon.
Iran was certainty anti-Soviet at that time.

The body of one Soviet hostage was found a few days later in
Beirut. At once the Soviets hastily evacuated their overstaffed
embassy. According to PLO sources, a male relative of Sheikh
Fadlallah was kidnapped and killed, and his private parts, in a
cellophane bag with an explanatory medical note, were sent to
the sheikh. The other three Soviet hostages were immediately
released. No more Soviets were taken hostage in Lebanon. A
point had certainly been made, but one that was far too medieval for Western states to contemplate, anxious as they were
to exhibit clean hands and avoid the stigma of dirty tricks.

TERRY WAITE

Terry Waite, the personal envoy of the British Archbishop of
Canterbury and accredited with successfully negotiating the
release of British detainees in Libya in August 1985, appeared
on the Lebanese hostage scene, visiting dignitaries and
making contact with kidnappers. He claimed to have been involved in the release of Benjamin Weir. Waite generated a
great deal of personal publicity and seemed to make more
enemies than friends. In the United States Waite had briefed
George Bush, then US vice president, but he was rejected by
the Kuwaiti authorities.

SYRIAN CHANGE OF POLICY

At first some hostages were hidden in parts of West Beirut,
which in 1985 degenerated into a chaotic district in which
armed militias, including Amal and Hezbollah, struggled for

existence, influence and territory, and in which kidnapping was rife. Savouring the attendant publicity and the growing helplessness and frustration of certain Western powers, Hezbollah was in no hurry to release its hostages, let alone abandon the practice.

Embarrassed by external pressure and Western allegations that it was a state supporting terrorism, on 22 February 1986 the Syrian army, which still occupied parts of northern and eastern Lebanon, swept into West Beirut, overcoming militia resistance by force. Hezbollah was not excluded, and in one incident Syrian troops bombarded a building occupied by Hezbollah, which would neither surrender nor withdraw, killing 22 Hezbollah personnel. Hezbollah hastily withdrew with its hostages into southern Beirut, a largely slum area controlled partially by Nabih Berri's Amal militia. Syrian forces remained in control of much of west Beirut, and the airport.

Saiqa, Syria's main intelligence agency (Syria was a country of semi-independent intelligence agencies) continued to liaise with Hezbollah and other militias, but relations between them, which had been deteriorating since the TWA hijacking, were cool. Nabih Berri too remained at loggerheads with Hezbollah. This tended to restrict Hezbollah's former free-ranging activities in Lebanon. The significance of this re-arrangement of local power did not appear to be appreciated by the Tehran authorities, as was later demonstrated by the blundering Kuwaiti hijacking exploit in 1988.

THE HEZBOLLAH COALITION

By this time Hezbollah had developed into a terrorist coalition, directed and funded by Ayatollah Khomeini, it being openly admitted that he was its supreme guide. Several terrorist groups and factions operated within the coalition, pooling intelligence and resources and developing international contacts. The main leaders were still Abbas Moussawi, Mohammed Hussein Fadlallah and Sobhi Tufeili, the latter appearing to be responsible for terrorist activities. It had formed a consultative council, an executive committee and an administrative framework for its various other religious, social and welfare activities. It remained autonomous, with a direct line to

Khomeini, although several Iranian personalities tried to 'get a piece' of the command structure. Hezbollah continued to have a foothold in several camps, occasionally cooperating with the most unlikely bedfellows.

EXECUTIONS: 1986

On 5 March 1986 Islamic Jihad announced it had executed Michel Seurat, on the ground that he had 'supplied French intelligence with research on the Middle East, and on Islamic movements in Lebanon'. On the 10th a photograph was released of Seurat's body. That day, Islamic Jihad denied any involvement in the kidnapping of a French TV crew (Philippe Rochot, Georges Hansen, Aurel Cornea and Jean-Louis Normandin), which had been seized in West Beirut after filming a Hezbollah rally.

Previously, secret negotiations between France and Iran for the release of French hostages held in Lebanon had been unsuccessful, and so this process had lapsed. When Jacques Chirac's government came to power in March 1986 the secret contact was resumed.

On the 14th the Revolutionary Justice Organisation (RJO), which was probably Dawa-based, claimed it was holding the TV crew and released photocopies of their identity cards. The kidnapping was taken to be a reprisal for the expulsion of two pro-Iranian Iraqi dissidents (Fawzi Harmza and Hassan Kheir al-Din) from France to Iraq. A report that one had been executed later proved false, as on 12 March both were released and produced for the media in Baghdad, having received a pardon from Saddam Hussein.

A video film was released by Islamic Jihad of the French nationals still held (Marcel Fontaine, Marcel Carton, Georges Hansen and Jean-Paul Kauffmann), who criticised French policy in the Middle East. On 9 April Michel Brian, a French schoolteacher, was kidnapped in Beirut, but was freed two days later by 'hunters' in the Bekaa Valley. Later, on 30 August an elderly Frenchman, Camille Sontag, was seized in Beirut.

Meanwhile, on 11 April, Brian Keenan of Ireland was kidnapped in Beirut. On 17 April (two days after US warplanes raided Libya) two British teachers , Leigh Douglas and Philip Padfield, who had been kidnapped on 28 March, and Peter Kilburn of the United States were found shot dead, a note on their bodies stating that the 'Arab Command Cells' claimed responsibility, and that their deaths were in revenge for the US action against Libya. Also on 17 April John McCarthy, the British acting Bureau chief for *World Wide Television News*, was kidnapped in Beirut.

The ROSM released a video on 23 April showing the execution by hanging of Alec Collett, said to have taken place on the 16th. The ROSM claimed the execution was in revenge for the 'joint American–British raid' on Libya (the US warplanes had flown from Britain).

On 13 May Hezbollah issued a statement denying it had kidnapped the British teachers, saying it was a conspiracy against education in Lebanon. Islamic Jihad warned the media in Beirut that if 'America, France, or any Arab country' exerted pressure to gain the release of the hostages, the hostages would be killed. The American CBS TV network reported on 29 May that the French government had secretly offered to pay $1 million to Iran, and a smaller amount to the kidnappers, if the release of the hostages could be secured, but France denied this.

On 29 June the Frenchmen Rochot and Hansen were released unharmed in West Beirut, and at a press conference said they had been well treated. The RJO asked the French government to give proof of its goodwill by revising its undertaking to give aid to Iraq, so that other hostages could be released.

The Iranian deputy foreign minister for international economic affairs stated on 26 June that Iran 'had played a vital and constructive role' in the release of the French hostages, 'thanks to our ideological links with groups in Lebanon'. This was unusual, in that it was an admission of involvement instead of oft-repeated denials. He added that the same could be done for British hostages if Britain were to change its policy towards Iran. (Tehran Times). That month another American, Faik Wareh, was kidnapped.

Steven Donahue, an American who had been kidnapped by drug traffickers in the Bekaa Valley in August 1985, was released on 2 July, reportedly after a $400 000 ransom had been paid. Donahue's claim that he had been on a mission for the US Drug Enforcement Agency was denied by US officials.

Father Lawrence Jenco was released on 26 July, also in the Bekaa Valley. Terry Waite claimed to have played a major part in the negotiations. Jenco brought with him a video message from Terry Anderson, David Jacobsen and Thomas Sutherland, appealing to the US government to negotiate with their captors. This was rejected, a US presidential spokesman saying that the United States was 'not prepared to negotiate with terrorists'. However behind-the-scenes efforts were made by William Casey, head of the CIA, who had talks with President Assad during a secret visit to Damascus.

On 9 September 1986 Frank Reed, an American teacher and convert to Islam, was kidnapped by Islamic Jihad, followed on the 12th by Joseph Cicippio, another American convert to Islam. On the 24th the RJO announced it was holding Cicippio, as well as a Frenchman, Marcel Coudari, who had not previously been reported missing. The RJO also claimed responsibility for kidnapping another American, Edward Tracey, an author, on October.

In late October 1986 Terry Waite arrived back in Lebanon, saying that he was making progress in freeing the Western captives. It was later confirmed that he had been involved to some extent in a covert CIA operation aimed at securing the release of the American hostages.

On 2 November David Jacobsen was released, following a visit by Waite to Damascus, where he allegedly met Ali Akbar Vellayati, the Iranian foreign minister. Al-Jihad al-Islami stated that the US government had 'embarked on approaches that could lead, if continued, to a solution of the hostage crisis', a reference that was taken to mean 'arms for captives'. Iran's Speaker Rafsanjani entered the picture, stating that Iran was willing, under certain conditions, to advise groups holding US hostages to release them, but that the United States must support Lebanese Muslim demands for the release of detainees in Kuwait, Israel and France.

The RJO released the French hostages Camille Sontag and Marcel Coudari on the 11th. Jacques Chirac, the French prime minister, thanked the Syrian, Saudi Arabian and Algerian governments for their part in securing the release of these two men. There was some speculation that Coudari was in some way connected with the French intelligence service.

On 24 December 1986 the RJO released the French TV cameraman, Auriel Cornea. This followed the reported arrest in France of six Arab opponents of President Assad, and was thought to be due to cooperation between the French and Syrian security services. The French government confirmed on the 25th that expulsion orders had been served on three Jordanians and one Syrian. Almost openly some governments were making release arrangements to gain the liberty of captive nationals.

THE LONDON ACCORD: 1986

It soon became apparent that Western countries with nationals being held hostage in Lebanon had differing views on how to deal with the situation. Despite the facade of 'no deals with terrorists', some hostages were quietly released, some reputedly for huge sums of money and perhaps other undisclosed reasons, which caused bickering between the nations involved. At a European Economic Community summit in London on 12 December 1986 it was agreed that no concessions should be made under duress for the release of hostages in Lebanon, or elsewhere. This became known as the London Accord.

MORE HOSTAGES

Terry Waite returned to Lebanon on 13 January 1987. The same day a French photographer, Roger Auque, was kidnapped, soon after taking pictures of Waite, and on the 14th a Saudi Arabian diplomat was seized (Bakr Damanhouri). Damanhouri was released on 18 March, as was Khaled Deeb, another kidnapped Saudi Arabian. No explanations were offered. Waite held discussions with several leaders, including Fadlallah, and then on the 20th he disappeared and all contact with him was lost.

Waite was accused by Hezbollah of being an American spy in the pay of the CIA. PLO sources alleged that, when captured, Waite had had an electronic 'CIA bug' in his hair, which he denied on his eventual release.

On the 24th four academics were kidnapped from the Beirut University – three Americans (Alan Steen, Jesse Turner and Robert Polhill) and an Indian (Mithileshwar Singh) – for which dual claims of responsibility and dual demands were made. In response the US 6th Fleet moved towards the Lebanese coast, provoking threats from some kidnappers that hostages would be killed in the event of an attack on Beirut. Demands were made for the release of 400 prisoners in Israeli detention, and a list was produced of 310 Lebanese and 90 Palestinian names by the Islamic Jihad for the Liberation of Palestine.

Hezbollah and its constituent groups now held at least 16 Western hostages. There may have been more, as secrecy began to surround some cases, and not all were officially reported missing by those willing to pay ransoms or bargain with the terrorists. Western governments were still at loggerheads with each other over this issue. It seemed that in some instances Hezbollah deliberately selected hostages who worked for wealthy firms or organisations that were able and willing to pay large ransoms for the safe return of their employees.

SYRIAN ACTION: FEBRUARY 1987

By now West Beirut had deteriorated into a chaotic intermilitia melee of violence that coincided with the ongoing 'war of the camps' (the besieged Palestinian refugee camps). George Shultz, US secretary of state, described Beirut as 'a plague-infested place from the Middle Ages, which should be quarantined' (*New York Times*). The Syrian army moved in on 22 February 1987, deploying two brigades (7000 troops) plus a detachment of artillery in the overlooking hills, its stated aim being to 'take control of security in West Beirut for good', and to 'secure the release of all captives and hostages' (*The Times*). It drove factions from the streets and closed down their '75 militia offices' (*Le Quotidien*). By the end of the following day the Syrian army had taken over. Militiamen who defied Syria's order not to carry arms were shot dead on the streets.

On the 24th Syrian troops attacked a Hezbollah building whose occupants had refused to surrender. Twenty-six people were killed in the fighting – 18 Hezbollah guerrillas, five women and three Amal members (*The Times*). Their funerals were held the following day, and over 10 000 Hezbollah supporters turned out to demonstrate against the Syrians. This caused the Syrian military commander to announce lamely that 'there was no need to deploy into the southern suburbs', which were dominated by Hezbollah. This decision was probably reinforced by the presence in Damascus of Ali Akbar Vellayati, the Iranian foreign minister, and Mohsen Rafiqdust, the Revolutionary Guards minister, who were desperately striving to curb President Assad's anger and prevent Syrian troops from clearing and occupying the Bekaa Valley, which Iran wanted to remain a no man's land for its own purposes.

THE HAMADEI BROTHERS

On 13 January 1987 Mohammed Ali Hamadei, a Shia Lebanese member of Hezbollah, was arrested in Frankfurt when bottles of liquid explosives were found in his luggage. It was alleged that he was one of the team involved in the 1985 TWA hijacking, and that his fingerprints had been found on the aircraft. Later a former hostage identified him as one of the 'terrorists on the plane'. The United States immediately demanded his extradition, but the West German authorities hesitated, saying they would try him themselves. They needed a show trial for national morale purposes and to demonstrate they were being tough on terrorism, having not inconsiderable terrorist problems themselves.

A few days later a price was paid by the West German authorities for this decision as two West Germans (Rudolf Cordes and Alfred Schmidt) were kidnapped in Lebanon by Hezbollah. Next, on the 27th, Abbas Ali Hamadei (brother of Mohammed), who had become a West German citizen, was arrested in Frankfurt with explosives in his possession. Abbas Ali Hamadei was additionally charged with kidnapping the two West Germans. It was said that a third brother, Abdul Hadi was a security chief of Hezbollah.

During the somewhat lengthy argument over whether or not Mohammed Ali Hamadei should be extradited to the United States (capital punishment is practiced in the United States, but not in West Germany), an American journalist, Charles Glass, was kidnapped by Hezbollah in Beirut on 18 June. Glass had covered the TWA hijacking in 1985 and had obtained exclusive interviews with some of the hostages. It was assumed that Glass had been seized to prevent him from giving evidence at the West German trial of Mohammed Ali Hamadei.

West Germany decided not to extradite Hamadei to the United States and his trial proceeded. On 18 August Glass 'escaped' from an apartment building in southern Beirut, Syria alleging that this had been 'allowed to happen'. Next, on 2 September Alfred Schmidt, who had been periodically chained up in captivity, was released. The West German government expressed its thanks to both Iran and Syria. It was reported that a ransom of over $2 million, plus huge quantities of medical supplies, had been handed over to Hezbollah by the international firm that employed Schmidt, but this was denied by all involved. It was admitted in evidence at the later trial that death threats to Glass had prevented Mohammed Ali Hamadei's extradition to the United States. Rudolf Cordes was not released until 13 September 1988, when again rumours abounded of a huge ransom being paid.

On 27 January 1988 a West German, Ralph Schray, was kidnapped in West Beirut. This was linked to the ongoing trial in West Germany of Abbas Ali Hamadei for kidnapping the two West German citizens. Hezbollah was hoping for an exchange for Hamadei. This did not happen, but Schray was released on 3 March, supposedly following Syrian intervention. Both Syria and Iran professed to be working to gain the release of all Western hostages. The West German trials went ahead.

FRENCH DUPLICITY

In July 1987 the French security forces wanted to arrest an Iranian interpreter at the Iranian embassy in Paris, Vahid Gordji, who was suspected of being involved in a series of bombing incidents in the city the previous year, in which 14 people had been killed. Iran refused to surrender him, even though he did not have diplomatic immunity. French security forces besieged the Iranian embassy, and as a countermeasure the French embassy in Tehran was likewise besieged by a security ring. Secret negotiations continued as the diplomatic sieges dragged on.

Suddenly, on 27 November 1987 two French hostages, Roger Auque and Jean-Louis Normandin, were released. Vahid Gordji, after appearing briefly before a French examining magistrate, was freed and quickly deported, the official face-saving excuse being that 'it was purely a matter for the French judiciary'. The same day the restrictions on the Iranian embassy in Paris and the French embassy in Tehran were lifted. Exchanges of personnel took place at Karachi airport, bringing Pakistan, a country friendly to Iran, into the frame of suspicion.

It soon became apparent that the French had made considerable concessions to obtain the release of these two hostages (three still remained in Hezbollah captivity). A very large ransom had been paid by someone in France to the RJO. In addition the French government had agreed to slow down the rate of its arms deliveries to Iraq (still at war with Iran), which referred to promised delivery dates for some 20 Mirage F-1 combat aircraft; to reduce its naval contribution to the Allied Gulf embargo fleet (the aircraft carrier *Clemenceau* was withdrawn); to stop making threats against Iran; and to repay a huge cash instalment of a billion-dollar loan contracted by the Shah.

First West Germany and now France, almost openly and blatantly, for selfish national interests, had shattered the unity of the London Accord. Britain had just praised France for its fight against terrorism by intercepting a ship carrying Libyan arms to the Irish Republican Army. This was compounded by another breach of the London Accord on 4 May 1988, when the three remaining French hostages in Lebanon (Marcel Carton, Marcel Fontaine and Jean-Paul Kauffmann), were released. The price was believed to have been another huge repayment instalment on the shah's loan. Prime Minister Jacques Chirac welcomed the hostages home and thanked the Iranian government for their release.

COLONEL HIGGINS

Foreigners avoided Beirut and Lebanon if they could, and those unable to do so took careful security precautions. Even so kidnapping continued, although somewhat less frequently. One high-profile example was Lieutenant-Colonel William Higgins – the newly arrived American head of the UN Truce Supervision Organisation (UNTSO), attached to the UN Interim Force in Lebanon (UNIFIL) – who was abducted on 17 February 1988 near Beirut, in an area where the Amal militia and Hezbollah were competing for domination. He was accused of being a CIA spy.

AMAL–HEZBOLLAH CLASHES

Relations between Nabih Berri's Amal militia and the aggressive, expansionist Hezbollah coalition in Lebanon had been abrasive for some time. During the latter part of 1987 Hezbollah, having ample funds from Iran, expanded its realm of influence, especially in the poorer Shia areas of southern Lebanon, the eastern Bekaa Valley and south Beirut. This was largely achieved at the expense of the Amal militia, which could not compete with Hezbollah's generous welfare programme. Soon Hezbollah committees were controlling groups of villages and doling out subsistence payments to poor families, while in south Beirut it operated subsidised supermarkets and pharmacies.

Armed clashes broke out between the two militias in early September 1987 in areas south of Beirut in Shia-inhabited terrain. Such clashes rumbled uneasily on, until a sharp bout of intermilitia fighting in south Beirut began in May 1988. This lasted for several days, during which time over 400 people were killed and over 1000 were injured (*The Times*). The Amal militia fared badly in this fighting, being 'driven out of nine of the ten localities' it had controlled (*Le Quotidien*). With Iran's reluctant agreement, Syrian troops stepped in to stop the fighting and prevent further bloodshed.

On 3 June Nabih Berri, now immersed in Lebanese politics, announced the disbandment of his Amal militia in all areas except southern Lebanon. He urged his militiamen to join the Lebanese army, meaning the mainly Shia 6th Brigade. Berri said he would devote his energies to political activities. Sporadic clashes continued, there being outbreaks in August and again in October. Hezbollah was spreading its wings over a large section of Lebanon, which gave its terrorists considerable mobility and sanctuary, as Syrian troops hesitated to enter such areas. Relations between Syria and Lebanon were fragile, but each retained a foot in the other's camp.

Fighting between the two rival militias broke out again in south Beirut in January 1989, and on the 13th a bomb exploded during a Hezbollah parade, killing seven people. On the 30th a 'peace accord' was drawn up between the two sides, under which Hezbollah recognised the 'Amal militia's primacy in southern Lebanon, but reserved the right to maintain bases there'. This uneasy live-and-let-live arrangement continued for the remainder of the year, until fighting erupted yet again, this time in the western Bekaa Valley, and continued intermittently. Clashes also reoccurred in west Beirut, and once again Syrian troops stepped in to restore order.

In May 1989 two West Germans, Thomas Kemptner and Heinrich Strubig, were seized in Lebanon, the hope being to exchange them for the two Hamadei brothers held in West Germany.

ISRAELIS CAPTURE OBEID

Meanwhile Hezbollah militias were launching frequent attacks in the Israeli security zone in southern Lebanon. On 28 July 1989 a helicopter-borne Israeli commando group raided the home of Sheikh Abdul Karim Obeid in Dibchit, just north of the Israeli security zone. They seized the sheikh and two of his bodyguards, shot dead a neighbour who intervened and flew Obeid back to detention in Israel. Israel alleged that Obeid was a senior Hezbollah executive in charge of operations against Israel, and was also responsible for the kidnapping of Colonel Higgins. Others suggested that Obeid was only a minor cleric, that he was not part of Hezbollah's leadership and just happened to be a convenient target.

In Tehran, Ali Akbar Mohtashemi, the hardline minister of the interior, called this an Israeli 'terrorist act' and threatened that both the United States and Israel would pay dearly for it.

The Organisation for the Oppressed of the Earth, the Hezbollah code name for the Higgins seizure, threatened to hang Higgins unless Obeid was released.

Just after the deadline on 31 July, a message was sent to the media in Beirut, accompanied by a video of the event, saying that Higgins had been executed. There was lingering doubt about the claim owing to the poor definition of the video images. Israeli sources suggested that Higgins might have been hanged as early as April 1988, and that the video recording had been withheld for a such an opportunity.

Nearly three months earlier, on 4 May 1989, three West Germans working for the Humanitas Relief Agency had been kidnapped near Sidon (Lebanon), but two had been released the following day with a message that the West German government should deal leniently with Mohammed Ali Hamadei (then on trial in Frankfurt for involvement in the 1985 TWA hijacking). The third had been released on the 14th. All three had again been kidnapped on 17 May, together with another West German, one of whom had been released the following day. On 13 May Jackie Mann, a British expatriate, had been kidnapped in Beirut.

Speaker Rafsanjani had already said (in February 1989) that he would work towards freeing the Western hostages in Lebanon, which indicated that power in Tehran still remained divided, and that a top-level struggle was pending at a time when Ayatollah Khomeini was becoming enfeebled. Rafsanjani was looking towards the future. The war against Iraq had ended in August 1988, with what was virtually an Iranian defeat. The task ahead was to rebuild Iran's shattered economy. Rafsanjani wanted Western credit for the Iranian reconstruction process, which was being withheld while the hostage problem remained. He also wanted to undermine his powerful, radical, Islamic fundamentalist rivals, one of whom was the recently out-of-Office ex-interior minister, Ali Akbar Mohtashemi, a claimed founder member of Hezbollah.

THE TAIF ACCORD

Lebanese National Assembly deputies met on 30 September 1989 in Taif, Saudi Arabia, several being too scared to return from exile to meet in their native country. Agreements were made that became known as the Taif Accords. These were supported by Saudi Arabia and eventually led to the emergence of the 'Lebanese Second Republic', which began to come into effect the following year. A Lebanese government was formed by Prime Minister Rafiq al-Hariri, with Nabih Berri as speaker of the Assembly, which slowly managed to stabilise the economy, consolidate peace and launch a spectacular, grandiose, 25-year plan for rebuilding war-shattered Beirut. Within two years it claimed to have repatriated about 200 000 refugees to their original homes. However parts of the Bekaa Valley had to be 'shared' with Hezbollah, while the extreme south of the country remained a Hezbollah–Israeli battlefield.

Syria now began more openly to support the Amal militia in its battles against Iranian-supported Hezbollah in southern Lebanon. Both countries now had obviously opposing agendas, but retained formal contact with each other. Both had clenched teeth but smiling faces.

On 30 April 1990 the American hostage Frank Reed was released by Hezbollah, and the US president (now George Bush) thanked Syria and, for the first time, Iran. Robert Polhill had been released on 22 April.

SYRIAN–LEBANESE TREATY

On 22 May 1991 the Syrian–Lebanese Treaty of 'brotherhood, cooperation and coordination' was signed in Damascus. A few days later Rafsanjani, now President of Iran, visited Damascus and Lebanon and talked to Hezbollah leaders. Rafsanjani had to tread carefully to get his way, as many hardliners in Hezbollah had taken a liking to kidnapping Western hostages, which gave them a sense of smug self-satisfaction. It delighted them to see the pompous West wriggle ineffectually under their pressure.

The secretary general of Hezbollah, Sheikh Sobhi Tufeili, who had held that position since 1989 and was thought to be in charge of the operations section, was pushed aside and replaced by Sheikh Abbas Moussawi, who was expected to phase out hostage taking and direct all Hezbollah's energies against the Israelis. Rafsanjani was concentrating on improving relations with the West. A British minister visited Lebanon in June, and was assured that the three remaining British hostages (Mann, McCarthy and Waite) were in good health.

In mid-July fighting broke out again between Syrian-backed Amal militia and Iranian-backed Hezbollah, said to be started by Hezbollah. During the fighting a Palestinian faction briefly allied itself with Amal, whose intention had been to wreck the Taif Accord peace process. Israel, which wanted to keep the Palestinians and Amal at each other's throats, briefly allowed the hard-pressed Hezbollah to resupply some of its forward elements over Israeli-held terrain, but the same day bombed Hezbollah camps in the Bekaa Valley. An Amal–Hezbollah ceasefire came into effect on 2 September, and a confirming agreement was signed by both sides in Damascus on the 9th.

RELEASE OF THE WESTERN HOSTAGES

Brian Keenan, the Irish hostage, was freed on 24 August 1990. According to Hezbollah, his release had been delayed by the Amal–Hezbollah fighting. Keenan's release was a Rafsanjani victory; the latter certainly claimed all the credit, but at the same time continued to demand the release of the prisoners held by Israel.

On 8 August 1991 John McCarthy was freed, carrying with him a letter for the UN secretary general calling for the release of the prisoners in Israel, and for UN negotiations to free the remaining Western hostages. On the 11th the American Edward Tracey was freed.

A UN negotiator, Giandomenico Picco, had been very active in trying to obtain the release of the Western hostages in Lebanon, working quietly and effectively in several cases. He deserves more acclaim than most of the publicity-seeking statesmen, politicians and others who sought to overshadow his achievements.

Within a few weeks most of the remaining Western hostages were freed. Jackie Mann was released on 24 September; on 21 October the American Jesse Turner was set free amid a spate of Israeli exchanges, and Terry Waite on 18 November. Joseph Cicippio was released on 4 December, the United States reputedly paying Iran $278 million in compensation for arms impounded in 1979; as were Alan Steen and Terry Anderson on the 4th. This cleared most of the high-profile Western hostages, although two remained in captivity – the Germans Kemptner and Strubig, who were being held by the 'Hamadei faction' of Hezbollah. The two Hamadei brothers were now serving prison sentences in Germany, and Hezbollah was hoping for some trade-off, and all were eventually released by 17 June 1992.

ASSASSINATION OF SHEIKH MOUSSAWI

On 16 February 1992 Sheikh Abbas Moussawi, secretary general of Hezbollah since May 1991, was killed by an Israeli helicopter raid on his motorcade when returning to Beirut from a Hezbollah rally in Dibchit, southern Lebanon, the main Hezbollah base. Two helicopters strafed the vehicles. Guided missiles killed Moussawi, his wife and son, and five bodyguards. The attack was the culmination of a series of Israeli air raids on Hezbollah positions in Lebanon to avenge the death of three Israeli soldiers in an assault on an Israeli military camp on the 14th. Some 50 000 Shias attended Moussawi's funeral in Beirut.

THE END OF THE WESTERN HOSTAGE SAGA

Moussawi was replaced as secretary general of Hezbollah by Sheikh Hassan Nasrallah, who hurried off to Tehran for talks with President Rafsanjani and other influential Iranian leaders. Nasrallah then announced there would be no more kidnapping of Westerners, and the Western hostage saga passed into history. Giandomenico Picco, when he later left UN employment, bemoaned the fact that although few if any Westerners remained in captivity in Lebanon, the same could not be said of non-Westerners as the practice continued, but with little publicity as this was of less interest to the Western media. He also remarked that a main culprit was Israel, which continued to hold hundreds of prisoners without trial.

The first Western hostage to be taken had been an American, Frank Regler, who had been seized in Beirut in

February 1984 and released some two months later. The last had been two Swiss nationals, taken in May 1989 and eventually released in June 1992, after which the EC authorised economic aid to Iran to the tune of $212 million. During this dramatic eight-year period, watched in fascination by the world, it is probable that more than 100 hostages were kidnapped (not all Westerners); no one seems to know exactly (Lebanese government sources). At least ten died in captivity, and about half a dozen were thought to have escaped. At least 17 different organisations claimed responsibility, the best known being Islamic Jihad. The remains of Buckley and Higgins were recovered, but no trace of either Collett or Seurat was found.

This dramatic saga had thwarted and humiliated certain Western governments, some of which had falsely denied they 'would not deal with terrorists'. Hezbollah gained massive and continual international media coverage, the 'lifeblood of terrorism', while Iran gained more covert political and financial concessions than Western countries were prepared to admit. Eventually the terrorists choked on this form of warfare, like a cat on cream: Hezbollah sought more of this exhilarating diet, but the Iranian government, faced with reconstruction problems after its eight-year war with Iraq, had to moderate its ideological rantings in order to establish good relations with the nations that held the international purse strings.

Although the Iranian government generously financed Hezbollah throughout, it never had full control of Hezbollah's activities owing to the latter's 'hot line' to Khomeini. Also, members of several Hezbollah executive committees had their own varying agendas, and some of the extreme constituent groups, such as Dawa, managed to retain virtual independence of action. Only after Khomeini's death was Rafsanjani able to change, or modify, Hezbollah policies. When he became president his policy was to direct Hezbollah's energy into anti-Israel resistance activity.

The Hezbollah coalition was amazed at its own success, and astounded that the United States, a world superpower, and Britain and France, two former major colonial powers that for decades had been held in some awe in the Middle East, were so helpless and impotent in the face of this form of naked terrorism.

PEACE IN LEBANON

A Lebanese military court ruled on 24 May 1993 that the 'National General Assembly Amnesty for War Crimes' (of 1991) included those responsible for bombing the US embassy in Beirut in 1983. This upset the United States, which closed down the New York office of Middle East Airlines, the Lebanese air carrier.

Two months later a severe bout of fighting erupted in southern Lebanon near the Israeli security zone, causing Israel to launch 'Operation Accountability', which included air strikes on Hezbollah and other terrorist bases, while Israeli gunboats fired at targets near Tyre and Sidon. Hezbollah ordered full mobilisation. Later the Lebanese government reported that about '130 people had been killed and 470 injured', and that some 300 000 had been uprooted and 30 000 houses destroyed. A ceasefire was brokered by the United States on the understanding that both Syria and Lebanon would restrain the activities of Hezbollah; but it did not call for Hezbollah to be disarmed, as Israel was insisting. Syria retained 35 000 troops in Lebanon, but still only controlled parts of the Bekaa Valley.

On 24 May 1994 in the Bekaa Valley, Israeli helicopters snatched Mustafa al-Dirani, leader of a small Shia terrorist group known as the 'Faithful Resistance', suspecting he was holding Ron Arad, a missing Israeli airman. Israeli sources later stated that Arad had been held by al-Dirani for two years, and then had been 'sold' to the Iranian Pasdaran in 1989 for $300 000. Hezbollah remained active against the Israelis, causing a small, but constant, toll of casualties.

At the meeting he addressed an hour or so before he was assassinated by an Israeli helicopter raid, Sheikh Abbas Moussawi had enunciated the Hezbollah dictum that 'we are not fighting so that the enemy recognises us, and offers us something. We are fighting to wipe out the enemy' (Taheri, 1987).

The calm in the sea of terrorism was shattered in Lebanon in January 1994 by Abu Nidal, when a group of his terrorists killed Naeb Imran Maytah (a Jordanian embassy official) in Beirut, its first assassination of a foreign diplomat since 1990. Seven accused were placed on trial in October 1994. All were sentenced to long terms of imprisonment, some *in absentia*.

The trial was notable in that one of the assassins, Yousef Shaaban, a Palestinian, claimed he had also been responsible for blowing up Pan Am Flight 103 over Lockerbie in Scotland in December 1988. Two hundred and seventy lives had been lost, for which the United States, and Britain, blamed Libya.

This claim was ridiculed by the court, the Lebanese government and the international media, but provoked thought among those who suspected that the United States was presupposing Libyan guilt without having any proof. According to Israeli media reports, Iran was the culprit, having paid a large sum of money to Abu Nidal to blow up the aircraft in mid-air in revenge for when the USS *Vincennes* shot down (by mistake) an Iranian airliner in the Gulf with the loss of 290 lives.

7 The Enemy Within

As the birth pangs of the Islamic revolution in Iran subsided, Ayatollah Khomeini became a leader with two main problems: he had to survive in power, and he had to impose Islamic fundamentalism on his country, which was not universally welcomed. He began by assembling the structures and pillars of state, as he wanted to make sure the revolution remained in safe Shia hands.

Khomeini had one major advantage over his internal enemies, which was a power-base network of 120 000 Shia mullahs in 80 000 mosques scattered nationwide. Under the shahist regime, Shia mullahs had been studiously cold-shouldered, and so almost to a man they rushed to support Khomeini, looking to him for recognition, leadership and guidance. Khomeini did not disappoint them, even though he was not the most senior Ayatollah by any means, nor was he the Marja Taqlid (the supreme leader of Shia Muslims everywhere), but he was vibrant and politically ambitious, and he had come amongst them.

Khomeini wanted a veil of democracy to cover his government, but of Islamic form, not that of the West. Elections were scheduled for the 270-seat Majlis, but every candidate was carefully vetted for his beliefs and attitude, and the rejection rate was very high indeed.

The new constitution for the country was put to a general referendum during the first two days of December 1979, and was accepted by an 'overwhelming majority'. This gave Khomeini and his Islamic clergy considerable powers, and virtually transformed Iran into a theocracy. He had achieved his declared ambition – now he had to enforce it upon the people, not all of whom were in favour.

In January 1980 the presidential election was held. This was won by Abdol Hassan Bani-Sadr, a non-cleric, who was confirmed in office by Khomeini, who tended to take a lofty back seat. Bani-Sadr was also appointed commander-in-chief. He took his military duties seriously and hoped, especially when the war with Iraq began in September, to turn the rehabilitated armed forces into a power base for himself, something he lacked. He ran into opposition from the mullahs and had a hard time. He also faced a major internal security problem as armed parties and factions were struggling against each other, and against his government, using violence and terrorism.

As the months passed Khomeini became somewhat dismayed by the number of non-clerics being appointed to senior government positions, as in his view they tended to be over-imbued with Western liberalism. Khomeini's original thinking had been that the senior Islamic clergy would be in supervisory or adjudicatory roles, the business of government being left to reliable and experienced Muslim layman.

Ayatollah Mohammed Husseini Beheshti, leader of the IRP, became involved in a power struggle with President Bani-Sadr, and by Spring 1981 had gained control of the Majlis. Eventually, on 20 June 1981 Bani-Sadr, who had been losing his struggle against the mullahs, was impeached but escaped. Khomeini appointed a three-man Presidential Council, consisting of Beheshti, Prime Minister Mohammed Ali Radjai and Hashemi Ali Akbar Rafsanjani, to share presidential power between them for the time being. That day Rafsanjani was made speaker of the Majlis, a most important and powerful office of state. On the 24th Radjai was elected president of Iran.

THE OPPOSITION

Active opposition to the Islamic regime came from political groups wanting to eliminate Khomeini and take his place, including the Mujahedeen Khalk, the Fedayeen Khalk, the powerful, Soviet-supported Tudeh (Communist Party), the some six million separatist Kurds in the north-western provinces; and the left-wing Komala, which had a Kurdish communist majority.

The Mujahedeen Khalk, soon to become known as the Mujahedeen Khalk Organisation (MKO) within in Iran, was led by one of its founding members, Masoud Rajavi. Under his leadership the Mujahedeen Khalk had been very effective in the underground struggle against the shah, who had referred to the organisation as a 'bunch of Islamic Marxists'. Its platform was to establish a form of Islamic–Marxist society in Iran – a curious contradiction of philosophies.

Although originally comparatively small in size – probably fewer than 2000 members – it became powerful after the revolution. Five of its executive committee had seats on the IRP, and Ahmad Khomeini (the Ayatollah's son) was a member. In addition its deputy secretary general, Nuraddin Kianouri, was also secretary general of the Tudeh. This was a brief era of confusing dual appointments in intertwining groups, when all were nominally 'legal'. The MKO mounted spasmodic bomb attacks against the Islamic authorities, and was referred to generally as the 'Monafeqin', or less formally as 'American mercenaries', during the initial period of hysterical anti-US hatred.

On 20 June 1981 the MKO, now allied to six smaller left-wing groups, declared war on the Islamic government. It launched a series of terrorist explosions in Tehran, which caused loss of life, injury and material damage. The government fought back in like vein, using the Pasdaran, now expanded and fairly well armed, and Hezbollah, the military arm of the IRP, which it was thought mustered about 20 000 armed activists.

A vicious civil war erupted, and by the end of August it was estimated by one authority (Amnesty International) that the government had executed over 600 rebels. The MKO put the figure at 872 (Free Voice of Iran).

On 28 June 1981 in Tehran, a massive explosion demolished the building in which a meeting of the top layer of the Islamic Republican Party was being held, killing 74 people and injuring many more. The dead included Ayatollah Beheshti, leader of the IRP, twelve government ministers and 28 Majlis deputies. The government automatically blamed the MKO, although at the time this was not fully accepted in some circles. The IRP had so many enemies. Whenever terrorist incidents occurred, everyone blamed everyone else, and many allegations and acceptances of responsibility had dubious foundations. The struggle between the Pasdaran, aided by Hezbollah, and the MKO continued, not only in Tehran but also in several provincial cities.

Much later (in 1994), in a book written by a defecting former senior Iranian diplomat who had served in the London embassy (Mir Ali Asghar Montazam), Speaker Rafsanjani was linked to this high-profile bomb explosion. The publishers (Anglo-European) claimed that a diplomat from the Iranian embassy in Bonn had wanted to buy up the whole print run. The Iranian embassy confirmed this contact, but denied it wanted to prevent the book from being circulated, stating 'It is not correct that the embassy has tried to stop the distribution of the book, as its contents cannot be proved'.

It was certainly odd that Rafsanjani had somehow avoided being at the fatal meeting at that vital moment. Another character who left the vital IRP meeting before the explosion was Javid Bahonar. Montazam goes on to allege that the Iranian prosecutor general, Ayatollah Ali Qoddusi, was assassinated a few days before he could present to the Majlis his findings on the incident, in which it was alleged he accused Rafsanjani of being responsible.

MEDIA CLAMP-DOWN

The fact that Reuters published details of the death of Ayatollah Beheshti and the other IRP members hours before the news was carried by the Iranian media caused some government chagrin and embarrassment, which resulted in a sharp clamp-down on the foreign media in Iran. Reuters staff were expelled from Tehran. The IRP newspaper *Jumhuri Islami* (Official Islamic Word) alleged there were about '1000 foreign journalists in Iran gathering information, whose espionage is a most important source of information to the enemy'. No American and very few European journalists remained in Tehran.

Khomeini urged everyone to be alert and to become vigilantes, reporting any subversive acts, or gossip, to the authorities. More newspapers were banned, including the *Islamic Revolution*, Bani-Sadr's media organ, and other left-wing ones. The Voice and Vision of the Islamic Revolution was under IRP control and had a virtual monopoly of TV and radio, while the FARS news agency, which had operated under the shah, had tamely come to heel.

DEATH OF THE PRESIDENT AND PRIME MINISTER

Bani-Sadr's impeachment was in hand and a presidential election was held quickly to replace him, Khomeini urging all to vote so that a new president could get on with governing the country. Mohammed Ali Radjai (one of four candidates) was elected president on 24 July, supported by the Islamic clergy and gaining some 90 per cent of the votes. Radjai, a teacher, was regarded as a somewhat drab compromise choice, but he had the almost essential qualification of having been imprisoned under the shah for his 'religious beliefs'.

On 30 August 1981 in Tehran, a bomb exploded at a cabinet meeting, killing President Radjai, Prime Minister Javid Bahonar and several others; more were injured. The MKO was blamed.

This had happened during a weekend of violence in the capital. There were two other large terrorist explosions, one mullah was assassinated, eleven Pasdaran members were killed in street fighting, and 46 people were executed by firing squad. This violent terrorist opposition campaign against the government was being fought out against the backdrop of the war with Iraq, which initially Iran seemed to be losing. Iran was now fighting on two fronts, one external and the other internal.

President Brezhnev of the USSR sent a message of sympathy to Ayatollah Khomeini, describing the killings as acts of terrorism. The Soviets were trying hard to woo the Iranian government, but were becoming disillusioned by the mass execution of left-wing Iranians. A Tass report called for economic reform in Iran and for the standard of living of its rural people to be raised, this being the first open Soviet criticism. Previous Iranian events had been reported starkly in the Soviet media, without comment.

The Soviet Union, wanting stability along its frontiers and to prevent the United States from reestablishing its position of influence in Iran, had initially supported Khomeini in the hope that the Tudeh could eventually achieve power.

EVIN PRISON DEATH

Another casualty at about this time was the governor of the notorious Evin Prison, a so-called model prison built by the Shah on a hill overlooking Tehran, where it was reckoned that during the first two years of the Islamic revolution over 200 executions had taken place. The governor, Mohammed Katchu, aged 31 years, was shot by a discontented Pasdaran member, whom he had dismissed for having 'bad morals'. The assassin died in hospital.

Katchu had boasted that he was an enlightened governor who had abolished torture and allowed prisoners family and conjugal visits. On the other hand he had fully implemented Koranic punishments, especially the lashing of women and threatening them with death for a second offence of adultery. His philosophy had been the Koranic dictum that 'corrupt elements on earth must be annihilated, both men and women'. This attitude had been adopted by many clerics newly finding themselves in positions of secular authority.

Katchu, who had himself been imprisoned in Evin Prison under the Shah and claimed to have been tortured for religious activities, had said 'There is repentance and forgiveness in Islam, but that does not mean that a person who repents and receives forgiveness should not be punished. Repentance is for Allah'. The assassin's six collaborators disappeared from view into Evin Prison, where there 'had been 40 executions in the previous eight days' (Amit Roy) (*Daily Telegraph*).

MUJAHEDEEN KHALK ORGANISATION

During 1982 the Islamic authorities intensified their action against the Mujahedeen Khalk Organisation and were determined to destroy it completely. They ruthlessly employed bomb attacks, mass arrests, assassinations and executions, but this served to heighten rather than lessen the tempo of the civil conflict. For example, on 2 October a massive explosion in Imam Square, Tehran, killed more than 60 people and probably injured more than 700; and on the 15th in a mosque in Kermanshah, an MKO suicide bomber with a grenade walked towards Ayatollah Ashrafi Isfahani, a close friend of Khomeini. The grenade went off, killing both the bomber and the ayatollah, and injuring others. The MKO had accused the ayatollah of being responsible for the execution of hundreds of people in Western Iranian cities.

In an effort to root out MKO guerrillas the government suddenly issued new identity cards, which resulted in more mass arrests. It was announced in the Majlis on 3 January 1983 that the security forces had 'raided 20 groups of Mujahedeen, in which 80 had been killed or arrested' (Amit Roy'). The Iranian security forces, mainly Pasdaran, shot first and asked questions afterwards.

FEDAYEEN KHALK

The other major anti-Khomeini organisation was the Fedayeen Khalk (Sazman-e Fedayeen-e Khalk-e Iran), a Marxist–Leninist movement led by Mustafa Madani. The Fedayeen Khalk had a probable membership of 5000 or more, and reputedly could muster up to 50 000 people for a political demonstration. It came increasingly into conflict with the Pasdaran. Ayatollah Khomeini continually appealed to these and other warring factions to stop fighting each other and work together, but to no avail. The shah had referred to the Fedayeen Khalk as 'the Unholy Alliance of Islamic Marxists'.

FORQAN

Another organisation, much smaller but no less deadly, was the right-wing Forqan group, which was embarked on a pro-gramme of assassination. Its first VIP victim was General Mohammed Vali Qarani – who had been appointed army chief of staff in February 1979, only to be dismissed a month later – who was assassinated on 23 April 1979. This was followed in May by the assassination of Ayatollah Morteza Motahari, a member of the IRP; another senior mullah and the head of re-ligious broadcasting in July; a newspaper magnate in August; and a German businessman in October. Other assassinations followed at intervals. The office of the Iranian prosecutor general stated that Forqan members frequently posed as mullahs in order to infiltrate revolutionary circles.

On 18 January 1980 a group of Forqan members, including their leader, Akbar Goudarzin, were arrested after a shootout with the Pasdaran. Most were convicted of murder and were executed within days. That month an attempted military coup against the Khomeini regime was briefly mentioned, but without details, adding that those responsible had already been executed.

Several groups, small and less virile but hungry for publicity, often claimed responsibility for terrorist incidents to boost their tiny reputations. They often gave themselves flamboyant titles, and tended to hamper identification of who was doing what.

THE ARYA

A major incident occurred on 3 August 1984, when a bomb exploded outside a principle railway station in Tehran at the height of the morning rush hour, killing 18 people and injuring over 300. Responsibility was claimed by the 'Arya' organisation, an exiled shahist group based in Paris. Speaker Rafsanjani blamed the French for this incident, condemning them for 'giving asylum and other facilities, and support to criminal leaders'. However Rafsanjani also suggested the bomb explosion could have been a response by Kurdish groups to 'recent victories of Islamic forces in Kurdistan' (IRNA), where the Pasdaran had been successfully campaigning.

THE KURDS

Kurds in the north west had been in rebellion against the central government in Tehran since 1978 or earlier, autonomy being their minimum demand. They had originally supported Khomeini to oust the Shah, thinking that would lead to their demands being met, but when they discovered Khomeini was a rigid centralist who had no intention of loosening their link to Tehran, they turned against him. Owing to military weakness the central government had to leave them to their own devices for a couple of years or so until the Pasdaran became strong enough to attempt to bring them to heel.

The main opposition group was the Kurdistan Democratic Party of Iran (KDPI), led by Abdul Rahman Glassemlou. Another, smaller Kurdish group was the Marxist-orientated Komala. There was rivalry and occasional fighting between these two groups, but both continued spasmodically to wage a partisan war against government forces in their own territory. The government claimed that large numbers of Kurds surrendered periodically, including KDPI leaders, but these claims were usually overstated. The Kurdish insurgency dragged on during 1984 and 1985, although the number of incidents tended to be fewer than in previous years, and periodic fighting between the KDPI and the Komola broke out occasionally.

The Pasdaran was still used in anti-insurgency operations in Iranian Kurdistan, partly because the government still did not completely trust the military in an internal security role, and partly because of reluctance on the part of senior army officers to again become involved in the shooting of Iranian citizens, which Kurds technically were. Every single soldier was wanted at the front to fight against Iraq, as although the tide of defeat had been stayed, a trench warfare situation had set in, and this was sucking in all available manpower. Also, Ayatollah Khomeini frowned on the use of troops for internal security missions. As the Pasdaran had limited manpower, the Kurdish insurrection simmered on.

Iran's enemy, Iraq also had a northern Kurdish problem, so the Tehran government did its best to incite and help Iraqi Kurds to fight against their own government. The Iraqi Patriotic Union of Kurdistan (PUK), led by Jalal Talabani, was based in and supported by Iran. In response the Baghdad government gave similar support to the Iranian KDPI.

A spokesman for the National Iranian Resistance Movement in Paris stated in April 1985 that the KDPI had been expelled from the alliance, having been accused by the Mujahedeen Khalk of negotiating with the Tehran government. The Kurdish problem formed a tangled web for both governments throughout the Iran–Iraq War, neither of which obtained any real advantages in this issue. Later another Kurdish rising occurred, in September and October 1989 after the war with Iraq had ended and Khomeini had died, which President Rafsanjani crushed harshly. It was admitted that the government forces incurred heavy casualties in this operation. The Kurds quietened down again, but their leadership had to operate from abroad.

THE TUDEH

In early 1983 Nuraddin Kianouri, secretary general of the communist Tudeh, and other senior Tudeh officials were captured, and several made televised 'confessions'. Their trial was set for November 1984, and then postponed indefinitely. Some alleged this was because the government feared that evidence produced at the trial would also reveal state crimes, while others attributed it to Soviet intervention. Certainly, negotiations did take place about that time between the Soviet charge d'affaires in Tehran and the Iranian foreign minister, Ali Akbar Vellayati. Iran, then at war, wanted Soviet assistance, but the Soviets had a price. The clamp-down on the Tudeh, conducted so viciously in the early months of the revolution, had been eased, seemingly due to Soviet pressure.

MKO PROTESTS

Allegations were made by several opposition groups that the authorities were torturing and executing activists, and on 7 September 1984 the MKO presented a letter to the UN secretary general alleging that the regime had 'executed 10 031 people since June 1981, of whom 9000 were MKO members or sympathisers'. A year later the Mujahedeen, also in a letter to the UN secretary general, updated the figure to approximately 12 000 executed. It also alleged that a further 120 000 people were currently in detention for political reasons.

The Fedayeen Khalk too made allegations, claiming on 3 March 1985 to have obtained 'leaked government papers' that revealed that since September 1984 168 soldiers had been executed for spying or engaging in counterrevolutionary activities. The Bahai Information Office in France alleged that 18 Bahais had been executed in a six-month period, and that all Bahais had been dismissed from government service.

On the government side, on 28 August 1985 Ayatollah Reyshahri, the new intelligence and security minister, reported that 494 people had been arrested since September 1984 in connection with terrorist activities. He went on to say that during that period there had been 36 attacks against government officials, and that security forces had dismantled 39 terrorist groups. This gives some idea of Iran's ongoing internal security problems.

Meanwhile terrorist explosions, many of which were car bombs, continued. In March 1985 an explosion at Tehran

University killed six people, including the terrorist who was planting the bomb. A car-bomb explosion in May, in Tehran's central market, killed 15 people and injured over 50; another in June killed four people. An explosion in June near a Tehran bank killed three people and injured five. A car bomb in August injured over 30 people; another at Tehran University injured twelve people; and so on. In the main the authorities blamed the MKO, but this was invariably denied, the MKO insisting that it only struck at military targets.

This spasmodic violence continued into 1986, and in August of that year Ayatollah Reyshahri announced that during the previous 12 months 50 assassination squads, responsible for 22 deaths, had been broken up, and that 86 of their members had either been killed or arrested. He added that three men accused of a bombing incident in Qom had admitted to the offence, and had been executed.

THE FREEDOM MOVEMENT

Beginning in mid-1985, as it was feeling more secure and confident, the Islamic regime began cautiously to permit a limited amount of political discussion, and in this new atmosphere the 'Freedom Movement' acquired a semi-legal status and began to utter mild criticisms. However it was not formally recognised as a political party. The Freedom Movement (Nezat-e-azadi), more properly named the Association for the Defence of the Freedom and Sovereignty of the Iranian Nation, had been formed by by Mehdi Bazarghan and its platform was to support the Islamic revolution and the constitution, opposing only the war with Iraq. It was regarded with suspicion by the Tehran leadership, but in view of the new spirit of moderation, verging on tolerance, it was left alone. Bazarghan was able to visit Tehran in May 1986, but while there was briefly kidnapped and threatened. He hastened back into exile.

In December the UN General Assembly expressed its deep concern about allegations of human rights abuses in Iran. This seems to have upset the Iranian leadership, which thought it was smoothly and openly relaxing its former hardline attitude towards opposition.

AYATOLLAH MONTAZERI

In November 1985 Ayatollah Hussein Ali Montazeri was nominated as Khomeini's successor as supreme guide of Iran. In June the following year Montazeri ordered the release of all those political prisoners who were no longer considered to be a threat to the regime. A special team was formed to implement this decision. However Montazeri fell out with Khomeini, and a campaign was launched to discredit him. He was placed under virtual house arrest in Qom.

As the feud between the two ayatollahs worsened, Khomeini accused Montazeri's followers of smuggling explosives into Saudi Arabia. Some of these followers were executed, and in early 1989 Khomeini published his letters to Montazeri in a volume called *The Book of Sufferings*. Khomeini was anxious to get his side of the story over to the Iranian people before he died. In March 1989 Montazeri resigned as the nominated successor to Khomeini.

ELECTIONS 1988

In April and May 1988, elections were held for the third Majlis. The elections were run on non-party lines, the IRP having been disbanded the previous year. The only party to be recognised was the Freedom Movement, which boycotted the elections. In its place two 'groups' began to take shape, the 'reformists' and the 'conservatives'. The reformists gained the most ground, opening the way for reformist economic legislation. On 2 June Rafsanjani was again elected speaker, as well as acting commander-in-chief.

END OF THE IRAN–IRAQ WAR

The Iran–Iraq War, which had begun in 1980, ended suddenly on 18 June 1988 when Ayatollah Khomeini made a dramatic statement that he would 'drink from a poison cup' and accept UN Security Council Resolution 598 for a ceasefire, which came into effect on 20 August. His armed forces had been unable to break though the entrenched Iraqi lines, and Iran's military and economic strength was being drained away for no purpose. Faced with the massive burden of reconstructing its shattered economy, Iran started to look around for friends in the international arena to help with this stupendous task, but found few.

DEATH OF KHOMEINI

Ayatollah Khomeini died on 3 June 1989. The news was broken the next morning by his son, Ahmad Khomeini, in a radio broadcast to the nation. The Assembly of Experts went into secret session, and a majority of 60 of the the 74 members present voted for President Ali Akbar Khamenei as Khomeini's successor. Khamenei had entered the session as a middle-ranking hojatolislam, but emerged as an ayatollah, the degree of eminence required by the constitution for the position of Wali Faqir, (supreme guide).

The funeral of Khomeini was dramatic. His glass-encased body was displayed in public in Tehran on the 5th, and the crowd became so dense that eight people were crushed to death and over 50 were injured. At his burial on the 6th, hysterical mourners grabbed at his shroud and his body fell to the ground.

Many ambitious, high-profile leaders in Iran had been waiting impatiently for Khomeini to die, after which they hoped to be able to implement or operate their own agendas. When the mourning period was over, they anticipated a reversal of some of Khomeini's policies, slowly at first, but then more quickly. All had expected Khomeini's funeral to be well attended by the masses, but all were surprised at just how many came. Mullahs led their flocks into Tehran in their hundreds of thousands to pay their last respects. This unexpected depth of feeling indicated that any radical programmes to unravel Khomeini's dictum would meet with fierce opposition from the mullahs. Thus for the pragmatists, of whom Rafsanjani was one, it turned out to be a slow march forward.

PRESIDENT RAFSANJANI

On 24 July 1989 Hashemi Ali Akbar Rafsanjani, aged 55, was elected the fourth president of Iran. The voters also approved wide-ranging constitutional amendments that were put to a referendum on the same voting paper. About 80 hopefuls had registered as presidential candidates, but the monitoring Council of Constitutional Guardians had disqualified all but two – Rafsanjani and a weak opponent.

The post of prime minister was abolished, thus giving Rafsanjani exclusive executive power, while Khamenei held supreme Islamic power. Both were regarded as pragmatists, but they were uneasy partners. Ayatollah Mehdi Karubi was appointed as speaker of the Majlis, now a much lower-profile position than formerly. President Rafsanjani declared that his foremost policy objectives were to improve the economy of the country, which had been shattered by Iran's disastrous war with Iraq, and increase industrial output.

Ayatollah Khomeini had said that 'Economics are a matter for donkeys' (Heikal, 1982), but Rafsanjani was reputed to be earnestly studying Western textbooks on economics and allied subjects. His 'economic liberalisation' policy became known as 'Islamic capitalism' by his enemies. Iran was short of hard currency, its short-term loans amounted to about $35 billion, and the standard of living had fallen to 50 per cent of what it had been in the shah's days. Economists said that only a significant rise in the world price of oil could resolve the Iranian economic problem (*Middle East Economic Digest*). Many Iranians had to work at two jobs, some even three, to get by.

As far as can be judged, like his predecessor President Rafsanjani adopted a direct 'hands on' approach towards the Ministry of Intelligence and Security. He confirmed the late Ayatollah's fatwa on Salman Rushdie. The Council of Guardians ensured that all legislation conformed with the Islamic constitution, and they also had the power to veto candidates for high office.

Post-Khomeini legislation included the passing of a bill in August 1989 to merge the Pasdaran, Khomeini's favourite tool, into the single Ministry of Defence and Army Forces Logistics, thus reducing its former autonomy. Following US legislation allowing US armed forces to arrest 'terrorists anywhere in the world', the Iranian president was authorised to arrest and punish any US citizen found guilty of anti-Iranian terrorism anywhere in the world.

An election for the 83-member Assembly of Experts, which was empowered to interpret the Islamic constitution, took place on 8 October. In the run-up to the election arguments were aired between the 'radicals' (an expression used to describe Islamic fundamentalists) and the pragmatists. In this election the radicals lost influence, and a split began to show.

INTERNAL TERRORISM CONTINUES

Iran's reputation overseas remained black. For example Amnesty International stated that during 1988 at least 1200 people had been executed in Iran, and other human rights organisations made similar condemnations. Iran also had a huge drug problem. It was admitted that there were over one million drug addicts in the country, and that over '900 drug dealers had been executed in 1989' (IRNA). The government complained that 'secret agencies of enemy powers' were behind the massive drug problem of the country (*Kayhan*). In a report published in December 1989 Galindo Pohl, the UN special envoy on human rights, stated that 'more than 5,000 people had been executed in three years'. Later, in November 1993, he accused Iran of holding 20 000 political prisoners, and wrote that 'torture was common throughout Iran' (UN reports).

In May 1989 the Tehran government claimed it had broken a spy ring that had been supplying 'sensitive information to the Iraqi Baathist Party and other foreign agencies' (IRNA). Eleven suspects were arrested, including Masoud Dalvand, the alleged leader of the group and said to be a leading member of the Paris-based NIRM. Some of the suspects made televised 'confessions', a procedure favoured by the authorities in Tehran during that time to concetrate public attention on such issues, and probably divert it from other unpleasant ones. At the subsequent trial, four of the suspects were found guilty. They were hanged on 4 November, when Hojatolislam Mohtashemi harangued the mob.

A proclamation was issued that 4 November 1991 was to be a 'National Day of Struggle against World Arrogance'. This was also the year in which 884 death sentences were passed for drug offences in Iran (IRNA). On 2 December the Iranian

VVIR reported that over recent months 300 people had been arrested. The detainees allegedly belonged to four different underground organisations, named as 'monarchists, SAVAK, the Mujahedeen, and a group for financial corruption'.

RIOTING IN MASHHAD AND ELSEWHERE

In November 1992 reports came in of rioting in the cities of Mashhad, Shiraz and Arak, caused by a 'small number of subversive counterrevolutionaries', and it was thought that up to a dozen ringleaders were executed. An uneasy feeling of general discontent was apparent in Iran during that year, and this continued into 1993, mainly due to a combination of inflation, falling oil prices, and an expansion of the population, the latter having risen from about 32 million in 1978 to over 60 million. The Iranian First Five Year Plan (1988–93) had not been adequate.

ATTACKS ON RAFSANJANI

On 10 February 1993 an attempt was made to assassinate President Rafsanjani. His motorcade ran into an ambush at a crossroads near Tehran, and in the firefight that erupted at least five of the attackers were killed. Three were arrested. In a communique, responsibility was claimed by the Babak Khorramdin, a comparatively new covert organisation that was opposed to the Islamic regime. It was said that three members of the attacking commando were former army officers and two had been members of Pasdaran, indicating a rumble of discontent within the ranks of these two defence forces.

In February 1994 another assassination attempt was made against President Rafsanjani at a mass rally in Tehran. Some 20 suspects were arrested, and responsibility was claimed by the 'Free Officers of the Revolutionary Guards', another comparatively new covert group. A government communique said it had been 'a well planned and prepared plot by foreign powers'. The seized assassin was Kouresh Nikahtar, said to be a Pasdaran reject. This indicated a split in the Pasdaran's ranks, a section of whom disliked the new policies of the 'moderates'.

(This was the third known attempt on Rafsanjani's life, the first being in 1979, when he was shot in the stomach.)

On 11 June 1993 Rafsanjani was re-elected president for a second four-year term. The 2700 polling stations were heavily guarded, and all vehicles had to be parked some distance away for fear of car bombs. In the run-up to the election Rafsanjani had done his best to reduce the influence of the radical element, and in this he was supported to a degree by Ayatollah Khamenei, the supreme guide, who perhaps by the nature of his absolute position was becoming more radical himself. Rafsanjani was losing popularity. His anticorruption campaign – launched the previous May and relaunched in June, which amongst other things had banned officials at state-run institutions from accepting 'commissions', from which many clergy had benefited personally – had not been successful. Rafsanjani said of the clergy: 'they have gone off course, and the authorities have not behaved well'. Later Rafsanjani's brother, Mohammed Hashemi, who was in charge of the VVIR, was abruptly dismissed by Khamenei – the split between Islamic and secular power was widening.

Rafsanjani was accused of failing to stem the tide of creeping Westernisation. Indeed in June he had arrested a number of vigilantes, both men and women, of the 'Squad for the Propagation of Virtue and the Elimination of Vice', which sought to enforce the Islamic dress code and Islamic behaviour in public. Ayatollah Khamenei ordered their release, and decreed that the organisation should establish headquarters in each province. Previously, when Rafsanjani had attempted to prevent casual Islamic groups from harassing the public on this issue, Ayatollah Khamenei had ordered the reconstitution of the youthful Baseej organisation, which had played such a dramatic part on the battlefield in the war with Iraq, and had given them the authority to police Islamic conduct in public.

To shore up and strengthen his Islamic credentials, Rafsanjani officially received Sheikh Hassan Nasrallah of the Lebanese-based Hezbollah. This provoked Western criticism, as did his allowing Bakhtiar's assassins to be promoted within the intelligence service. In the United States Secretary of State Warren Christopher was insisting that Iran was 'one of the principal sources of support for terrorist groups around the world' (Congress records).

ATTACKS ON CHRISTIANS

On 30 January 1994 Haik Honsepian Mehr, an Armenian bishop, was found murdered in a street in Tehran. Mehr had obtained the release from prison of Mehdi Dibaj, a Muslim who had abandoned his faith and become a Christian. For this he had been sentenced to death by an Iranian court, but this had been commuted to a term of imprisonment. At one time there were 310 000 Christians in Iran (1976 census), but as subsequent census forms did not pose the same questions under the Islamic regime, it was suspected that this number had decreased. Only four minority religions – Zoroastrianism, Judaism, Armenian Christianity and Assyrian Christianity – were permitted under the Islamic constitution.

Later in the year two more Christians were murdered in Tehran: Tateds Michaelian on 29 June, and Mehdi Dibaj on 3 July. On 8 July two women were arrested and accused of planning to bomb the tomb of Khomeini and murdering an unnamed Christian. On the 13th one of these women confessed to the murder of Michaelian.

MORE PROVINCIAL DISTURBANCES

Intermittent unrest surfaced again in certain provinces. In February 1994 in Zahedan (the provincial capital of Sistan-Baluchistan), which had a Sunni majority, disturbances broke out following the destruction by the Shia authorities of the Sunni Sheikh Fayed Mosque. This was a somewhat unusual example of Shia–Sunni differences expressing themselves in violence. The government blamed 'foreigners and antirevolutionary' protestors. Eventually Bahran Assazaseh, an MKO member, was arrested and accused of planning the explosion that destroyed the mosque. He was convicted and hanged in public on 13 August.

In Mashhad (the provincial capital of Khoristan) on 20 June there was an explosion in the Hussein Mosque, which was filled with worshippers on the Shia Day of Mourning of Ashura – 25 people were killed and over 100 injured. The government again blamed the MKO, and named Mehdi Navi as the organiser of the incident, which vaguely surprised the security forces as formerly the MKO had operated only in Tehran and the western provinces. Navi was eventually arrested, and on 1 August was fatally wounded while attempting to escape. Before he died he was interviewed in his hospital bed by a TV reporter, and admitted he had been responsible for the Mashhad bombing. The MKO denied he had been a member.

The Tehran government alleged that the Saudi-backed extremist Sunni Anjuman Sispah-i Sahaba group was implicated in attacks from Pakistan into Iran, and in particular had been involved in the Zahedan disturbances.

In August 1994, riots erupted in Zanjan province over the proposed separation of the Qazvin region from the Farsi-speaking part of the province, the inhabitants resenting being administered by Azeri-speaking Zanjanis.

INTERNAL TERRORISM IN IRAN: 1994

Internal terrorism continued to plague the Tehran government during 1994, which named the three main active terrorist groups as the MKO, the KDPI and the MPRP (Muslim People's Republican Party), the latter led by Hussein Farish. Also named were two newly formed groups: the Babak Khorrandin and the 'Free Officers of the Revolutionary Guard' (FORG). The main incident of the year, on 19 April, was a bomb explosion in the centre of Tehran that injured over 20 people. Responsibility was claimed by the al-Haraka al-Islamiya, whose communiques referred to the destruction of the Sheikh Fayed Mosque in Mashhad, so it was assumed either to be a code name of the Saudi Anjuman Sispah-i Sahaba organisation, or a new Sunni anti-Iranian-government one.

SATELLITE-LINKED TV

The Islamic authorities in Iran became obsessed by pernicious Westernisation seeping into their culture, and in particular they were alarmed by the mushroom growth of satellite TV dishes in Tehran and other major cities. Satellite-linked TV was enabling Iranians to obtain a view of the world outside the narrow confines of their own Islamic one. On 5 April the government banned the unauthorised use of satellite linked dishes to gain access to foreign TV, as they 'infringed our people's national and religious culture'. Throughout the year the Islamic authorities and mullahs campaigned for this insidious form of Western counterpropaganda to be banned, but still satellite dishes arrived in Tehran by the thousands.

It was not until January 1995 that the Majlis passed legislation, approved by the monitoring Council of Guardians, that enabled the Ministry of National Guidance to ban the dishes in order to 'safeguard the cultural boundaries of the country, and of its families against destructive and indecent satellite programmes'.

It was estimated that there were already over 250 000 satellite dishes in Tehran, and more in other provincial cities and across the country, and that more than three million people regularly tuned into Western broadcasts (*The Times*). Satellite dishes were to be removed, their importation was forbidden and heavy fines were imposed for failure to comply. Opposition came from educated and middle-class elements, and those who thought the ban would lead to clandestine viewing rather than stopping it completely, especially as technical progress meant that dishes were becoming smaller and programmes were multiplying in number and variety.

8 Iranian Terrorist Tentacles

On 31 December 1979, at a press conference in Qom, Ayatollah Sadiq Khalkhali, who as head of the Revolutionary Courts had already sentenced scores of victims to death, crowed that he had sent death squads to London to deal with enemies of the revolution, and that Ayatollah Khomeini had approved his action. This boastful statement was made in the full flush of the Islamic Revolution, at a time when it was for some reason generally thought that most escaping shahist leaders and followers were flocking to Britain for sanctuary. It seemed to take some time for it to be realised that France was the main country to offer political asylum, whereupon the 'death squads' were presumably relocated. Certainly, at that time the forceful Khalkhali was garnering power for himself in the maelstrom of the political struggles for survival and power in Tehran. It is probable that he became the first patron of the Iranian terrorist tentacles that began to penetrate beyond Iran's borders in search of the Islamic Republic's enemies.

It can be said with some certainty that a government-directed, government-funded-covert assassination network was developing. One of its first prominent victims was Captain Mustafa Chahryar Chafik, a nephew of the shah, who was killed in Paris on 7 December 1979, even though he had adopted a false identity. Responsibility for this assassination was accorded by Khalkhali – who had repeatedly called for the death of the shah and his family – to the Fedayeen Islam, a group of extreme, integrationist Muslims. Khalkhali warned that this organisation would continue its activities in Europe and the United States against the former shah, his relatives and associates. The assassination of Chafik was the first battle honour in the Iranian covert assassination programme.

EXPANSIONARY ISLAMIC FERVOUR

The desire to carry the Islamic fundamentalist revolutionary banner beyond the borders of Iran was frequently and

145

boastfully expressed. On 5 December 1979 Sheikh Abbas Mohammed Montazeri, son of Ayatollah Hussein Montazeri, a prominent member of the IRC, announced that he proposed to send 1700 volunteers to fight for the Palestinian cause in Lebanon, that the first contingent was due to reach that country on the 8th, and that it would 'enter by force if necessary'. The Lebanese government closed its air space to prevent this, and so to save face Ayatollah Khomeini cancelled the project. However this did nothing to damp enthusiasm.

The Islamic Revolutionary Students too had expansionary zeal, despite their ongoing involvement with the American embassy hostages and their internecine squabbles. They organised a conference of representatives of 'liberation movements from 17 Islamic countries', which was addressed on 11 December by Ayatollah Montazeri. The object of the conference was 'to combine in revolutionary unity' in order to export the Iranian Islamic fundamentalist revolution to other parts of the world.

ATTEMPTED ASSASSINATION OF BAKHTIAR

As the Iranian death squads continued their covert external operations, a window on their activities and methods was opened on 18 July 1980 when one squad failed to eliminate Shahpour Bakhtiar, the shah's former prime minister, who was living in exile in Paris. Posing as journalists, a five-man team of hired terrorists – led by Anis Naccache, an internationally known Lebanese terrorist who was reputed to be member of Fatah and used the code name 'Abu Mazen' – entered the apartment block where Bakhtiar was living. In the subsequent shoot-out Bakhtiar escaped injury, but a French policeman and a woman resident were killed, and three other people were injured. Three of the terrorists were arrested on the spot. The other two fled, but were quickly apprehended.

Anis Naccache told the French police that his group (four Arabs and one Iranian) had been given money and weapons by Iranian officials and sent to Paris to kill Bakhtiar, arriving from different European capitals the previous day. He claimed that Yasser Arafat, leader of both the Palestine Liberation Organisation and Fatah, one of its constituents, had personally ordered the operation, and that 'it had been requested by the Iranian authorities without specifying who they were' (*Le Quotidien*).

Speaking on French TV, Bakhtiar said he had received a series of death threats, and that the previous month Ayatollah Khalkhali had announced that orders had been given for his assassination. Radio Tehran reported that a group called the Guardians of the Islamic Revolution had claimed responsibility. The Palestinian Fatah organisation denied any involvement.

Sadiq Gotbzadeh, the Iranian foreign minister, happened to be passing through Paris at the time, and he vigorously denied (also on French TV) any official Iranian involvement in the incident, alleging that the murder attempt had been a put-up job by Iranian exiles enjoying safe asylum in France. Previously French relations with the Islamic Republic of Iran had been good; and the French, who had sheltered Khomeini in exile, were anticipating lucrative commercial contracts. Relations had begun to deteriorate when the French government, adhering to the country's long tradition of liberal political asylum, refused to extradite Bakhtiar at Iran's request.

The deduction from this Bakhtiar incident can only be that the Iranian government was operating a covert policy to assassinate prominent, exiled, pro-shah leaders, and that it was employing mercenary international terrorists to carry out the operations in order to distance itself from the odium, while consistently and vigorously denying any involvement.

NATIONAL IRANIAN RESISTANCE MOVEMENT

Paris became a hotbed of Iranian political exiles of all shades of opinion. In August 1981 Shahpour Bakhtiar announced the formation of the National Iranian Resistance Movement, whose aim was to overthrow the Islamic regime in Tehran; to put Ali Pahlavi Shah, the son of Mohammed Reza Pahlavi Shah (who 'had died in exile in Egypt in July 1980) on the Peacock Throne; and to establish a secular democratic government, with himself as prime minister. Bakhtiar surrounded himself with prominent monarchists. The NIRM included the Kurdish KDPI, but its relationship within this coalition was an uneasy one. Eventually, in April 1985 an NIRM spokesman announced in Paris that the KDPI had been expelled from the alliance, having been accused of negotiating with the Tehran government.

PROVISIONAL GOVERNMENT AND NATIONAL RESISTANCE COUNCIL

The other main Iranian exiled opposition groups in France announced their existence on 1 October 1981: The Provisional Government of the Democratic Republic of Iran, with Bani-Sadr as its president; and the National Resistance Council (NRC), headed by Masoud Rajavi, leader of the Mujahedeen Khalk. The two men, who had fled from Iran in July in a commandeered air force plane, agreed to work together, but would have nothing to do with any of the other resistance groups, especially monarchist ones. The NIRM and the NRC conducted their own individual propaganda and covert campaigns against the Tehran regime, and although there was some cooperation between them, it was not overdone. Each leader had his own secret agenda.

HEZBOLLAH IN LEBANON

From 1982 onwards the Tehran government's main covert external terrorist effort was conducted through Hezbollah and other groups it was supporting and activating in Lebanon, which accounts for a seeming slackening off of overseas assassinations and other allied covert projects.

THE BUTCHER OF TEHRAN

However assassination overseas was retained as a terrorist tool, and on 7 February 1984 General Gholam Ali Oveissi was killed in Paris by four men, the Lebanese-based al-Jihad al-Islami claiming responsibility. Oveissi, a former military governor of Tehran under the shah, had become known as the 'Butcher of Tehran' for opening fire on demonstrators in 1978. A week after his death (the 14th) Hojatolislam Ali Akbar Mohtashemi, the Iranian Ambassador to Syria, was injured by a parcel bomb in Damascus. Tehran put the blame on Iranian exiles.

NATIONAL RESISTANCE COUNCIL

The partnership between Bani-Sadr and Masoud Rajavi did not last long as Rajavi began to establish links with Iraq. This was abhorrent to the patriotic Bani-Sadr, and the two men parted company in April 1984. In June 1986 Rajavi, leader of the National Resistance Council, of which the Mujahedeen Khalk Organisation (MKO) was the military arm, was pressed to leave France. He had been wearing out his welcome in France for some time as he was raising a body of guerrillas, which he referred to as his National Liberation Army (NLA). Anxious to gain the release of French hostages in Lebanon, and wanting to improve its standing with the Iranian government, France ejected Rajavi and his NLA, who were then invited to Iraq.

President Saddam Hussein of Iraq recognised the propaganda value of having an anti-Tehran Iranian military force, no matter how tiny, on Iraqi soil to fight side-by-side with Iraqis against Iran. He agreed that Rajavi should be allowed to 'administer Mehran as Iranian territory' – Mehran being a part of Iran just captured by Iraq – in order to attract anti-Khomeini Iranians. Unfortunately for Rajavi he was unable to take up this prestige offer as a successful Iranian counteroffensive (Operation Karbala-1) resulted in the recapture of Mehran on 20 June 1986. Rajavi's NRA had to be located nearby, where for propaganda purposes it was said to be 'holding part of the Iraqi front line'.

SHIA ASCENDANCY

In the decades following the dissolution of the Ottoman Empire after the First World War, the spread of Western influence into the Middle East caused a decline in Islamic ascendancy and authority and the rise of secular and semisecular governments. During this period of Islamic decline, Middle Eastern Muslims tended to look towards Saudi Arabia as the repository of Islamic authority and tradition. Islam had after all originated in what was now Saudi Arabia, which also contained the two most holy Islamic cities: Mecca and Medina. This orientation was strengthened by the annual pilgrimage, or hajj, which all good Muslims should make at least once during their lifetime. Saudi Arabia, a monarchical Islamic theocracy, developed the hajj, which became so popular (and profitable to Saudi Arabia) that countries were confined to 'quotas' of pilgrims, dictated by the Riyadh authorities, which sometimes caused friction.

As the Tehran regime began to consolidate Iran as an Islamic fundamentalist republic, Ayatollah Khomeini sought to assume the mantle of 'marja taqlid', that is, leader of the reputedly 100-million-strong Shia branch of Islam, even though the present incumbent, an elderly Iranian cleric, was much senior to himself in the heirarchy. Khomeini sought to impose his personality and authority on a wider section of Islam outside Iran's borders. He set his sights on Saudi Arabia, in spite of that country being coldly hostile to him and having only a small Shia population. Khomeini was particularly incensed when in October 1986 King Fahd of Saudi Arabia assumed the title 'Custodian of the Two Holy Places', meaning the holy cities of Mecca and Medina. This title had a proprietorial ring to Khomeini's ears that slighted his dignity.

The next annual hajj took place in July 1987. The large Iranian contingent (about 154 000 pilgrims) contained a small group of political activists and members of the Pasdaran, who chanted political slogans, not only against Western imperialists, but also against King Fahd and the Saudi regime.

On 31 July these political pilgrims clashed with Saudi security forces, which were blocking their way to the Grand Mosque. The outcome was disastrous. Iran subsequently claimed that over 600 pilgrims had been killed, many by gunfire, although it later admitted that most had died as a result of being trampled underfoot by panicking pilgrims hemmed into a confined space. The Saudi authorities put the death toll at 402, of whom 85 were Saudi security personnel and civilians, 275 were Iranian pilgrims and 42 pilgrims of other nationalities. A further 649 people had been injured. Later the Iranian authorities stated that 230 bodies had been returned, but that a further 90 had been withheld as they 'bore bullet wounds' (IRNA).

This Iranian political march had been well organised and was prepared for trouble. Many of the pilgrims had carried political banners, which was forbidden by Saudi regulations. Stones had been thrown from house tops on to the Iranians, who at one point were said to have been incensed by reports that Batoul (Khomeini's wife, who was on the hajj) had been attacked and beheaded by a Saudi policeman, who then displayed her head on a pole. Other bloodthirsty incidents were subsequently related by both sides. The Jordanian anti-terrorist '101 Battalion' was deployed at Mecca at the time, but the authorities remain silent about whether or not it was involved in this major incident (*Financial Times*).

Previously, on 28 July, Khomeini had addressed the world's Muslims, calling on all hajj pilgrims to rid their Islamic lands of the forces of Satan, and pointing out that it was wrong for Islamic countries to allow foreigners 'to penetrate the secret military centres of Muslims', the latter statement being aimed against the Saudi regime. The following day Ayatollah Mehdi Karubi, leader of the Iranian Haj pilgrims and later to become speaker of the Majlis, warned the Saudi minister of pilgrimage and religious endowments who had rejected the request for what was obviously a political march to the Grand Mosque that he was responsible for keeping order. Prince Nayef ibn Abdul Aziz, the Saudi interior minister, later stated that Karubi had assured him the march would end at a certain point, but as the demonstrators had continued on to the Grand Mosque the Saudi security forces had had to take restricting action.

On 1 August 1987 the Saudi and Kuwaiti embassies in Tehran were stormed by organised mobs, and 2 August was designated by the Iranian media as a 'day of hate'. Speaker Rafsanjani called for revenge and the freeing of the Holy Shrines from the wicked Wahabis (the sect to which the Saudi royal family belonged). The Saudi authorities accused Iran of deliberate provocation, and an Iranian investigative team was refused access to the country. The Iranian Ministry of Intelligence and Security was behind the hajj provocations.

Most Arab countries voiced their open support for King Fahd – even Syria, normally an ally of Iran. Most Lebanese Muslims supported the Saudis, although there was an explossion outside the vacated Saudi embassy in Beirut and pro-Iranian demonstrations occurred in parts of the Bekaa Valley.

Colonel Gaddafi of Libya suggested that the two Islamic holy cities should be placed under international Islamic control, which pleased neither Fahd nor Khomeini. Yasser Arafat too supported Saudi Arabia.

Saudi Arabia also revealed that the previous year Iranian hajj pilgrims had been discovered carrying explosives, but that nothing had been said at the time because Ayatollah Khomeini had apologised and blamed it on Mehdi Hashemi, an Iranian who was later executed.

General Ulrich Wegener, who had been head of the West German GSG-9 counterterrorist force when it rescued the hostages of the Mogadishu hijacking in 1977, was appointed head of the Saudi task force to oversee security arrangements in Mecca for future hajj pilgrimages.

The Saudi authorities sharply reduced the Iranian quota of pilgrims, causing the Tehran government to boycott the hajj in 1988 and 1989, and to sever diplomatic relations with Saudi Arabia. Khomeini and his statesmen continued to hurl insults at King Fahd, who kept a dignified silence.

Ayatollah Mehdi Karubi sought other means of distressing the Saudis. On 10 July 1989 a bomb exploded near the Grand Mosque in Mecca, killing one pilgrim and injuring others. Several arrests were made. The following day responsibility was claimed in Beirut by the Generation of Arab Anger, a Dawa code name. On 21 September, 16 Kuwaiti Shia Muslims (ten of whom were said to be of Iranian descent) were convicted of involvement. They were publicly beheaded by the sword. Of twenty others convicted, one received 20 years' imprisonment and 1500 lashes; the remainder were given shorter terms of imprisonment and 1000 lashes, the corporal punishment being administered in public.

These were official Saudi announcements, but one wonders whether the corporal punishments were actually carried out in full, or even in part, or whether they had been made up to deter others. Khomeini, himself an exponent of naked terrorism, said nothing about this Saudi capital and corporal response, although the decapitated were hailed as Shia martyrs.

Iranian hajj pilgrimages were resumed, but in 1993 Saudi Arabia again complained that the police had had to disperse an unruly Iranian mob of pilgrims at the Grand Mosque in Mecca. Mohammed Reyshahri, still in charge of hajj arrangements, loftily replied that 'It was a minor issue' (IRNA). Iranian–Saudi relations remained tense and poor. In March 1994 Ayatollah Khamenei, the Iranian supreme guide, accused the Saudis of obstructing Iranian pilgrims on the hajj, adding the accusation that the Saudi-backed Sunni extremist group, the Anjuman Sipahah-i Sahaba, had been involved in attacks from Pakistan into Iran, and that it had also been responsible for instigating disturbances in the Sunni Zahedan province.

THE RUSHDIE FATWA

On 14 February 1989, in the final months of his life, Ayatollah Khomeini created a wave of terror that reached far into the Western world. Khomeini issued a fatwa (a religious edict, although some Islamic purists doubt its ultimate validity) condemning Salman Rushdie, the Indian-born British author of *The Satanic Verses*, to death for blasphemy and forcing him into hiding. The implication was that any good Muslim should kill him (and his publishers) on sight, wherever in the world he happened to be. The following day a senior Muslim cleric in Tehran put a multi-million dollar price on Rushdie's head. *The Satanic Verses*, which was published in September 1988, was banned in India and then in some other Muslim countries as it was considered offensive to Islam.

On 18 February 1989 Rushdie expressed his regret, but made no apology, causing Khomeini to reaffirm his fatwa. On 7 March Iran severed diplomatic relations with Britain (they were restored in September 1990 upon the outbreak of the Gulf War over Kuwait). On 30 March, Sheikh Abdullah al-Ahdam – imam at the main mosque in Brussels and opponent of Khomeini's fatwa – and his assistant were shot dead, even though on the 14th the Islamic Conference Organisation had dismissed the fatwa by a majority vote.

On 24 December Rushdie announced he had embraced Islam and withdrawn his permission for the book to be published – but this was not enough. Although Khomeini had died in July 1989, his fatwa lived on as his legacy, exuding terrorism from the grave as it was indefinitely enforceable in the Islamic sense, and seemingly could not be reversed – or more accurately, no one wanted to do anything about rescinding it.

Senior Islamic clerics and many others barely concealed their smiles of satisfaction, rather enjoying the alarm and distress Khomeini had inflicted, and was still inflicting, on the West.

In February 1990 Ayatollah Khameini, Khomeini's successor, reaffirmed the Rushdie fatwa, although in a sermon later that month President Rafsanjani gave a hint that some compromise might be reached, if only Britain would respect Islam.

Britain took this fatwa very seriously, and in June 1989 deported three Iranians suspected of anti-Rushdie activities. Nine more were deported in December (including the head of the *IRNA* bureau), followed by another nine in February 1991. In response the Iranian government announced it had closed down the 'BBC bureau in Tehran' (IRNA). The BBC quietly replied that it had no bureau in Tehran, only a part-time Iranian journalist. In 1992 Britain expelled three Iranians for being involved in intelligence activities, meaning they were searching for Rushdie's hiding place.

In July 1991 Rushdie's Japanese translator was stabbed to death in Tokyo. That month Ayatollah Hassan Sanei, head of the foundation of the 15th Khoirdad, a private organisation, offered a reward of $2 million plus expenses for anyone who killed Rushdie. In July 1993 an attempt was made to assassinate Rushdie's Italian translator in Milan, and also his publisher in Tokyo, while in Oslo another attempt was made on the life of his Norwegian publisher. More Muslim countries, or those with a sizable Islamic minority, banned *The Satanic Verses*. Sweden ejected three Iranian diplomats for 'harassing Iranian refugees', and in turn Iran ejected three Swedish diplomats,

In February 1993 Ayatollah Khamenei called on Britain to hand over Rushdie to Iran. The following month Norway expelled two Iranian diplomats alleged to have been involved in the attack on Rushdie's publisher.

At the time of writing the fatwa on Rushdie remained in force. Rushdie remained alive, but in semi-hiding, emerging to meet President Clinton, Prime Minister Major and other Western VIPs in order to cock a snook at the Iranian Islamic fundamentalist establishment; and on certain other publicity occasions, to indicate condemnation against the Islamic death threat, which was generally regarded in the Western world as an unwanted harassment. Some major airlines refused to carry

Rushdie as a passenger, despite official pressure to do so, for fear of Islamic retribution.

ASSASSINATION OF KURDISH LEADERS

The Tehran government continued spasmodically with its covert assassination policy against opposition leaders in exile, and in particular Kurdish leaders were marked out. On 13 July 1989 Abdul Rahman Ghassemlou, secretary general of the KDPI, together with two aides, was killed in an apartment in Vienna whilst conducting secret peace talks with an Iranian government delegation. It was suggested that if the KDPI supported the central government, accepted its sovereignty and ceased its dissident activities it could be formally recognised as a normal Iranian political party. In return development projects would be carried out in devastated Kurdish areas.

These negotiations had been authorised by Speaker Rafsanjani and organised by Jalal Talabani, the Iranian-based leader of Iraqi Patriotic Union of Kurdistan, and were attended by a senior Pasdaran commander, Mohammed Jafari Sahrarodi, and other Iranian officials. Sahrarodi was wounded by the assassins.

The Austrian authorities blamed 'Iranian intelligence agents' and arrest warrants were issued for two alleged members of the Iranian Intelligence and Security Ministry (one was named as Mansour Bozorgian), both of whom had disappeared. These negotiations were taking place in an uncertain semi-power vacuum in Tehran (Ayatollah Khomeini had died the previous month) in which there was much jostling for power.

Rafsanjani wanted peace with the unruly Kurds, but others did not. It seems that Ayatollah Reyshahri, as minister of intelligence and security, caused, or was persuaded to cause, triggers to be pulled to scupper the proposed deal, which had been favoured by both Rafsanjani and the Pasdaran. It was thought that Reyshahri did not have a sufficient following to be a credible principal contender in any covert power play, and therefore he was backing someone else against Rafsanjani, who was about to stand for the presidency. Theories abounded, but none were convincing.

The following month (on 26 August) Bahman Javadi, a Kurdish leader in the Komala left-wing organisation, was shot dead in Larnaca, Cyprus. 'Iranian intelligence agents' were blamed. On 18 April 1991 Abdul Rahman Broumand, a senior member of Bakhtiar's NIRM was killed in Paris. 'Iranian agents' were again blamed by the police. The NIRM continually claimed that the Iranian government was funding 'death squads' that were roaming Europe looking for opposition leaders. On 6 June 1993 Mohammed Hassan Arbab, an MKO leader, was assassinated in Karachi, Pakistan.

The next assassination of KDPI leaders occurred in a restaurant in Berlin in September 1992, when four were shot dead, one of whom was its new secretary general, Sadeg Sarafkandi. Again 'Iranian agents' were blamed. Eventually five people were arrested by the German police. Their trial began in October 1993 and immediately ran into controversy, it being alleged that details of the case had been discussed with Iran during 'security cooperation' processes.

GERMAN–IRANIAN COLLABORATION

German–Iranian covert collaboration began in 1991. At the time Germany was trying to secure the release of two hostages being held by Hezbollah in Lebanon, who were eventually released. As part of the deal, some time later Germany freed Abbas Ali Hamadei, who had been convicted in 1988 of kidnapping two German businessmen in Beirut. Hamadei had served only half his ten-year sentence when he was released in August 1993. The United States suspected that Germany was about to release Hamadei's brother, Mohammed Ali, (who was also serving a prison sentence in Germany for killing an American passenger in the 1985 TWA hijacking), and protested. Mohammed Ali Hamadei remained in prison. The German authorities said they were merely trying to obtain information from Iran about Ron Arad, a 'missing' Israeli airman who had been shot down over Lebanon and fallen into Hezbollah hands in 1986, and insisted that their contact with Iran was solely for humanitarian reasons.

Germany claimed its close liaison with Iran was producing results, and that already two German hostages had been released, but the United States disagreed, its policy being to isolate Iran and bring pressure on its allies to do likewise.

In October 1993 Ali Fallahyan, Iran's minister of intelligence and security, visited Germany. It was secretly agreed that Germany would provide Iran with sophisticated spying equipment, including computers, to enable it to keep track of Iranian dissidents, both in Iran and abroad, as part of an intelligence information and training package. He was given a list of Iranian exiles in Germany and agreed to expand German–Iranian intelligence contact. In return Fallahyan promised to stop attacking Iranian dissidents on German soil (Ken Tommerman, US arms control expert). Western intelligence agencies by this time had labelled Fallahyan as the chief instigator of exported Iranian terrorism and the suppression of dissidents in Iran.

Fallahyan's visit to Germany was controversial, indeed it was reported that the chief federal prosecutor wanted to arrest him but had been ordered not to do so. Instead Fallahyan was given VIP treatment. He was allowed to meet Bernd Schmidtbauer, a minister who answered directly to Chancellor Kohl on security matters, and also to talk to security officials. Fallahyan's visit coincided with the trial of the assassins of the KDPI officials in Berlin in 1992.

A few days after Fallahyan's return home a German businessman, Gerhard Bachmann, was arrested in Iran and accused of 'making unauthorised contact with the military', which was taken to be a warning to Germany not to renege on its secret computer deal and tracking arrangement. Iran had just passed a law banning officials from making unauthorised contact with foreigners. Neither trusted the other. US security agencies said 'I told you so', in bitter recrimination. Bachmann was released on 4 November.

On 5 January 1994 Iran passed the death sentence on Helmut Szimkus, a German engineer who had been arrested in 1988 and charged with passing security documents to the Iraqi army. This coincided with the KDPI assassination trial in Germany of five men – one Iranian and four Lebanese Shias. Helmut Szimkus was pardoned on 14 June and released on the 30th after a visit to Germany by Ali Akbar Vellayati, the Iranian foreign minister. Germany and Iran were playing a deadly cat-and-mouse game with each other.

FRENCH–IRANIAN COLLABORATION

The French were secretly negotiating with the Iranian government for an $18 billion helicopter deal, and in addition
French representatives had secretly visited Iran to discuss the
provision of spare parts for Mirage fighter aircraft. Although
the Iranian government openly declared its priority was to
rebuild its economy and industry, it was at the same time
thinking well ahead and covertly creating large and powerful
armed forces. It was also playing the game both ways.

French suspicions had been aroused back in July 1989,
when a Lebanese Shia student named 'Bassam M' was suspected of intending to bomb targets in Paris. The French security forces carried out a series of searches in Paris and
other parts of the country, including the Marseilles, Lyons
and Grenoble areas, during which an alleged Shia Lebanese
terrorist network was uncovered. In early November large
quantities of explosives and bomb-making material were discovered in a container that arrived at Marseilles. This caused
the French authorities to fear that another spasm of Middle
Eastern violence was about to hit the streets of Paris and
other French cities. Further arms caches were unearthed
and eight people were arrested, one being the ringleader,
Fouard Ali Saleh, who was said to have masterminded several
terrorist incidents in Paris in 1986. The French security
forces stated that the 'Iranian connection was obvious'. This
was a severe setback to Iranian terrorism in France
(*Le Quotidien*).

IRANIAN DENIALS

In January 1992 a Tehran government spokesman again
denied US allegations that it was providing funds to groups
holding foreign hostages in Lebanon and receiving a share of
the reputedly large sums of money extracted as ransom, but
for the first time did admit, on TV, that it had 'a special
influence in Lebanon'. Amnesty International expressed
concern at the increase in extrajudicial killing in Iran and of
Iranians living abroad, suggesting they had been approved by
the Tehran government.

In February 1993 President Rafsanjani gave a high-profile speech to the diplomatic corps in Tehran, calling on 'world thinkers' to change their attitude towards Iran and rejecting Western allegations of Iranian support for terrorism. The following month Iran again vigorously rejected the US allegation that it was the 'world's most dangerous state sponsor of terrorism'.

ASSASSINATION OF BAKHTIAR

On 6 August 1991 Shahpour Bakhtiar, the shah's last prime minister, and his secretary, Sorouch Katibek, were assassinated in their apartment in Paris. It was a tale of treachery and deceit, for which a French examining magistrate later blamed Ali Fallahyan, the Iranian minister of intelligence and security, and Mohammed Gharrazi, minister of telecommunications. Bakhtiar had been given French state protection – a squad of gendarmes had guarded his residence and immediate area, and visitors had been rigorously monitored. His son Guy was a serving French police officer and had been involved in his father's security arrangements.

The Trojan Horse turned out to be Farqsoum Boyer Ahmadi, a family friend recruited by VEVAK, who had wormed his way into Bakhtiar's confidence. Although some of Bakhtiar's colleagues had pointed the finger of suspicion at Ahmadi, Bakhtiar had not listened to them. The two assassins were Mohammed Azadi and Ali Vakili Rad, who had flown into Paris on the day of the assassination. Their entry visas had been granted on the recommendation of Katieb Massoud Hendi, an Iranian businessman who resided in France and was in on the plot. They were met at the airport by Ahmadi, who took them to Bakhtiar's apartment. There he vouched for the two, who were posing as members of Bakhtiar's National Iranian Resistance Movement. Before being allowed in all three were searched by the gendarmes on duty and surrendered their identity documents.

The visitors said they had come to discuss the filling of a vacancy on the NIRM Executive Council, caused by the assassination of a member some days previously. They presented Bakhtiar with a gift – a picture illustrating a scene from Omar

Khayyam's Rubaiyat. While they talked Ahmadi went into the kitchen and returned with two large kitchen knives. These he gave to the assassins, who stabbed Bakhtiar several times and then sawed off his head. Katibek came into the room at that moment, and he too was stabbed to death.

The telephone lines were cut, the body was covered with a tablecloth and the three calmly departed, collecting their identity documents from the gendarmes, who suspected nothing. Ahmadi reported back to VEVAK 'mission accomplished'. The bodies were not discovered until over 30 hours later, when Guy Bakhtiar, unable to reach his father on the telephone, visited the apartment to see what was wrong. For almost two days the crime remained unreported in the media. An interesting point was that the absence of media coverage worried VEVAK, and according to one source (*L' Express*) the British SIS monitoring station in Cyprus picked up messages from VEVAK to the Iranian embassy asking for confirmation that the deed had been done.

The French police arrested eleven suspects, of whom five were Iranian. One assassin, Rad, fled across the border into Switzerland, but was caught and deported back to France because his documents were not in order. He managed to recross the border, only to be arrested again when the Bakhtiar murder became general knowledge. He was found hiding on a boat on Lake Leman and was extradited to France.

Back in Tehran, Fallahyan was publicly thanked by Khomeini for his 'great achievements in combating and uprooting the enemies of Islam, inside and outside the country' (IRNA). It was said that all Iranian embassies, banks, airlines and cultural centres in Western Europe were ordered to destroy any documents that could link Iran with the Bakhtiar assassination. It was also probable that the sudden release of the captive John McCarthy on 8 August had been to distract attention, while the kidnapping of the Frenchman Jerome Leyraud on the same date was to obtain a convenient hostage counter to bargain with if necessary.

Eventually, in November 1994 three people were brought to trial in Paris for involvement in the Bakhtiar assassination: Ali Vakili Rad, charged with murder; Katieb Massoud Hendi, charged with complicity; and Zeynal Abedine Sarhadi, charged with involvement. Arraigned *in absentia* were Mohammed Azadi, the traitor, and Farqsoum Boyer Ahmadi, the other assassin, both of whom had succeeded in fleeing France. Tension arose over the fact that Sarhadi was a close relative of President Rafsanjani.

Rad was sentenced to life imprisonment and Hendi to ten years' imprisonment, but Sarhadi, who was alleged to have been a contact man in the plot, was acquitted. Tension between France and Iran subsided somewhat. The French government was still trying to convince itself that President Rafsanjani was not involved. France, already the fourth largest supplier of civilian materials to Iran, was angling for additional lucrative commercial contracts. Commerce and propriety jostled with each other, but another of the Iranian Islamic regime's major enemies in exile had fallen.

IRAN–IRA COLLABORATION

In April 1994 the British government accused Iran of forging links with the Irish Republican Army (IRA), and as a consequence the Iranian charge d'affaires was expelled. President Rafsanjani complained that the British intelligence services were bugging the Iranian embassy in London.

The Iranian Ministry of Intelligence and Security had first come into contact with the IRA when it began to organise international terrorist seminars. Representatives of Sinn Fein, the political wing of the IRA, sometimes attended in the hope of attracting money and arms for its terrorist campaign in Northern Ireland. In 1980 Hadi Ghaffari, then in charge of the Iranian Hezbollah, told a rally in Tehran that 'We are ready to blow up British factories and ships. Now is the time for the death of Mrs Thatcher' (IRNA). These expressed Iranian sentiments formed the basis of Iran's future association with the IRA. Ghaffari, then known as the 'Machine-gun Mullah' for boasting that he had killed up to 60 ex-shahist officials, visited Ireland covertly to meet members of Sinn Fein, and reputedly offended them by refusing to pay for their drinks at a lunch provided by him. However the two sides' differing views on the consumption of alcohol did not disrupt the tentative liaison.

The first overt indication of this liaison was when an Iranian diplomat attended the funeral of Bobby Sands, the first IRA hunger striker to die (in May 1981). Iran changed the name of Churchill Avenue in Tehran, which runs outside the British embassy, to 'Bobby Sands Avenue'. Iran–IRA links slowly developed from that date. The following month, when the top echelon of the IRP was removed by a bomb explosion in Tehran, the IRA sent a message of condolence.

A Sinn Fein delegate attended the Conference of World Movements, meaning international terrorist movements, in Tehran in 1982, and the Intelligence and Security Ministry sent congratulatory messages to the IRA's annual Ard Feis (convention) in Dublin, but the relationship remained largely political as Libya was then providing the IRA with more arms than it could handle.

More positive cooperation dated from December 1987, when Gerry Adams, president of Sinn Fein, was invited to Tehran as an official guest and was given VIP treatment. This caused the British MI5 and MI6 to turn their attention to surveillance of the movements of known IRA terrorists and their meetings with Iranian diplomats in London, Paris, Bonn and the Hague.

Apart from Ghaffari, three other key Iranians involved in IRA liaison activities were identified and tracked by Western intelligence services: Ali Reza Hakikian, a diplomat based in Bonn until 1993; Vahid Attarian, Hakikian's replacement and responsible for coordinating Iranian operatives in Europe; and Amir Eravani, the contact between the Bonn embassy and Tehran. British intelligence interest was heightened by an incident in Greece in 1993, when Jurgens Merx and his wife Anet were arrested in Athens for smuggling huge quantities of heroin to Britain and came under suspicion of generating funds for the IRA.

A large, well-attended meeting of international terrorist leaders or their senior representatives took place in November 1993 at the Feirouzi Palace, Tehran, at the behest of their occasional Iranian paymaster. The organisations attending included the IRA, Hezbollah (Lebanese branch), the Revolutionary Council of Fatah, the Euskasi Ta Askentasvna (ETA – the Basque terrorist organisation) and the Japanese Red Army. Present were Abu Nidal and Gerry Adams. The gathering was hosted by Muhsin Rezai, Commander of the Pasdaran (James Adams, *The Sunday Times*).

The object of the conference was to gain support for a plan by Iran to fund and arm a 'New Terrorist International', which was to launch attacks against Western targets and cause devastation in Western capitals by coordinated bombing attacks. The intention was to fuel revolution in Europe and extract a heavy price from all those supporting US policies in the Middle East. Gerry Adams was there to ask for money and sophisticated weapons, including detonators and ground-to-air missiles – Libya, the IRA's former paymaster and arms supplier, having been frozen out. Adams received generous promises from Iran.

However Western intelligence agencies were on to this 'New Terrorist International' project, and mounted combined counteroffensives involving satellite surveillance, the interception of Iranian communications and bugging (James Adams). Action was taken against Iranian diplomats suspected of involvement, and several were expelled.

ARMS TO BOSNIA

In April 1994 Britain accused Iran of breaking UN embargos and sending arms to Bosnia-Hercegovina, which was denied. Wherever there was a chance to nibble away at the credibility of the West, and in particular to embarrass the Great Satan and its allies, the Iranian Intelligence and Security Ministry was ever eager to have a go. Its attention became focused on Bosnia-Hercegovina, which had been accorded sovereign independence in March 1992 in the wake of the collapse of the former Socialist Federal Republic of Yugoslavia, which promptly devolved into a state of civil war. This caused an arms embargo to be imposed on the former republics of Yugoslavia. US warships were sent to the Adriatic Sea to enforce the embargo.

Iran was in sympathy with the embattled Bosnian (mainly Muslim) government, which was facing insurrection by the better-armed Serbs. Iran sent humanitarian aid and funds, but was also suspected of sending illegal arms in small quantities. The story of arms smuggling into Bosnia during the period

1992–95, and of telescopes being put to blind UN eyes, is yet to be told in full.

A cargo of illicit arms for Bosnia, said to include 4000 AK-47 automatic weapons and one million rounds of ammunition, was seized at Zagreb airport in Croatia from an Iranian jumbo jet on 4 September 1992. The cargo was impounded, but the aircraft was allowed to return to Iran. This incident was kept under wraps for a few days, waiting for a suitably acceptable denial by Iran. None came.

This was the first hard evidence of Iranian arms smuggling to fellow Muslims in Bosnia. The odd feature about this seizure was that the detection was not the work of UN embargo monitors on duty at Zagreb airport, but was a result of information provided by the US CIA. It was suspected that similar flights had slipped through on several previous occasions, the cargoes being unloaded at night and quickly whisked away without passing through the normal customs channels.

Any subsequent Iranian arms smuggling activities were less obvious and blatant, as thereafter the smugglers' expertise became more finely honed. 'Sanction-busting' became a fairly risk-free occupation, in which the Tehran government showed a deep interest.

THE BANGKOK PLOT

Iran's terrorist tentacles also reached into Southern Asia. On 3 March 1994 the police in Thailand discovered a plot to bomb the Israeli embassy in Bangkok. Three Iranians were arrested: Hussein Shariari Farr, Babak Tahiri and Basr Kazemi. Farr was charged with the murder of a Thai truck driver, and the other two with falsifying documents. A fourth man, an Iranian named as Mohammed Lotfollar, was also sought. The Thai government issued a statement denying that Iran had protested against these arrests, but the Iranian embassy in Bangkok had preempted this by urging the Thai police to be 'more vigilant about attempts to damage Iranian prestige' (*The Times*).

THE FILIPINO PLOT

In January 1995 the Pope paid a ceremonial visit to South-East Asia. He spent five days in Manila, capital of the Philippines, a mainly Roman Catholic country but one that had a Muslim insurgent problem in its southern islands. Muslims form less than 10 per cent of the 65 million population. Two days before the Pope arrived, two Iranians were arrested in a hotel room containing explosives, detonators, pictures of the Pope and clerical robes. (Earlier, in 1970, a Bolivian terrorist disguised as a Roman Catholic priest had tried to attack a previous Pope at Manila airport.)

As the activities and exploits of Ramiz Ahmad Yousef (the alleged mastermind of the World Trade Centre bombing in New York) during his brief sojourn in Manila at that time came to light, the reasons for the arrests become clear. Many Western intelligence agencies tend to believe that Iran's terrorist tentacles extend to wherever there is an Iranian embassy. There is one in Manila.

9 Hamas

It was announced on 16 November 1992 that 'Hamas', an Arabic acronym for the Palestinian Covenant of the Islamic Resistance Movement, had formally entered into an alliance with Iran, the latter promising to provide financial and political backing to Hamas in its 'war to liberate Palestine'. The covenant stated that 'Israel will exist, and will continue to exist, until Islam obliterates it, just as it has obliterated others before it'. This statement merely formalised an established fact, as the Tehran government had already been heavily supporting Hamas.

Ibrahim Ghoseh, the Hamas representative in Jordan, said that this formal alliance had been the result of a series of meetings in Iran in October 1991, adding that Hamas intended to strengthen its ties with the Iranian-backed Hezbollah in Lebanon. Talks between Yasser Arafat, leader of the semi-secular PLO, and Ibrahim Ghoseh of the Islamic fundamentalist Hamas were brusque and showed little prospect of the two groups working together, let alone existing peacefully side by side.

Founded on 14 December 1987, the nucleus of Hamas was a small group of extremist fundamentalist Sunni Palestinians, who aimed to emulate the Shia Hezbollah in their struggle against Israel. This was a little unusual in one respect. It was tacitly assumed, but seldom voiced, that because of their indoctrination only Shias were psychologically capable of being turned into 'suicide killers', and that Sunni suicide bombers were the exception rather than the rule. For the first three years or so of the existence of Hamas there was no reason to question this assumption.

Sheikh Ahmad Yassin, founder and leader of Hamas, had been captured by Israel in May 1989. On 16 October 1991 he was sentenced by a Gaza military court to life imprisonment 'plus 15 years', having allegedly confessed to being the leader and founder of a 'hostile (to Israel) organisation', ordering the murder of Palestinians alleged to have cooperated with the Israeli authorities, and possession of illegal arms. Yassin left behind many able and active lieutenants to carry on the fight against Israel.

At first Hamas, which remained completely independent and had nothing to do with other Palestinian resistance or political groups, contented itself with issuing anti-Israeli propaganda. It concentrated mainly on providing religious, social and welfare programmes for Palestinians in the occupied territories in order to build a power base for itself, although it openly admitted that its ultimate aim was the destruction of the state of Israel and the formation of an Islamic fundamentalist Palestine state. Its early terrorist activities consisted of attacks on Israeli soldiers and settlers in the occupied territories, but there were bunglings and failures.

At first the Israeli authorities did not consider Hamas to be dangerous, feeling it was more concerned with rhetoric than with action. In fact Israel even gave it some covert support, thinking it could develop Hamas as a counter to Arafat's Fatah organisation. Senior Israeli security officers described Hamas as 'a surprisingly unprofessional bunch. They had no training, and acted without specific instructions' (*New York Times*). Despite its failures, Hamas's zeal and determination, together with its Islamic fundamentalist persuasion, attracted the attention of the Iranian VEVAK. The Tehran government had no time for Arafat, or indeed any of the Palestinian resistance groups, but did want to gain a foothold in the Palestinian occupied territories, and Hamas seemed to be be an ideal medium. Financial help from Iran arrived in 1990, perhaps just before, and some Israeli sources said this amounted to at least $50 million for each of three years. Iran then began to provide arms as well as money, and it opened its training camps to Hamas guerrillas.

Arafat continually tried to persuade Hamas to concentrate on a political role and join him in the ever ongoing, but seemingly negative, Middle East peace process. From the beginning Hamas, firmly committed as it was to the armed struggle, was against all peaceful compromise solutions. Consequently Fatah and Hamas had conflicting agendas, and there was constant friction between them as Hamas sought to wrest control and influence over Palestinians in the occupied territories from Fatah's grasp.

In mid-1991 Hamas became more competent at acts of violence via its military arm, the Izzeddin al-Qassam units, which came to be known as the Qassam, or Qassam Brigades. Hamas became a very tight, closed organisation consisting of tiny cells of two or three activists only, the identity of whom was known by no one but its controller. Israeli intelligence put its maximum strength at about 80 only, but admitted that the Qassam Brigades were hard to penetrate.

During 1991 the Qassam Brigades made a series of hit-and-run attacks against civil and military Israeli targets in the occupied territories. Instances occurred of hitch-hiking Israeli soldiers being snatched. Such hitch-hikers were a fairly common sight and were easy prey. They were subsequently killed, as at that time Hamas had nowhere to hide hostages and was unable to develop a hostage-taking operation like the one being conducted by Hezbollah in Lebanon.

HAMAS LEADERSHIP

After the capture of Sheikh Ahmad Yassin, the hard core of the Hamas leadership command stayed in exile, shuttling between Jordan, Iran, Syria and Sudan. According to Israeli sources key Hamas leaders included Musa Abu Marzouk, head of the Hamas political bureau; Emad Alami, Hamas's representative in Tehran; and Mohammed Kassem Saulha, who was regarded as the military commander. There was also an overt side to Hamas that sought to gain influence in such local and municipal elections as were held, and it was also prominent in Bir Zeit University's political activities.

Hamas attacks against Israeli targets increased. On 11 October 1992, for example, a Hamas member drove a stolen van into a group of Israeli soldiers, killing two and injuring eleven. This was claimed to be a reprisal for the killing of 17 Arabs in October 1990 on the Temple Mount in Jerusalem.

THE PALESTINE LIBERATION ORGANISATION

Yasser Arafat, leader of Fatah and chairman of the Palestine Liberation Organisation (PLO), of which Fatah was the largest constituent member, was involved in peace talks with Israel, sponsored by the United States. In this he failed to gain total Palestinian support, as some factions felt he was betraying the cause by compromising with Israel, and that the 'war of liberation' should continue by all means possible. Armed Palestinian factions came to blows over this issue, Hamas Qassam Brigades being pitched against the 'Fatah Hawks'. Another extremist Fatah armed group – the Black Panthers – was active against both Israel and Hamas, and become a particular target for undercover Israeli gunmen.

Arafat was prepared to accept a form of self-government in the occupied territories as a first step towards independence. He wanted Hamas to come under the PLO umbrella, or at least to accept some form of partnership with him. However Hamas was now fully supported by the Tehran government, which had visions of an Islamic fundamentalist Palestine and espoused the glory of a military victory as a significant milestone on the much vaunted 'Road to Jerusalem'.

HAMAS–FATAH CLASHES

During June 1992 armed clashes between Hamas and Fatah reached a crescendo, especially in Palestinian refugee camps in the Gaza Strip. On 13 July a Fatah–Hamas peace accord was signed, but this only produced a momentary pause in the hostilities. A further skirmish broke out between them on 30 September in the Khan Younis refugee camp, where over 70 people were injured. The fighting erupted after Hamas activists fire-bombed a house.

Arafat, who had already met Hamas leaders several times to try to entice them to co-operate, tried again in November. The two sides met in Sudan, but were unable to reach an agreement. Arafat commented several times that he 'could not fight Hamas' as that would be fighting Islam, the religion followed by the majority of Palestinians.

On 7 December in the crowded Gaza Strip, which was packed with some 850 000 Palestinians, most of them in long-stay refugee camps, a Qassam section ambushed an Israeli military patrol and shot dead three Israeli soldiers, the largest number killed in one incident since the Palestinian intifada began in 1987. The Qassam had recently been receiving better weaponry from Iran. This worried the IDF, which was responsible for keeping the peace in the occupied territories. The IDF stated that so far in 1992 there had been 340 shootings, compared with only 38 in 1988.

ISLAMIC JIHAD

On 11 December 1992 Israeli armed forces attacked a West-Bank house that was occupied by a 'wanted' Islamic Jihad guerrilla, Issam Barahma. A seven-hour battle ensued in which Barahma was killed, as was one Israeli soldier. Three others were injured. 'Islamic Jihad', a Palestinian extremist resistance organisation with fundamentalist ambitions, was waging a terrorist war against the Israeli occupation authorities.

THE TOLEDANO INCIDENT

On 12 December 1992 Hamas organised demonstrations against the IDF, in which over 100 Palestinians were injured. Two were killed in the Gaza Strip and one on the West Bank. On the 13th the Qassam Brigade shot dead an Israeli soldier near Hebron. On the same day the Qassam abducted an Israeli border policeman, Nissim Toledano, from his home near Lod and threatened to kill him unless Israel released Sheikh Ahmad Yassin, the imprisoned Hamas leader, and other detained Palestinians. Israel sealed off the occupied territories and conducted widespread but unsuccessful searches. On the 15th Toledano's bound body was found: he had been strangled and stabbed. The Israeli prime minister, Itzhak Rabin, promised a 'merciless campaign against Hamas', but insisted that the disrupted Middle East peace talks should continue (*Jerusalem Post*).

HAMAS DEPORTATION

That day, with the approval of the Israeli cabinet, 415 Palestinians – mainly Hamas members, supporters or

sympathisers, and mainly clerics, professional men or intellec-
tuals – were bundled into buses for deportation. Bound and
blindfolded, they were driven to the northern Israeli border.
There they halted for some 30 hours, still in the buses under
the same uncomfortable conditions, while civil rights lawyers
made last-ditch efforts to prevent their deportation. When this
failed the 415 were taken into the Israeli security zone in
southern Lebanon, where at dawn they were debussed and on
the 18th forced into territory nominally controlled by the
Lebanese government.

This time the Lebanese government, which since the beginning of the intifada had accepted some 67 Palestinian deportees, being physically incapable of taking action to stave off
such Israeli actions, refused to cooperate with Israel. On
21 December 1992 Lebanese troops were deployed to push
the deportees back into the security zone, thus preventing
them from entering Lebanese villages. Soldiers of the Israeli-
controlled South Lebanese Army, which policed the security
zone, fired at the returning deportees, wounding two and
stranding them all in winter weather on a tiny barren scrap of
no man's land known as Mari al-Zuhour.

The Lebanese government refused to allow any supplies to
be sent through its territory to the deportees; so with tents
provided by the Red Cross they huddled down in the miser-
able conditions, to remain for many months. This gave
Hamas, which was little known outside the narrow Middle
Eastern arena, tremendous international publicity. The Israeli
government, which did not seem to have anticipated the
Lebanese government's lack of cooperation, was hugely embarrassed. Israel had miscalculated, and the Tehran government, the sponsor of Hamas, rejoiced.

After the deportation had taken place, UN Resolution 799
was approved (18th), by the Security Council condemning the
Israeli government's decision and ordering it to abandon the
project. Despite strong objections from the United States and
a visit to Israel by James Jonah, a UN undersecretary, to try to
bring about a change of mind, on the 20th the Israeli cabinet
reaffirmed its decision. The Lebanese prime minister, Rafik al-
Hariri, heading a predominantly Muslim government, also
stood firm, refusing to see the UN under secretary and blocking all attempts by the UN and other international aid

organisations to send food and other necessities through Lebanon to the deportees.

Since the Lebanese–Syrian Treaty of May 1991, the Lebanese Hairi government had developed a more resolute stance, and its rejection was a sign of new self-confidence, a factor the Israeli prime minister had not counted on. Israel lost out badly on this one.

Spasms of unrest broke out in the occupied territories, and on the 19th, in the Khan Younis refugee camp area, Israeli troops shot dead six Palestinians, including a nine-year-old girl, and killed another Palestinian on the West Bank. On the 23rd two more Palestinians were shot dead in the Gaza Strip, and over 40 were injured in a fresh bout of violence. The eighth round of the bilateral Middle East peace talks, which had opened in Washington on 7 December, were halted.

PLO and Hamas leaders held talks with each other in Tunis, still the PLO HQ base. Both agreed that something must be done to repatriate the deportees, but neither could agree on what that something should be.

On the 29th Israel permitted ten of the deportees to return, insisting they should never have been deported in the first place, but it was not until 1 February 1993 that they agreed to the repatriation of a further 101 deportees. The terms of exile for the remaining 304 were reduced to allow them to return to their homes by the end of 1993. This was rejected by Hamas as it fell far short of the conditions laid down in UN Resolution 799.

Israel tried again on 10 May, offering to add a further 25 to the proposed 101, but this too was rejected. It was not until 9 September that over 180 deportees returned; and not until 15 December that the remainder followed suit, by which time Hamas was well and truly on the Middle Eastern map.

In October 1993 the so-called Taba Talks were held to discuss the release of Palestinians in Israeli detention, attended by Dennis Ross, US special coordinator for the Middle East peace talks. Differences arose over whether Hamas members should be included. The PLO negotiators demanded they should, but Israel objected. Eventually 617 'low-risk' Palestinians were released on the 25th and 26th – Hamas members were not included.

ISRAELI REACTION

Rabin stuck to his hard line, and the Israeli security forces clamped down firmly on Hamas during the first half of 1993. In June an official spokesman claimed that in a 'two-month operation against Hamas, Israeli security forces had destroyed 15 Hamas cells and arrested 120 Hamas activists' (*Jerusalem Post*), including four accused of Toledano's murder and others of its 'East Jerusalem cell', which had probably been formed especially for the Toledano killing. It was further alleged in a *Middle East Watch* report on 29 June that Israeli undercover agents had killed over 60 Palestinians during 1992. It was a dirty war in the occupied territories, in which Israel relied heavily on informers and collaborators.

DECLARATION OF PRINCIPLES

On 13 September 1993 a further stage in the Middle East peace process, the so-called Declaration of Principles, was signed on the lawn of the White House in Washington DC by Israeli Foreign Minister Shimon Peres, Mahmoud Abbas (Abu Mazan) on behalf of the PLO, and Norwegian Foreign Minister Johan Joergen Holst, under the auspices of President Bill Clinton. Secret negotiations had previously taken place in Norway, and had become known as the 'Oslo Line'. This was an Israel–PLO peace agreement, but the PLO faced opposition in the form of a ten-party Palestinian Rejection Front, based in Damascus, which included both Hamas and Islamic Jihad.

HAMAS'S REACTION

The reaction of Hamas to the Declaration of Principles was to intensify its war against Israel, threatening to 'turn Gaza into a mass graveyard for Israeli settlers and soldiers' (*New York Times*). On 4 October 1993 a Hamas suicide bomber drove his car into a bus near the Israeli settlement of Beit El, injuring 32 Israeli settlers. On the 15th Hamas killed four 'collaborators', including two Fatah members'; on the 24th Hamas killed two Israeli soldiers; and on the 29th an Israeli settler was killed in the Gaza Strip. Hamas's pattern of violence developed. Israel hit back hard. On 24 November IDF troops killed Imad Akel, leader of a Qassam cell, and on the 26th Khaled Zer, leader of another Qassam cell, was shot dead, allegedly by an undercover Israeli agent.

ANOTHER FATAH–HAMAS PEACE ACCORD

Another peace accord was signed on 22 April 1994 between the Fatah Hawks, the military arm of Fatah, and the Hamas Qassam Brigades. Both agreed to end their violent attacks on each other; to establish a joint committee to resolve the differences between them; and to grant a one-month amnesty to Palestinian 'collaborators' so that they could renounce their cooperation with Israel. This slackened the incidence of clashes between them somewhat, but it did not last. They were soon pummelling each other again.

The Tehran government, Hamas's paymaster, had been behind this accord, wanting it as a propaganda veil. It certainly did not want Fatah and Hamas to sink their differences and work together to help Arafat become the first president of an Arab Palestine. The Iranian government could not make up its mind which it disliked the most – Arafat or the Israelis. It decided to regard Arafat as the immediate problem to be dealt with first, and Israel as a longer-term one that could be put on the back burner for the time being.

THE HEBRON MASSACRE

On 25 February 1994, dressed in an Israeli reservist army uniform an Israeli settler – Baruck Goldstein from the Kirayat Arba settlement near Hebron, and a member of Kach, an ultramilitant Zionist party – entered the Ibrahimi Mosque (Tomb of the Patriarchs) in Hebron during prayers and sprayed the congregation with automatic weapon fire, killing 48 worshippers and injuring scores more. Goldstein was killed by the congregation.

Hamas swore it would exact revenge by committing five similar attacks on Israelis. On 6 April in Afula, inside the

Green Line (the boundary separating Israel from the occupied territories), a Hamas suicide bomber drove his car into a
bus, killing himself and seven Israelis and injuring 52. The
next Hamas incident occurred on the 17th in the northern
town of Hadera. A suicide bomber entered a bus and detonated an explosion that killed himself and five Israelis and
injured 30.

Hamas's tactics then changed from hitting Israeli targets in
the occupied territories, which brought reprisals on unfortunate local Palestinians, including women and children, to one
of suicide attacks inside Israel proper. This shocked the Israeli
government as little could be done to stop determined suicide
attacks, apart from taking conventional security precautions.
The IDF established security cordons to keep Palestinians
inside the occupied territories, especially around the explosive
Gaza Strip. Questions arose in Israel of the efficiency of this
military precaution.

On 24 November 1994 Said Badarneh, a Hamas member,
was sentenced to death by an Israeli military court for involvement in the Hadera incident. There had only been one instance of the death penalty being awarded and carried out
since Israel had come into existence as a modern state. That
was of Adolf Eichmann, the Nazi war criminal who was hanged
in 1962. Israelis were generally against the death penalty so
Badarneh's sentence caused some controversy. It had been
imposed as a warning to Hamas, and was generally expected
to be commuted to life imprisonment in due course – but
emotion in Israel over Hamas killings was such that no one
could be sure.

Next, on 9 October 1994 Hamas kidnapped a young Israeli
soldier, Nachshom Wachsmann. He was shown on TV being
threatened with death unless Sheikh Ahmad Yassin and some
200 other Palestinians were released by Israel. The kidnappers
and their hostage were traced to a building in the village of
Bir Naballah, near Tel Aviv, again inside the Green Line. In
the subsequent attack Wachsmann was killed, as were three
Qassam kidnappers and the Israeli commando leader.

On 19 October, in Tel Aviv during the morning rush hour, a
Qassam suicide bomber boarded a bus. His bomb exploded,
killing himself and 22 people on the vehicle, and injuring 47
others. Hamas claimed responsibility for these four incidents.

Not to be outdone, on 17 November Islamic Jihad claimed it had recruited 50 volunteers for suicide attacks. Israel waited apprehensively for the promised fifth revenge attack by Hamas to happen. It came on 27 November, when Hamas gunmen fired on a car near Hebron, killing a Rabbi settler, Ami Ulami, to mark the first anniversary of the death of Khaled Zit, a Hamas commander who had been killed by Israeli troops. A Hamas spokesman stated that it was also in memory of Imad Akel, another Hamas leader killed a year previously; and that its jihad against Israel would continue. The previous day Hamas had mustered some 40 000 supporters for a demonstration in Gaza.

FATAH–HAMAS

The deadly Fatah–Hamas feud worried the Palestinian leaders, especially Yasser Arafat, who did what he could to heal it. Arafat also wanted to bring Hamas into his Palestine National Authority (PNA) administration, which technically came into being on 17 May 1994, although Arafat did not feel confident enough to set foot in the Gaza Strip until 1 July, the first time he had been there in 25 years. Hamas described Arafat's arrival as 'shameful and humiliating' (Hamas communique).

On 14 August Hamas killed an Israeli settler in Gaza, the fourth death since the formation of the PNA. Arafat's Palestinian police arrested some 44 Hamas members the following day, but released them soon after. The arrest had been a gesture to placate the Israeli government, which was sneering that Arafat was unable to control the members of the PNA. On the 26th Hamas killed two more Israelis inside Israel, and said it would continue to do so until the Hebron massacre score was levelled.

Slowly the PNA administration took shape and attempts were made to form freely elected town councils. On 28 August a Hamas member joined the Jericho town council. This was the first Hamas activist to participate in the PNA self-rule administration, which pleased Arafat and caused speculation as to whether Hamas was really thinking about developing a political wing to compete in the December elections. It was, but not to participate in the Western-type democracy Arafat was trying to institute.

On 9 December 1994 a nine-member peace forum gathered in Gaza, where an accord was signed by representatives of Fatah, Hamas and Islamic Jihad, although in fact this meant little.

A TEST OF WILL AND STRENGTH

Under pressure from Tehran to seize an opportunity to supplant Arafat while his position in the PNA was desperately weak, Hamas organised a massive anti-Arafat demonstration to take place in Gaza on 18 November 1994 after Friday Prayers, the secret objective being to make Gaza ungovernable. Officially Hamas claimed to be protesting against the PLO–Israeli peace deal, which it alleged was opposed by 30 per cent of the Gaza Strip's 850 000 Arabs, many of whom were unemployed as Israel's borders were now closed to them (at least 120 000 Palestinians had formerly crossed the Green Line into Israel each day for employment). Hamas was trying to run Arafat out of Gaza. It was the first test for both Arafat and his new PNA police, which responded by firing on the mobs, killing 14 people and injuring over 200. Hamas backed away, leaving Arafat as victor in this small field.

The Tehran government was thwarted and angry. Ali Akbar Mohtashemi, the former minister of the interior, called on Muslims everywhere to avenge the Gaza killings, and to single out President Clinton, Israeli leaders and Arafat. He demanded that 'The revenge should target the real terrorists, who are criminal Americans and the Zionists. Arafat and his clique come next in line' (*Kayhan*).

HAMAS CHANGES ITS TACTICS

During 1994 Hamas's tactics underwent a drastic change from attacking Israeli settlers, soldiers and other targets in the occupied territories to suicide bombing inside Israel, claiming that its strikes were now aimed at Israelis, not Palestinians. Hamas was now operating a two-pronged policy, the first being to continue violent terrorism against Israel in the form of suicide bombing, to cause panic and despair. The other was to work at local levels by entering the electoral processes, taking them over and sweeping the ground from under Arafat's feet.

On 25 December 1994 a bomb carried by a Hamas suicide bomber at a busy bus stop in Jerusalem exploded, killing the bomber and injuring eleven Israelis. It was thought that the explosion had been premature, and that the bomber – named as the 'Martyr Aymas Radi', who had worked as a traffic policemen – had intended it to explode once he had boarded a very crowded bus in a repeat of the October Tel Aviv bus explosion. The Israeli people asked anxious questions about the effectiveness of the military security cordon that was designed to contain Palestinian terrorists.

Hamas now began to describe itself as 'moderate', being aware of the publicity value of such a label. It stated it would not interfere directly with the PNA administration, and might be willing to cooperate with Arafat on certain issues. Having received a bloodied nose at the hands of Arafat's PNA police, and realising that Arafat had the will to use them again if necessary, Hamas appears to have decided to avoid another head-on confrontation for the time being, and opted instead for a form of open cooperation to disguise its covert push for power through the masses to obtain an Islamic fundamentalist Palestine with its capital in Jerusalem.

The point at which Hamas and the Tehran government will cross paths and cross swords in the future remains a matter of speculation. What is more certain is that a local battle in the civil war that is renting the body of Islam is being fought out in the occupied territories of Palestine, so it remains to be seen how long comrades-in-arms on the 'Road to Jerusalem' will remain fraternal in their Islamic quest.

THE NETANYA MASSACRE

On 22 January 1995 two almost simultaneous explosions occurred at the Beit Lid road junction on the outskirts of the coastal town of Netanya, just north of Tel Aviv and well inside Israel. Both were detonated by suicide bombers. Twenty-one people were killed and over 60 injured, mainly soldiers waiting at a bus stop to return to their camps after Sabbath leave. In Israel this is known as the Beit Lid Massacre. Responsibility was claimed by Islamic Jihad, which named the assassins as Anwar Sukkar and Saleh Shaker, both from the Gaza Strip. The object was to fracture the peace process and avenge the killing of three PNA policemen by Israeli soldiers.

The Israeli government closed the frontier along the Green Line with the occupied territories, suspended talks on the release of Palestinian prisoners and arrangements for 'safe passage' between the Gaza and Jericho entities in the PNA, but decided the peace process must continue, despite huge popular opposition. Even Ezer Weizmann, the Israeli president and well-known peace advocate, called for it to be abandoned for the time being

The date was most significant to Israel, as it was the one chosen for Israel's official commemoration of the 50th Anniversary of the liberation of the Auschwitz death camp. Prime Minister Itzhak Rabin cancelled his planned address at the Yad Vashem Holocaust Memorial in Jerusalem so that he could visit the scene of the massacre, which was only a short distance from the prison holding Sheikh Ahmad Yassin, the leader of Hamas.

Rabin stated his belief that the best long-term solution would be complete separation between Israelis and Palestinians, something often thought of but seldom spoken aloud by ministers in office. It had been discussed before but had ran into certain problems, the first being the as yet undefined boundary between Israel proper and Arafat's PNA. Another was that Israel, with its precarious economy, was still heavily dependent upon cheap Palestinian labour, and the third was that it would exclude some '141 000 Israeli settlers in 141 settlements' (*Maariv*), who would be left defenceless. However a committee was formed to report on this project, which would require a 90-mile security fence costing over $200 million and taking over a year to complete. This came in for condemnation as a form of 'apartheid', while the PLO called it a 'land-grabbing idea'.

Arafat sent a message of condolence to Rabin and condemned the incident, as did King Hussein of Jordan, who had just signed a peace treaty with Israel. In Gaza, Arafat's PNA police made a few token arrests, including that of Sheikh Abdullah al-Shami, leader of Islamic Jihad, whose offices were searched and closed down. In Tehran there was

jubilation. The VVIR praised the 'martyrs' and Islamic Jihad,
while condemning both Israel and Arafat. The Israeli media
noted that this massacre had brought the number of Israelis
killed since the signing of the Peace Accords with the PLO to
over 100.

Rabin, in an angry mood, made threats against Islamic fundamentalism (meaning Iran), saying 'We will continue with
the peace process and at the same time strike you. We will
chase after you. No border will stand as an obstacle. We will
wipe you out and defeat you'. (Reuters). This was taken as a
hint that there might be increased Mossad activity overseas.
The Israeli government authorised a three-month extension
of a dispensation order for Shin Bet to continue to use 'moderate physical force' when interrogating prisoners, against
which Israeli human rights activists had been protesting,
calling it 'legalised torture'. The Head of Shin Bet (still not
named in Israel) had boasted that tougher interrogation
techniques had helped foil several recent attacks (*Jerusalem
Post*).

In the Gaza Strip there was mass exultation, which rather
shocked the people of Israel, especially those who hoped it
might be possible to work with Palestinians in the future. The
following day, at the funerals in Gaza, Sheikh Abdullah Shami
promised the father of one of the 'martyrs' that 'the jihad
against the enemy will continue, and will not stop', boasting
that he had scores of would-be martyrs standing by.

The Israeli security forces arrested over 60 Palestinian suspects and issued the name and photographs of the terrorist
they sought. He was Yehia Ayash, a 29-year-old Palestinian
whose suicide killers had killed 56 people, and injured over
200 in 18 months. He had studied electrical engineering at Bir
Zeit University on the West Bank, and then spent some time in
Iranian training camps in 1992. Israeli security sources stated
that Islamic Jihad worked closely with Hamas, and had about
50 suicide bombers available for action, but had only limited
quantities of suitable explosives.

In an interview in a Lebanese newspaper (*al-Hayat*),
Ibrahim Ghoseh said that Israel was holding over '4000 Hamas
members, of whom 1500 have been arrested since the Beit Lid
massacre', and complained that this was 'causing problems for
the group'. He alleged that this was being done as Prime

Minister Rabin's political career depended upon the destruction of Hamas.

PALESTINIAN OPPOSITION TO ARAFAT

On 7 February 1995 an Israeli tanker convoy was ambushed near Gaza. A civilian Israeli security guard was killed and another was wounded. Also, bomb explosions occurred near Israeli settlements. Responsibility was claimed by the Democratic Front for the Liberation of Palestine, led by Nayef Hawatmeh, a member of the ten-party, Damascus-based Rejection Front. This caused Yasser Arafat to clamp down on this organisation and arrest about 100 antipeace-process activists. He also established a State Security Court to try Palestinian activists operating within his PNA, on the lines of the Egyptian military courts that dealt with terrorists.

Acts of terrorism continue today in the PNA area, the occupied territories and Israel proper, and unfortunately this seems likely to remain the case as those involved have developed a rigid mind-set that excludes compromise and toleration, while in the dark background lurks the ever-active, insidious and malevolent VEVAK.

ISLAMIC FRONT FOR THE SALVATION OF PALESTINE

Arafat, desperately striving to maintain his position and policy, is beset by several hostile factions, but he has shown himself to be a survivor, so there is hope that the PLO peace process will not founder.

Additional opposition to Arafat's administration arose in March 1995 with the appearance of the Islamic Front for the Salvation of Palestine, whose policy is to impose on Palestinians strict observation of Islamic customs and behaviour, which includes keeping women in their Islamic role. Traditionally Palestinian Muslims have been 'moderate' and semisecular, a heritage from the days of the British mandate, but the arrival of Arafat and his followers from Tunis, where the atmosphere is cosmopolitan, tended to bring an even more relaxing influence. Instances quoted including the abandonment of the traditional head scarves worn by women, the staging of a women's fashion show at a hotel, and a more liberal policy on the sale of alcohol. Little is yet known about this new organisation, but from its announced policy it is not hard to guess that its funding comes from Tehran.

Israel may tend to see this new fundamentalist Islamic organisation as a blessing in disguise, as it will cause internal dissent amongst Palestinians and thus further disunite them. Nonetheless it will remain cautious until it finds out whether the organisation has any anti-Israeli terrorist teeth, in which event it could be a double-edged sword, especially if it is the advanced guard of an Iranian-orchestrated group that is determined to carry hostilities into Israel. Hamas and Islamic Jihad take Iranian money, but they tend to put their own interpretations on their paymaster's expectations and do not want to become part of an Iranian empire.

US PRESIDENTIAL EXECUTIVE ORDER

On 24 January 1995 President Clinton issued a presidential executive order freezing the US assets of 12 groups and 18 individuals suspected of being involved in terrorism aimed at disrupting the Middle East peace process. They included Hamas and Islamic Jihad, Black September, the Democratic Front for the Liberation of Palestine (Nayef Hawatmeh), Hezbollah in Lebanon (Sheikh Mahmoud Hussein Fadlallah), the Palestine Liberation Front (Abu Abbas), the Popular Front for the Liberation of Palestine (George Habash), the Popular Front for the Liberation of Palestine-General Command (Ahmad Jabril), the Revolutionary Council of Fatah (Abu Nidal), Gama Islamiya (Sheikh Omar Abdul Rahman) and the extreme Zionist Kach. But much more than this is needed, especially as long as Iran remains a secret, and selective, terrorist paymaster.

10 Algerian and Other Problems

On the morning of 24 December 1994 at Houari Boumedienne Airport, Algiers, an Air France Airbus 300, flight number 8969, was on the tarmac boarding its last passengers when four hijackers dressed in Air France uniforms drove up to the aircraft. Posing as cleaning staff, they went aboard and mingled with the passengers. Once loading had been completed they showed themselves, produced weapons and took over radio communication with the control tower. They declared that all on board (227 passengers and 12 crew), had been taken hostage and demanded the release of two imprisoned leaders of the Islamic Salvation Front (FIS – Front Islamique du Salut). The hijackers were members of the hardline Armed Islamic Group (GIA, Groupe Islamique Arme). Both the FIS and the GIA were in open rebellion against the Algerian government and cooperated with each other occasionally.

The Algerian government refused to accede to the demand and negotiations continued. The hijackers freed 19 women and children at about mid-day, but the negotiations stalled and in the evening they shot and killed two passengers, one of Vietnamese extraction and the other an Algerian. Around midnight more women and children were released. The negotiations remained stagnant the following day, so in the evening the hijackers shot and killed another hostage, a French embassy employee.

As several of the passengers were French, the French government took a direct interest in the situation and tried to persuade the Algerian president, Lamine Zeroual, head of the military government, to allow the French GIGN (Groupe d'Intervention, Gendarmerie Nationale) antiterrorist squad to storm the plane. The GIGN had already been dispatched to Palma in Majorca in readiness to join the scene. The French request was refused as Zeroual was hoping the incident would be resolved peacefully.

Both Beirut and Tehran airports refused to accept the hijacked plane as neither government wanted to become openly involved. The French prime minister, Edouard Balladur, indicated he would welcome the hijacked plane at Marseilles, but nowhere else in France, having an antiterrorist exercise in mind. At this stage the hijackers seemed to be entertaining the idea of a dramatic press conference in Paris. The Algerian struggle had a low priority rating in the international media, compared with that of Egypt for example.

French officials were incensed by the attitude of the Algerian government, which refused to pass on any information about the hijacking situation. A French minister later said 'They lied to us all the time' (*The Times*). It was only when the French threatened to cut off all aid to Algeria if its government did not fully cooperate that Zeroual agreed to allow the plane to leave Algiers. Just after midnight it departed, with 172 hostages on board, ostensibly en route to Paris via Marseilles airport to refuel. The GIGN squad was heading that way too.

At Marseilles the hijackers produced 20 sticks of dynamite and wired them up in the pilot's cabin. Two elderly passengers were released. A couple of hours later the hijackers broke off radio communication and the airport was evacuated.

Shortly afterwards, some 54 hours since the incident began, French GIGN commandos stormed the aircraft, and in a 24-minute shoot-out killed the four terrorists and brought the hijacking to a successful conclusion. Nine commandos, three air crew and 13 passengers were injured during the confrontation. Charles Pasqua – French interior minister and a hardliner who frequently commented that 'There is no such thing as a moderate Fundamentalist' – stated that the hijackers had intended to turn the aircraft into a 'flying bomb to explode and set Paris ablaze' (*Le Parisien*).

Three of the hijackers were named as Abdul Salim Yaya, Makhlous Ben Guettaf and Selim Layadi, all Algerians. The fourth member was not identified. The following day in Tizi Ouzou (some 70 miles east of Algiers) three Frenchmen and one Belgian priest were killed in revenge by the GIA. This was taken by some commentators to indicate the two groups were now working together.

It was revealed (*Le Figaro*) that another French aircraft had had a narrow escape from being included in the Algiers hijacking by arriving over half an hour late. Had it been on time it too would have been hijacked. This was an Air Inter airliner (flight number 4210) from Marseilles, which upon landing had been warned by an airport employee about what was happening. As soon as its passengers had disembarked the pilot had made an emergency turnaround and taken off, all baggage still on the plane and without the passengers who had been waiting in Algiers to board. The plane had returned safely to Marseilles.

OTHER ALGERIAN ISLAMIC HIJACKINGS

Two other Algerian Islamic fundamentalist hijackings occurred in 1994, both of which were far less dramatic than the one in December. The first took place on 28 February, when an Air Algerie Boeing 727 on an internal flight with 127 people on board was diverted to Alicante in Spain. The three hijackers demanded the release of Islamic prisoners being held by the Algerian government. At Alicante the hostages were freed and the hijackers surrendered to the police. They requested political asylum, but the Spanish authorities put them on trial for 'air piracy', a newly designated international crime.

The second happened on 13 November, when an Algerian Fokker 27 aircraft on an internal flight with 42 people on board was diverted to Majorca. The three hijackers, armed only with a knife and a 'coffee grinder', demanded the release of all political prisoners in Algeria and the holding of fresh elections. At Majorca they released their hostages unharmed and asked for political asylum.

ALGERIAN ISLAMIC FUNDAMENTALISM

Algeria was under French colonial rule or influence from 1831 until the Algerian War of Independence (1954–62) was won by the National Liberation Front (FLN). The FLN ruled the country until October 1988, when rioting and disturbances broke out, caused mainly by the dismal failure of its economic policies. President Bendjedid Chadli brought in the army to quell the unrest, promising reforms. In February 1989 voters approved a new constitution, drafted by the FLN, for a new multiparty political system, and within a year over 30 political parties declared themselves, including the FIS, the first legally recognised Islamic Fundamentalist party in the Arab world whose platform was an Islamic state.

The results of the first round of the elections in December 1991 showed that the FIS would win by a clear majority. When this was realised the remainder of the elections were cancelled. In this abrupt, non-democratic but nonetheless essential to the continuation of democracy decision, President Chadli had the full support of the French government, and perhaps secretly of other countries of the European Union, although some have since tried to distance themselves from the problem.

At the time there were over five million Muslims in France, the majority of whom were Algerian or of Algerian extraction. This caused the French government to conjure up a dark vision of a tide of Islamic fundamentalism originating in Iran and Afghanistan, sweeping into Egypt and Sudan and then into the Maghreb countries of Algeria, Morocco and Tunisia, prompting Algerian refugees to flood into France. Cancellation of the elections brought an angry, hostile response from the thwarted FIS, and from other groups with somewhat similiar programmes.

In January 1992 Chadli resigned, the National Popular Assembly (in which all deputies belonged to the FLN) was dissolved and a High Committee of State (HCS) was formed to rule the country. Not everyone in Algeria wanted the FIS to govern the country, as some were attracted to multi party politics and favoured a degree of Westernisation. Internecine disturbances began. The Algerian ambassador to Tehran was recalled, it being alleged by the Algerian prime minister that there was evidence of Iranian interference 'in Algerian affairs that was not confined to making a financial contribution to the FIS' (Agence France-Presse).

In February a state of emergency was declared. Extra powers were given to the security forces and a number of members of Takfir wal Higra, an underground extremist group, were arrested. Disturbances centred around mosques, where FIS imams (Algeria is a Muslim country with a Sunni majority, imams being the prayer leaders) were preaching subversive sermons, and many were detained. The government announced that some 5000 people had been deported to one of five detention camps in the southern Saharan region. The Religious Affairs Ministry stated it was having to appoint about 40 per cent new imams to the country's 9073 mosques, and complained that many had been taken over by unqualified individuals.

The FIS was dissolved by government decree in March for 'multiple violations' of the law, disregarding the conditions set out in the July 1989 Act, which among other things barred any party based exclusively on religion. Three members of the illegal Hezbollah organisation, which had failed to gain official party recognition, were sentenced to death. Back in June 1990, in local elections, the FIS had won control of 853 municipalities out of 1541 and 32 provinces out of 48, and in an attempt to break this stranglehold the government had suspended those held by FIS nominees and substituted government 'executive delegations' to administer them. During the initial peaceful penetration phase using democratic processes the FIS had been supported mainly by Saudi money, but as soon as violence erupted Iran began to show a keen interest.

In April 1992 the FIS leader, Abbasi Madani, and his deputy, Ali Belhadj, were arrested and charged with inciting armed rebellion. Both were eventually sentenced to 12 years' imprisonment. The arrest and trial of other FIS leaders followed, and many rank-and-file members were detained. Resistance violence was getting into full swing. Mohammed Boudiaf, president of the High Committee of State, was assassinated on 29 June. On that day he survived an explosion that injured 41 people, only to be shot at the scene by a gunman in military uniform.

ALGIERS AIRPORT EXPLOSION

A bomb explosion at Algiers airport on 26 August 1992 killed 10 people and injured 128. The finger of suspicion pointed at the FIS, which denied any involvement. Later, four FIS activists made full confessions on TV, and later still 38 FIS members were found guilty of involvement in the offence, of whom seven were executed.

The HCS, which had promised press freedom, began to close down newspapers. Curfews came into operation in the Algiers area and then in other major cities, and casualties mounted as Islamic fundamentalists clashed with security forces. Offers of amnesty were made, but rejected. The conflict developed into a bitter guerrilla-type civil war.

Occasional demonstrations against terrorism in Algiers (said to have been orchestrated by the government) met with Islamic hostility and violence. In addition there was opposition to the FIS, the major Islamic fundamentalist body, from the Berber minority then numbering about three million out of a population of 28.2 million: (IISS). Berbers are indigenous people living in the northern, mountainous area of Algeria. They are inherently hostile to the majority Arabs, who have never really conquered them.

Algeria severed diplomatic relations with Iran on 27 March 1993, and also recalled its ambassador from Sudan, alleging links between the FIS and Islamic fundamentalist organisations in those two countries.

THE GIA

The origins of the GIA are lost in a confused mist, but its leaders hint that its roots lie in resistance fighting during the war of independence. The relationship between the FIS and the GIA has never been made clear, although it is thought by many that the GIA is a splinter group that broke away from the FIS after it had become a completely separate organisation with a hard-line, 'no compromise' platform, the GIA objecting to the FIS's political activities. At times the GIA and the FIS seem to have remained comrades on the battlefield, but at others they have not.

The GIA was active in the 1980s, but was put out of action in 1986 when its leader, Mustafa Bouyali, was shot dead by the security forces. Most of his followers were arrested and sentenced to death, but were freed in 1990, due largely to pressure on the government from the FIS, which had reemerged in 1988.

The first GIA exploit since its reactivation was in November 1991, when it attacked an army outpost at Guemar in south-eastern Algeria, killing three soldiers. A spokesman at the time stated that 'foreigners were the main coronary artery of the plan to colonise the country with non-Muslim unbelievers'. The object of the GIA was to fight and kill them. It was also said that all GIA leaders had to take a direct part in violent operations to give them experience of battle, and to demonstrate they were killing God's enemies. Their leader was Cherif Gousmi, whose nom de guerre was Abu Abdullah (Reuters).

The GIA's declared programme in 1992 was to eliminate all enemies of Islamic fundamentalism, including 'Jews, Christians and infidels'. It went to work with deadly gusto, assassinating high-profile Algerian opponents, journalists and academics. For example on 21 August it ambushed and killed Kasdi Merbah, a Berber and former prime minister. The Islamic policy included inflicting damage on the country's economy, burning factories and devastating agriculture. In addition teachers and schools were targeted if they deviated from the narrow Islamic line. The FIS too was active in terrorism and destruction, but it frequently denied responsibility for such exploits.

The HCS tried to force a military solution, with a continuing welter of arrests, trials and detention. Shoot-outs were frequent, as Islamic fundamentalist groups hit back hard when cornered. In July 1993 it was reported (*Middle East Economic Digest*) that, since the beginning of the state of emergency, over '150 Islamists had been sentenced to death, six being executed in 1993, and that over 1,000' had died as result of the violence. The HCS was indecisive, swinging between hard repression and conciliation.

ASSASSINATION OF FOREIGNERS

The GIA began its campaign of assassinating foreigners on 20 September 1993, when two French surveyors were kidnapped. Their bodies were found the following day. On 19 October gunmen shot dead two Russian advisors at Lahouat in the Saharan region. Then three Italians were kidnapped, their bodies too being found the following day. On the 24th three French consulate workers were kidnapped by the GIA, but were freed after a shoot-out between the GIA and security forces, during which six GIA members were killed.

Attacks on French personnel in Algeria caused President Mitterrand to say he was considering evacuating French nationals from Algeria (Agence France-Presse). In France, on 9 November in a 'preventative operation', security forces scooped up some 88 alleged FIS members or sympathisers, prompting the FIS to threaten to strike at targets in France.

On 14 December twelve Croat and Bosnian workers were stabbed to death, the worst incident of this kind so far. The GIA claimed responsibility, declaring also that all foreigners must leave Algeria by the end of the month. As 1993 ended it was reported that over '2,780 Islamics are in detention' (*Middle East Economic Digest*). France recalled its ambassador from Algeria in January 1994, and reduced the size of its diplomatic mission there.

NATIONAL DIALOGUE COMMITTEE

Meanwhile, in October 1993, the month in which 13 Islamic activists were executed, the HCS established the National Dialogue Committee to attract political groups to work out a procedure to enable an elected government to be formed, but opposition parties refused to cooperate. Plans to hold a national referendum were abandoned. The HCS remained divided and hesitant, lacking firm political policies and relying entirely upon military means.

PRESIDENT LAMINE ZEROUAL

In January 1994 the HCS was abolished, and Defence Minister Lamine Zeroual became president of what was a military junta government. In March he tried to open a dialogue with the main political parties, and in May a 200-seat National Transition Council was established to formalise decrees. Zeroual was encouraged to some extent by a large demonstration in Algiers on the 8th by the FLN and other moderate political parties that were impatient with the delay in the progress of political dialogue. President Zeroual received financial and material support from the French government in his fight against Islamic fundamentalists, as well as arms and security equipment.

THE BLOODSHED CONTINUES

The GIA, whose members had become known locally as the 'Afghanis' as so many claimed to have fought in Afghanistan, had its share of setbacks, and on 27 February 1994 security forces in Algiers killed a senior leader, Mourad Si Ahmad. In July the bodies of another senior GIA leader, Abdul Kader Hattab, and nine of his guerrilla fighters were found hanging in a cave near Algiers. There was some speculation about who was to blame. The government announced that a 'Muslim group' was responsible, without naming it; others thought it had been an incident in the GIA–FIS struggle; while others blamed the government-controlled 'Ninjas', death squads involved in covert antiterrorist operations.

In May a French priest and a nun, who ran a library in Algiers, were shot dead. After this exploit the GIA – then in open opposition to the FIS and its AIS (Army of Islamic Salvation) – released a statement to the Algerian press. It claimed responsibility for the deaths, saying that 'Within the framework of the policy of the liquidation of Jews, Christians and miscreants from the Muslim land of Algeria, a GIA brigade organised an ambush in which it killed two Crusaders, who had passed long years in propagating evil in Algeria'. About 24 000 French citizens were living in Algeria at the time. The Algerian security forces launched a city-wide search for suspects, setting up road blocks and causing serious traffic congestion, but none were caught.

The GIA assassination campaign against foreigners continued during the summer of 1994. For example on 6 July seven Italian sailors asleep in their ship, which was docked in the port of Djendjen near Algiers, were killed. The government blamed the FIS, which denied responsibility, so it was probably the work of the GIA. In previous weeks Islamic guerrillas had stepped up their attacks on military targets, especially against conscripts.

On 15 July the GIA abducted the ambassadors of Yemen and Oman, and held them for seven days. On their release they passed on a message to President Zeroual, that if he agreed to free Abdullah Layada – a GIA member who had been arrested in Morocco in June 1993, repatriated, and sentenced to death by an Algerian military court – it would cease its activities.

GIA 'ISLAMIC GOVERNMENT'

During August 1994 several prominent FIS members defected to the GIA as they disliked the way the FIS seemed to be teetering towards a political dialogue with President Zeroual. In its efforts to achieve primacy in the field, and to capitalise on the situation, on the 26th the GIA announced the formation of an 'Algerian Islamic government', under its leader, Cherif Gousmi, who was accorded the grandiose title 'Commander of the Faithful'. However Gousmi did not last long, and was killed in a shoot-out with the security forces in Algiers on 26 September. The GIA's leaders were certainly leading from the front. Mohammed Said was nominated as Gousmi's replacement as Commander of the Faithful.

FRENCH REACTION

On 3 August 1994 five French nationals were shot dead in a GIA attack on the French embassy in Algiers, led by Djamel Zitouni, who was later accused of organising the December 1994 Algiers hijacking. This brought the number of French killed in the GIA campaign to 15, causing a knee-jerk reaction in France, where Charles Pasqua launched a crackdown on North Africans suspected of involvement with Algerian Islamic groups.

In France the FIS and GIA networks busied themselves among the huge Muslim population, extorting protection money and distributing Islamic fundamentalist propaganda. Their cadres searched for arms and bomb-making devices, usually from Middle Eastern sources. By way of Eastern Europe and then Germany, these were shipped from Hamburg and smuggled into Algerian ports.

A massive, high-profile security operation was launched in Paris, with security forces checking the identity of thousands of drivers and pedestrians. This caused massive traffic disruptions, delays and inconvenience, which continued for several nights in a row. Additionally, over a score of prominent members of the FIS were detained and held temporarily in a disused barracks in Folembray in northern France, it being the government's intention to deport them. No country would accept them, and Pasqua refused to allow them to return to Algeria. The Algerian fraternity in France called for the release of the 'Folembray-17', among whom were Djaffar el-Houari – head of the Algerian Brotherhood in France, which had close links with the FIS – and two imams. The FIS cried out that 'France has declared war on the FIS and on Algerian Muslims'.

Political opponents of Pasqua criticised his security operations, complaining they were infringing citizens' rights, while detainees' lawyers protested at being searched before visiting their clients. The French people, who were touchy about human rights issues but concerned about the rising crime rate, accepted some of Pasqua's tough measures, which included video surveillance and giving police the power to stop and search people on the streets without reasonable suspicion. This caused even President Mitterrand, a former member of the French Resistance, to mutter that they were interfering with the right of the French to demonstrate politically. In answer to complaints, Pasqua replied 'If you don't go fishing, you don't catch any fish. You have to terrorise the terrorists' (Reuters).

Pasqua was bitter about lack of support from the British and German governments, and their lax attitude towards 'Algerian Islamic subversives'. He accused them of allowing Muslim militants to 'engage in political activity, and make inflammatory declarations while in exile', complaining he had previously warned them of 'the gravity of the situation in Algeria' (Agence France-Presse). One French periodical (*L'Evenement du Jeudi*) claimed that Britain 'was stuffed with militant Islamists'. A very vocal FIS leader and spokesman in Germany was Anwar Hassam, but the German authorities refused to take action to detain him. Eventually some of the Folembray-17 were deported to the African state of Burkina Faso.

Pasqua organised another dragnet sweep in France in November, in which '95 Islamics were arrested in Paris' (*Le Figaro*) and quantities of arms and subversive literature discovered. He condemned the British government for permitting the International Muslim Khalifah to meet in London. The French government remained divided over its Algerian policy, with Alain Juppe, the foreign minister, being strongly in favour of negotiation in Algeria, and Pasqua remaining in favour of the military option.

NATIONAL DIALOGUE COMMITTEE

In September 1994 President Zeroual released Abbasi Madani, Ali Belhadj and three other FIS leaders from prison into house-arrest, in the hope they would join his National Dialogue Committee. Originally the FIS had not been asked, as Zeroual had obviously hoped he would be able to isolate it. The following day 16 beheaded bodies were discovered in three different parts of Algeria. This was taken to be the GIA's statement of protest against the National Dialogue Committee's processes.

The two FIS leaders refused to cooperate. Theirs was a strange partnership, as Madani was very politically orientated and wanted to get back into the Algerian political democratic process in order to subvert it, while Belhadj was an out-and-out, hard-line enthusiast for the armed struggle. On 29 October Zeroual admitted that his National Dialogue Committee had failed. He blamed Madani and Belhadj for 'encouraging violence and terrorism' (Agence France-Presse). It was said the real reason for the abrupt termination of the dialogue was that security personnel had found subversive literature from Iran in Belhadj's possession.

Madani and Belhadj were put back in prison. Even Algerian moderates had criticised the president for making such a 'unilateral concession'. In defence he said he had expected the FIS to respond with the offer of a truce.

Zeroual stated that since January 1992 the Islamic campaign of violence had claimed 10 000 lives, not 'only 4000' as previously officially stated; and that 60 foreigners had been killed. Amnesty International said the figure should be about 20 000, and went on to allege that the Algerian security forces were using 'terror, torture and unfair legal proceedings'. The Ninjas were certainly blamed for many killings.

The dirty war was getting dirtier, with reports that Islamic guerrillas were mutilating and beheading their victims, including a number of young girls, allegedly because they would not become 'wives' of FIS guerrillas. The FIS, operating in armed units of about 100 men, had turned a few sections of mountainous regions of the countryside into military no-go areas, but the government insisted it was in full control of the cities and much of the remainder of the country. Islamic activists still operated in Algiers, but covertly. For example on 12 October there were five separate car-bomb explosions.

Earlier, in March, there had been a prison breakout. FIS guerrillas had attacked a high-security jail and about 1000 inmates had escaped. Four days later 24 escapees had been killed, but only 114 recaptured. In November a mass prison escape was thwarted near Algiers, in which about 30 prisoners died and 60 were injured. This was only reported in one local Islamic newspaper, *al Watan*. Some newspapers had been closed down, and others had been warned about irresponsible reporting. By this time many incidents were unreported in the media. Foreign journalists had all but departed, and over 30 Algerian ones had been killed by the end of 1994. Those still working received threats from Islamic fundamentalists and the government alike, and were too scared to write anything that might upset either. This enabled the government to make its own news.

By the end of 1994 it is probable that only 11 500 French citizens remained in Algeria. The death toll since the state of emergency been declared was estimated at '25 000 civilians, 7000 terrorists and 2700 members of the security forces killed' (*Le Parisien*). It was said that up to 800 people were killed each week, over 600 schools had been destroyed and over 2000 teachers had fled. These figures are impossible to check, but more reliable ones do not exist.

CONTRARY WARNINGS

In mid November 1994 the FIS issued a statement that 'From January 1, 1995, suicide attacks will be carried out against French diplomatic missions and interests in the Arab world'. An unusually harsh warning from the FIS, which frequently denied being involved in terrorism and seemingly hankered after a more peaceful political takeover. It was speculated whether it was this that provoked the GIA, anxious to retain its deadly reputation, to stage the Algiers hijacking in December, so as not to be upstaged. After that hijacking Anwar Hassam, the FIS representative in Germany, stated 'we don't think that such acts can serve the just cause of the Arab people', which was almost a public reprimand.

On 24 December (the day of the hijacking) the GIA sent a letter to the British embassy in Berne, saying that if Britain did not close down its diplomatic mission in Algiers the personnel there would be killed. A similar letter was sent to the Germans. Security was tightened, but the staff of the British and German embassys in Algiers remained at their posts after the deadline had expired. On 30 January 1995 the FIS issued a bolder statement, virtually declaring war on France.

By this time Charles Pasqua was complaining that France would be unable to accommodate the anticipated 100 000 Algerian refugees, and would turn to his EU partners for help in such an eventuality. In Algeria, a ministerial committee was formed to prepare for the presidential elections.

An impromptu 'peace assembly' of Algerian opposition parties met in Rome, on 10 January 1995 to draft a proposal to end the civil war. The gathering was attended by Abdul Hamid Mehri, secretary general of the FLN, Hocine Ait Ahmad, leader of the Socialist Front Forces (SFS), and representatives of other secular groups. It was also attended by Anwar Hassam of the FIS. The government's reaction was that it would 'not tolerate any external interference in Algeria's internal affairs' (*The Times*). President Zeroual rejected this group's peace proposals out of hand, to the dismay of the United States, which had been pushing for a political solution, and also many in France. US statesmen and the US intelligence agencies were of the opinion that if the armed struggle continued, the FIS and the GIA would inevitably win, having the Iranian revolutionary pattern very much in mind.

EUROPEAN UNION PROBLEMS

The French were trying to persuade the German government to keep a much tighter rein on Rabah Kebir, an FIS leader in

Cologne who was organising the movement of arms, radio transmitters and detonators from Hamburg to Algeria. However Germany was loath to become involved in the Algerian Islamic fundamentalist problem, having some two-million Muslims of its own, mainly Turks. In addition it was apprehensive about what might happen after 1 April, when movement restrictions would be further relaxed between EU member countries. Kebir had been in Germany since 1992 and was seeking political asylum, on the ground that the 'FIS has chosen the peaceful political path'. The German counterespionage service reported it had identified '14 radical Muslim groups, and more than 22,000 active sympathisers in Germany' (*The Times*).

SUICIDE BOMBING AND MEDIEVAL SYMBOLS

The first suicide attack, for which the GIA claimed responsibility, occurred in the centre of Algiers near the main Police HQ on 30 January 1995, when a car, loaded with some 200 lbs of explosives, was driven into a building. As it occurred in the middle of the afternoon when the city was thronged with people, the result was devastating – 42 people were killed and over 280 injured. The previous day some 10 000 demonstrators had paraded through the city in support of President Zeroual, calling for 'Free democratic elections'. Terrorists alleged that the demonstration had been orchestrated by the government. On the same day the GIA had threatened it would step up the rate of killings.

On the 31st Ahmad Kasmi, a member of the FLN Executive Committee who had attended the Rome discussions, was kidnapped by the GIA. On 5 February his head was discovered in a railway station west of Algiers – a gruesome medieval symbol of terrorism. The GIA, and perhaps to a lesser extent the FIS, continued their campaign of high-profile assassination. Victims included TV presenters, teachers, journalists, entertainers and writers.

SATELLITE TV

An unexpected bonus for the Algerian government in its fight against fundamentalism has been the widespread purchase of satellite TV dishes by the people of Algeria: by the end of 1994 there were over 100 000 in the country, with hundreds more arriving every week (*Cable & Satellite Year Book: 1995*). Islamic fundamentalists have been slow to appreciate the power of satellite TV, which is detrimental to them, offering as it does several alternatives to the narrow Islamic TV channels. The fundamentalists are now condemning satellite dishes and demanding their removal.

IS VICTORY OR DEFEAT CERTAIN?

There is no doubt that Islamic fundamentalist terrorism has gained a grip on Algeria, but it is not all-embracing and is largely used in fear, rather than by choice. The pessimistic view, held particularly by the United States and increasingly by certain European countries, is that the FIS and the GIA cannot be defeated by military force. These Western countries strongly urge further negotiations and a political settlement, overlooking the fact that this is not what Islamic fundamentalists want – nor will they accept it, except as a stepping stone to total power.

The problems of anti-guerrilla warfare are often discussed. On the other hand the disadvantages experienced by the Algerian Islamic fundamentalists are seldom mentioned. There are several. For example Algeria's frontiers with Morocco and Tunisia are virtually closed, and so Algerian insurgents and their visitors are not able to cross the borders freely. Nor do they have easy access to international safe havens to flee to, use as training and rest centres, channel reinforcements and military supplies from and perhaps even obtain volunteer Islamic fighters. France, for example, has stopped issuing visas to Algerians.

The next problem is related to the first. The Islamic insurgents in Algeria need heavy anti-aircraft weapons to defend their few regional no-go areas in the mountains near Oran and elsewhere, but they are unlikely to get them. The closure of the frontiers has brought a virtual halt to the supply of heavy arms. The government security forces, however, have modern French helicopters, and more are on the way. These are being used to monitor insurgent movements and harass those in the no-go areas, as is artillery and aerial bombing.

Another drawback is their failure to gain the mass popular support that would enable them to muster huge demonstrations in the cities (on the pattern of the Iranian Islamic revolution), and thus harness the people to their cause and impress the watching world. This has been due largely to their inability to gain control over the Algerian media and the mosques, which to date has been prevented by strong government counteraction. They are starved of the 'lifeblood' of terrorism as much of what they do is not reported, while selected incidents of beheading, mutilation and other atrocities – the 'bad blood of terrorism' – are exploited by the government to frighten Algerians and negate public support. Mullahs and mosques brought Khomeini to power in Iran, but in Algeria they are of limited help to the Islamic fundamentalists as they control so few of them.

The mountainous northern region is inhabited by Berbers, who are hostile to both the fundamentalists and the central government. Perhaps the Algerian government will soon form and arm a Berber village home guard network to hinder Islamic fundamentalist expansion in the mountains. But the most powerful Western weapon of all is satellite TV, which apart from providing entertainment will spread universal enlightenment, education and knowledge.

It is true that Algeria's armed forces are undermanned (271 000, with reserves: IISS), that they are poorly equipped for such a task, and that the officer corps has both 'hawks' and 'doves', but morale seems to be sound and a military victory is anticipated – but this must depend upon French material and financial support.

MOROCCO

To the west of troubled Algeria lies the Kingdom of Morocco, which despite a veneer of democracy is ruled autocratically by King Hassan. Hassan is regarded as one of the more pro-Western Muslim leaders who keeps a sharp, wary eye on both his own Islamic fundamentalist problem and that of adjacent Algeria. He was quick to extradite the Algerian terrorist Abdullah Layada. Morocco and Algeria are not good friends, having a long-standing border dispute and holding conflicting views on the 'Polisario problem' (a dispute over the sovereignty of Western Sahara, a former Spanish colonial territory), which resulted in the joint frontier being closed from 1975 until 1988.

In early August 1994 two members of a group of Spanish tourists were killed when they were attacked in Marrakesh by French-based Muslim extremists, – members of the so-called 'disinherited youth'. These were recruited by Islamic fundamentalist organisations in France from amongst unemployed Muslim youth. They were indoctrinated, given guerrilla training in camps in Iran and Pakistan, and then sent on missions to destabilise the Moroccan economy.

King Hassan immediately accused the FIS of organising the Marrakesh exploit, and decreed that all Algerians visiting Morocco must first obtain a visa. Some three million Algerian tourists visited Morocco that year. In riposte the Algerian government clamped shut its border with Morocco, which was of considerable benefit in the general struggle against the spread of militant Islamic fundamentalism. In January 1995 seven men were arraigned in Fez for the Marrakesh incident. Two are facing the death penalty: Stephane Ait Idir and Hammadi Radouane.

TUNISIA

To the east of Algeria lies Tunisia, which probably has the most Western-orientated attitude of any Muslim country. The government of President Zine al-Abidine Ben-Ali – leader of the Ressemblement Constitutionnel Democratique party, which was returned to power in March 1994 with a comfortable majority – is anxiously watching events in Algeria; in case Islamic fundamentalism spills over into his own country. Ben-Ali's policy is dedicated to modernisation, tolerance, secularisation, education and women's rights, the latter being rather unusual in a Muslim state.

President Ben-Ali has closed his border with Algeria, and is constructing a strong security fence along it to prevent infiltration. Other security measures taken include refusal to issue work permits to Algerians, the withdrawal of those already issued, and the removal of Algerian workers from Tunisia generally. Islamic fundamentalists in Tunisia complain they are closely monitored and harassed by the authorities, but the government alleges that some slip through the fence into Algeria to gain battle experience, in preparation for insurgent activity in Tunisia some day.

SUDAN

On 19 August 1993 the US State Department put Sudan on its List of Countries Supporting Terrorism, accusing it of collaborating with Iran, and helping Gama al-Islamiya and other Islamic fundamentalist insurgent groups operating in Egypt. The role of Sudan in the Iranian Connection has perhaps been rather overstated by the United States in its zest to pillory it. Sudan's contribution to Islamic fundamentalist terrorism has been passive, merely providing bases, transit facilities and sanctuary. Sudan's economy is in dire straits – it is deeply in debt and, reliant as it is on imported fuel oil, has been penalised for non-payment by Libya, Saudi Arabia and Iran, all Muslim states.

Ruled by a military junta led by President Ahmed al-Bashir, Sudan is in confrontation with Egypt for supporting Islamic fundamentalist insurrection in that country, and is also engaged in a long-running civil war against southern Christian 'rebels'. In addition it has incurred Western hostility for its lack of liberal democracy and respect for human rights. Little real news comes out of Sudan due to internal censorship. It has a bad international press, most information about it emanating from Egyptian sources that are obviously interested in exaggerating Sudan's threat to the West. The CIA is supporting the Sudan People's Liberation Army, which is fighting for an independent Southern Sudan, operating by way of Uganda.

The second most powerful man in Sudan is Hassan al-Turabi, leader of the National Islamic Front (NIF), whose programme is to achieve a 'United Islamised Africa, where colonial borders are repressed' (*The Times*). Both he and al-Bashir are dedicated Islamic fundamentalists, one being concerned solely with Sudan and the other with a wider vision. Both are power contenders, but their exact relationship with each other is hard to define. For the moment at least they seem to be jogging along fairly smoothly together. The northern part of Sudan is in the process of being converted into a fundamentalist state: the southern part, which is mainly Christian or animist, is in revolt against the Khartoum government

Sudan's claim to international terrorist notoriety came in August 1994, when it suddenly admitted that its government had 'sold' Carlos the Jackal (Ilich Ramirez Sanchez, the renowned international terrorist, whom it was sheltering) to France for a reputed one million dollars and other vaguely hinted-at favours. Carlos remains in French custody, and Sudan remains a haven for wanted international terrorists, having a direct line to VEVAK in Tehran. One wonders which expendable international terrorist will be up for sale next.

EGYPT

In Egypt the government continues to use military force against Islamic fundamentalists. Its security forces conduct heavy-handed searches, curfews, detentions and trials in military courts. The fundamentalists have fought back whenever possible, involving both sides in a fierce cycle of terrorism and repression that shows no sign of faltering. Extremism has been strongest in southern Egypt, where hostility towards the Cairo government is traditional. One result of this is that the Egyptian tourist industry has fallen into decline.

President Mubarak puts the blame mainly on Iran, saying that militancy in Egypt will only calm down when external money and support ceases. However he also blames his traditional enemy, Sudan; and more recently, Saudi Arabia too, which he alleges is trying to force its own puritan brand of Islam on his country. The government claims that in a free election, the Islamic fundamentalists would be unlikely to obtain 10 per cent of the vote.

In January 1995 the new leader of Gama al-Islamiya, Mahmoud Selim, was shot dead by security forces. That month, in revenge for the death of six militant Islamists at the hands of the police in the southern Minya region, attacks were launched against the security forces – eight were killed near the southern town of Sohag. This brought to 568 the number of violent deaths since March 1992, when the Islamic fundamentalist campaign against the government began.

LIBYA

A few words must be said about Libya, which is still ruled autocratically by Colonel Moamer Gaddafi. Gaddafi has long been deeply involved in sponsoring and using terrorism, especially during the heyday of international hijacking (1968–86). He is still involved, but to a lesser extent, especially since his headquarters were attacked by American warplanes. For example he harbours George Habash, the veteran leader of the PFLP, and probably others. However he did refuse admission to Carlos, a former collaborator of his, when Syria was trying to get rid of him. Carlos eventually obtained sanctuary in South Yemen before moving on to Sudan.

Libya is a closed country, more noted for surmise about it than fact, but as far as can be ascertained there is little active Islamic fundamentalist agitation there. Libya is already an Islamic state, tailored according to Gaddafi's whims, as outlined in his Green Book.

The United States is pillorying Gaddafi intensively in the hope of bringing him down. It blames him for the Lockerbie air disaster of December 1988 and is demanding the extradition of two Libyan security personnel who are alleged to have been involved, which is being resisted. The United States is having difficulty in keeping its allies behind it on this issue, as concrete evidence is scant.

Egypt regards Gaddafi as a barrier against the spread of Islamic fundamentalism into North Africa, and for this reason alone is trying to persuade the United States to relax its pressure on him, as it sees him as the lesser of two evils. Egypt reckons it is better to have, and work with, the devil that is known, now somewhat chastened, than for him to be replaced by a raving fanatical Islamic fundamentalist leader. The United States may eventually go along with this reasoning, but it will be hard to persuade. Libya has European friends urging this course because, for example, it supplies oil at favourable rates to Italy and Germany. Neither want the Lockerbie show trial to take place. Gaddafi may have his uses.

BAHRAIN

The tiny Gulf state of Bahrain – an island of about 280 square miles, joined by a causeway to Saudi Arabia, with a population of about 458 000 – is facing an Islamic fundamentalist problem. It is the only other country in the world (Iran being the other) to have a Shia majority, the precise size of which is unclear as estimates vary between 60 per cent and 80 per cent which is barely represented in the Sunni administration. This traditional Arab state has a Sunni royal family, whose brief flirtation with Western democracy gave it a constitution and a National Assembly, but this was suspended in 1975 and has remained in abeyance since, to the chagrin and disappointment of the Shia majority, agitated by the Iranian Connection.

Shia opposition demonstrations erupted in December 1994, led by the youthful, 26-year-old Sheikh Ali Salman, who after studying in Qom for five years returned home in November 1992 to organise a petition for the reinstatement of the National Assembly, obtaining over 25 000 signatures. After the December (1992) disturbances, when it is thought that five Shias and one policeman were killed and over 450 Shias detained, a number of whom are expected to be put on trial, Sheikh Ali Salman and other leading Shia clerics were deported to Lebanon. They later turned up in London, where the Bahrain Freedom Movement had its base, seeking political asylum.

The crown prince of Bahrain accused Britain of becoming 'a haven for terrorists and saboteurs'. This was unusual, as relations between Britain and Bahrain were close and friendly, Britain benefiting considerably from its exports to that country, which allowed Western navies certain facilities. The ruling al-Khalifa family openly blame Iran for the Shia disturbances, and there has been a security crackdown since, with special surveillance on Shia clergy and their mosques. The trial of Shia demonstrators would inevitably trigger further Islamic fundamentalist activity, which could spread to other members of the Gulf Co-operation Council, which includes Kuwait, Oman, Qatar, Saudi Arabia and the United Arab Emirates. Bahrain has become an Islamic fundamentalist tinderbox.

TURKEY

A few comments must be added about the situation in Turkey, which has a growing Islamic fundamentalist problem to add to that of Kurdish insurgency in its south-eastern provinces. In the 1920s and 1930s Ataturk turned his country into a secular state, which it has precariously remained ever since. In recent years there has been growing influence by Refah (The Islamic Welfare Party), whose cover as a moderate religious party barely hides the anti-Western, pro-Islam stance that underlies its objective: to seize local power by force. Refah has become an election threat, and a future question may be: if Refah gains a working majority in the National Assembly, will the army, the traditional protector of Turkey, step in again and take over?

The IBSA-C (the Great Eastern Islamic Raiders Front) is even more openly and violently antagonistic than Refah to anything non-Islamic, targeting churches, places of entertainment, banks and even hospitals. Its aim had been to create a Federation of Islamic States by armed force by 1995. In the past the IBSA-C has not been considered dangerous to the state, although it has organised a few bomb explosions and committed a few assassinations. Nor has there been any sign of it having, or achieving, a popular following. All of a sudden the IBSA-C declared war on the Turkish government, and now presents a serious threat to stability. Turkey and Iran have never been real friends, their differences usually centring on border alignments and factional Kurdish border tribes, playing one against the other. But now the Iranian Connection has found a new contact in the IBSA-C.

11 International Terrorism Inc.

How does a dissident political group, or even a government for that matter, that wants someone leaned on or eliminated go about hiring a contract killer? Is there some shadowy, underworld hiring agency, a sort of rent-a-terrorist bureau, that will provide such services in return for a financial consideration? And if so, how does one get in touch with it? Is it a question of knowing the right fax number and code word? Drug barons and mafia godfathers, both in fiction and reality, seem to have plenty of hit men to dispose of rivals, informers and even government agents. Court trials of their lesser fry indicate that the laws of supply and demand throw up individuals who have an aptitude for such tasks. Money is the main motivation of both drug and crime syndicates and there is a philosophy that money can buy anything, particularly expendable hit men.

It must be much the same in the sphere of international terrorism, except that the main motivation is political rather than monetary. Even so many terrorist organisations resort to criminal activities, including protection rackets and robberies, to finance themselves, this being regarded simply as a means to the political end, not the end in itself. Nonetheless it is true that some fall by the wayside, with greed gaining the upper hand. Active terrorists are recruited by headhunters from among the small fry.

By the nature of their calling drug dealers and crime syndicates, as well as terrorists, operate in secrecy, away from the gaze of the media for their own security. They therefore tend to be shadowy, mysterious bodies in the public perception, of which just a few elusive activists at opportune moments kill a victim, plant a bomb or hijack an aircraft, and then disappear back into a misty underworld. There is obviously much more to it than that.

Terrorist groups come in all shades and sizes, ranging from very large to very small, but to operate and survive all need an organisational structure, an administration, specialised personnel, a political following and an income. In this way they resemble business concerns, or any large organisational body, with the performance of the chairman and the board of management determining how well or how badly they do, and whether they survive.

As in the commercial world, there is competition between terrorist groups, especially those with the same political objective, such as several in the Middle East region whose aim is to eliminate Israel. As in business, limited help is given to competitors. Indeed some terrorist resistance groups are hostile to each other, having contrary political creeds, some being right wing and religious, others secular and left wing, and others somewhere in between. In political struggles, prestige and one-upmanship are important, and this is especially so in the world of terrorism.

In the Middle East there is keen rivalry between terrorist groups. There are also expansions, amalgamations, mergers and takeovers, poaching of key personnel, desertions, internal sabotage, and occasionally physical scuffles and battles. Large terrorist groups grow larger, small ones survive precariously, or are swallowed up or eliminated, rather like the cutthroat fortunes and misfortunes of big business. All terrorist groups have to remain solvent and balance their books, and so most would be entitled to display 'Inc.', 'Ltd' or 'Plc' after their titles, should they so choose. Authors and TV scriptwriters frequently use 'Inc.', an American commercial suffix, as it gives the impression of a huge, powerful, multinational business organisation. As in the commercial sector, terrorist groups are vulnerable to financial mismanagement and internal fraud, sometimes on a massive scale.

The expression 'International Terrorism Inc.' has a dramatic ring about it that conjures up visions of national groups gathered together for a joint purpose. This is somewhat misleading as in the terrorists' case the expression 'international', as in commercial undertakings, simply means that they operate abroad and are not restricted to one country or locality in their movements, contacts and resources. Some may not be international when they begin, but they soon come to rely upon external support and sanctuary for sheer survival.

Countless small terrorist resistance groups have sprung into existence since the end of the Second World War in a wide variety of countries around the world, determined either to take over their government or to obtain independence, or variations of those two objectives, by force of arms. Some have been more visionary than practical, and many have failed, crushed by their own inadequacies or misfortunes in the face of established national resistance. On the other hand a few, by developing military muscle and know-how, have achieved their objectives.

Others, although unsuccessful in achieving their political aims, have managed to maintain their struggle, due mainly perhaps to their government's inability to eliminate them. Notorious survivors include the IRA, the Corsican Liberation Front, the Basque ETA, the French Action Directe, the Greek November 17 and the West German Red Army Faction, to name but half a dozen European ones. But many similar groups remain active, independent and separate entities in other parts of the world, despite adversity continually dogging their armed struggle.

Few are 'international' by inclination, and most remain focused on a narrow national objective, giving little or no thought to forming firm alliances with like-minded groups. In Iran, for example, the Mujahedeen Khalk, Fedayeen Khalk, Komala and Forqan all conducted separate terrorist campaigns against the shah, but showed little inclination to unite or even to cooperate with each other. They mostly kept their distance, although on occasion they jostled roughly together.

However even the most introspective and nationalist orientated groups have had to seek external comfort, aid and support, especially during their dull, discouraging 'long haul' periods, and so spasmodic forms of liaison have sometimes developed, for the sole reason that one day help may be required. This intercommunication has tended to develop into a sort of twilight intelligence world, which the KGB, the CIA and other national intelligence agencies have forever tried to tap into. Presumably drug barons, crime syndicates, smugglers, money launderers, illegal arms salesmen and others who conspire to defeat laws, tariffs, customs and embargoes, or who operate in nefarious or illegal trade of one sort or another, operate on the fringes of the mysterious, dark, international underworld of which they are part.

Terrorist leaders and masterminds do not like to be equated with business chairmen or managing directors, as they are basically political animals, being either secretary generals or members of a tightknit governing politburo, or a political organisation that of necessity has had to resort to terrorism. As they are engaged in an armed struggle they like to see themselves as generals leading armies, their key executives as captains on the battlefield, and their rank and file as soldiers, all marching and fighting for the cause.

Prestige comes to mean a lot to them, and with this usually comes – as it can to successful generals anywhere – a touch of megalomania. Most terrorist organisations have their publicity department, which carefully crafts communiques, demands and claims of responsibility. Some are better at this than others. A military atmosphere hovers over terrorist groups, and often a military esprit de corps develops, whereby defectors meet a traditional traitor's fate, or worse.

As the Cold War consolidated into two huge opposing blocs, both sides sought to bring Third World countries into their respective orbits by all possible means, including covert, subversive ones. Both the US CIA and the Soviet KGB realised the potential that the myriad of terrorist groups operating in Third World countries had to destabilise and embarrass one or other of the superpowers. Whenever possible terrorist groups were brought into superpower orbit, by bribery, blackmail and promises. In several instances, individual terrorist groups found themselves involved in a proxy war, in which they were fighting other terrorist groups on behalf of one or other of the superpowers.

Following the collapse of the USSR the story of Soviet support of national terrorist groups began gradually to be pieced together. KGB documents are being unearthed, translated and headlined in the Western media, although one should view them with caution as Cold War spies tended to exaggerate the importance of their intelligence finding to impress their paymasters. The espionage story of the CIA has yet to be told.

During the Cold War the KGB offered small sums of money to small, active terrorist groups to save them from extinction, aid that was extended to training facilities, arms and explosives. For example quantities of semtex explosive from the

Czechoslovakian factory reached terrorist groups by courtesy of the KGB.

The Soviets made contact with terrorist leaders of several different nationalities, especially Western ones. Some were taken to the USSR, where they were flattered, persuaded they were important and assured that their cause was worthy. The KGB hosted meetings and conferences for terrorist principals in Warsaw Pact countries, thus gaining a deep knowledge of them, their organisations and their strengths and weakness, which the KGB then exploited. Key terrorist activists moved, for example, from the Middle East, through Warsaw Pact countries into the West, by courtesy of the KGB and Soviet embassies and consulates, which provided false identities and passports, safe houses, travel arrangements and escape routes.

The notorious Lumumba University in Moscow, which catered for Third World students, was a fruitful recruiting and headhunting ground for Soviet agents, and a contact point for a wide variety of terrorists during the Cold War years. The CIA, although it had to be more furtive, was doing similar things, but on a more restricted scale. This meant there were two streams of terrorists, going to different meetings and training camps, both of which could to be regarded as 'international'.

The Palestinian–Israeli struggle was particularly relevant, as several Palestinian resistance groups arose, all pitched against Israel. Some had inauspicious beginnings, but a few developed into powerful organisations, their leaders becoming known in Western jargon as 'masterminds' because of the sophisticated daring of some of their exploits, which gave them notoriety status equivalent to that of drug barons or godfathers of crime syndicates.

The first to achieve such notoriety was George Habash, leader of the PFLP, who soon came to appreciate the value of international operations to attract attention to his cause. In the early days, when the Palestinians were losing out to Israel both in battle and in the field of propaganda, Habash quickly realised what an asset TV coverage would be, and his notoriety spread with the rapid expansion of media exposure.

In July 1968 the PFLP hijacked an Israeli airliner and diverted it to Algiers, where 12 Israelis were released in exchange for 16 Arab prisoners being held in Israel – a most unusual step as Israel had so far adamantly refused to bargain with terrorists. However Habash's TV spectacular occurred in August 1969, when the PFLP hijacked five international airliners, three of which ended up on a desert airstrip in Jordan. All on board were held hostage for days in front of international TV cameras, eventually the aircraft to be dramatically blown up. George Habash was now truly international.

Several other Palestinian terrorist groups were operating, and although most were grouped under the PLO umbrella they were in fact independent, and often in dispute with each other. The largest, Arafat's Fatah group, upstaged the PFLP in September 1972, when its Black September Organisation penetrated the athletes' village at the Munich Olympic Games and took the Israeli team hostage. The world's TV cameras focused on the drama, and fact surpassed fiction. Now Arafat too could be said to have gained international terrorist status.

Other Palestinian 'barons' with similar international terrorist status include Ahmad Jabril of the PFLP-GC, Abu Nidal of the Revolutionary Council of Fatah, and Nayef Hawatmeh of the DFLP. There have been others of somewhat lesser stature, but all their organisations have warranted the title 'International Terrorism Inc.'

One rare joint venture was between the PFLP and the Japanese Red Army, which was going international at the time. In May 1972, three JRA members fired automatic weapons and threw grenades into a crowded transit lounge at Lod Airport. One of the three, Kojo Okomoto, survived to become Israel's prize prisoner, after which the JRA faded from the Middle Eastern scene.

After the Iranian Islamic Revolution the pattern of terrorism changed in the Middle Eastern region. In 1982 the Iranian government established its Hezbollah umbrella organisation in the Bekaa Valley in Lebanon. From there it began to launch terrorist attacks against Israeli and Western targets on a grand scale, pushing other established Palestinian godfathers into the shadows.

The Iranian-backed Hezbollah could indeed be accurately referred to as International Terrorism Inc. as it gathered several individual terrorist groups under its control, headhunted operators and trained suicide bombers, weaving them into the Western Hostage Saga, dramatic hijacking exploits and terrorist activities against Israel and its supporters and sympathisers, producing such a comprehensive terrorist jamboree as had scarcely been seen before. The paymaster and instigator was Ayatollah Khomeini, operating through Department 15 of the Iranian Intelligence and Security Ministry. Khomeini's policy is continued even today by his clerical and political heirs and successors.

12 Epilogue

Is 'militant Islam', meaning Islamic fundamentalism, really an unstoppable juggernaut, an immediate threat to both moderate Muslim governments and Western ones? Can it be halted, or defeated? Or will it eventually burn itself out, only to be remembered as a hiccup in history? Its record during the past decade and a half is impressive, bloody and awe-inspiring. Ayatollah Khomeini's Islamic Revolution in Iran, which overturned a secular government, set the trend, giving encouragement, inspiration and some help to similar movements in other Islamic countries through its Iranian Connection.

The object of militant Islam is to turn countries into Islamic states, governed by the Sharia (Islamic law), by all means possible, including armed struggle. To many Westerners and moderate Muslims this means turning the calender back several centuries, reembracing and strengthening intolerance, and perpetuating the servile, lowly, uneducated position of women in society. An appalling thought, but this did happen in Iran and is happening now in Pakistan and Sudan. The justification given is that Islamic fundamentalism will oust corrupt and incompetent Westernised governments in Muslim countries and replace them with ones upholding traditional Islamic values.

Such fundamentalism can only operate in Islamic countries where a moderate Muslim population is available for conversion, and it does not seek – nor would it have any chance of success if it did, as universal Islam has little appeal to Westerners – a proselytising mission amongst non-Muslims. The danger to non-Muslim countries is that this religious struggle may spill over into them in that their Muslim minorities, including Muslim refugees, may become targets for intimidation and terrorist exploitation.

Western views on the threat of Islamic fundamentalism vary. Willy Claes, the new secretary general of NATO, stated in February 1995 that 'Islamic militancy has emerged as the greatest threat to Western security since the collapse of Communism'. He recommended that the NATO Partnership for Peace programme be extended to include not only Eastern European countries, but also North African and Middle Eastern ones too. Most Western governments consider Claes to be over-alarmist, suspecting him of seeking long-term job security for his organisation and looking for a replacement bogeyman.

The general attitude of Western governments towards Islamic fundamentalism is one of wariness, caution and restraint. None want to be caught up in its struggle for domination, and by keeping their distance they hope the heat will subside, while taking minimal measures to keep the situation as cool as possible.

Some Western countries occasionally find themselves in the firing line, owing to the main protagonist of this form of international terrorism, the Iranian government, striking at targets to demonstrate its potency and long-distance reach to blackmail, terrify or extract political concessions. The bombing of the World Trade Centre in New York and the Israeli embassies in London and Buenos Aires are cases in point. Added to that are the kidnapping of Western nationals to secure the release of terrorists from Western prisons, and the hijacking of aircraft for the same purpose.

Islamic fundamentalism is not a united pan-Muslim movement, but a collection of national ones within sovereign states, individually seeking to take over governments. To a minor extent they have been linked together by the Iranian Connection, developed by Ayatollah Khomeini, who had grandiose empirical ambitions. He would certainly have liked to have headed such a pan-Islamic movement, but he came to power late in life and had an overinflated opinion of his own capabilities, so died with such dreams unfulfilled. In any case Khomeini was a member of the minority Shia sect, and it was unlikely that he would have been accepted as the supreme Muslim leader by the majority Sunnis.

Individual Islamic fundamentalist movements accepted what aid and help they could obtain from the Iranian Connection, but there is little sign that any of them felt they were expected eventually to submerge themselves, if successful, into a Khomeini empire.

Islamic revolutionary doctrine had to be thrust on the people of Iran by force, and its grip maintained by violence, meeting vigorous opposition that had to be kept at bay. Terrorist opposition attacks have continually been made against the central government. Presidents and ministers have been assassinated, and antigovernment terrorism continues. It is by no means a popular government.

Khomeini's idea that Shia clergy should rule the country is beginning to wear a bit thin. Shia clergy in Iran, although permitted to participate in government and secular professions, generally have not done so, the Shia hierarchy usually standing aloof from government. It is suspected that many in Iran feel that the clergy in government have not been doing a very good job, but as yet few have dared to say so openly.

Ali Akbar Khamenei, who was dubiously elevated to the eminence of ayatollah to become president, had to back away from his attempt to seize the office of marja taqlid – that is, supreme leader of Shia Muslims everywhere – when the elderly incumbent died. Ayatollah Shariet-Madari, Khomeini's antagonist and senior, and now probably the most influential Shia cleric in Iran, has always stood aside from government, and seems to be encouraging his brother clerics to do the same, thus tending to take the 'Islam' out of Islamic administration. It seems probable that mosque and Majlis will gradually go their separate ways, which will allow pragmatists to rule the country. This could bring about changes in foreign policy. It could also mean that less interest will be shown in Islamic fundamentalist movements in other countries. If it wants to obtain a credible international standing, develop sound trading relations and attract international loans and support, Iran will have to drop its covert activities. The pendulum in Iran is starting to swing back again, but very slowly.

The views of moderate Muslim governments should be considered. These were expressed at the summit meeting of the Islamic Conference Organisation, held in Morocco in December 1994, which resolved to adopt a code of conduct committing members to refrain from supporting, either morally or financially, Muslim terrorists that oppose governments. The code was approved by 50 of the 52 members attending. This must represent the official opinion of the Muslim world, and surely should be welcomed by the West, as well as supported and perhaps rewarded. It could be true, of course, that not all the Muslim leaders who voted really meant what they said, having private reservations and agendas, but were voting with international credit and survival in mind.

Currently the fiercest battles being fought by Islamic fundamentalists are those in Algeria and Egypt. The governments of both countries are determined to crush them by military means, a process that is causing some Western governments qualms about lack of human rights, urging that negotiations replace military measures. Some Western governments are thinking of withdrawing assistance and aid from them, unless they 'fight with clean hands' and pay attention to human rights; some perhaps are uneasily aware of the dubious activities of their security forces in coping with their own terrorist and insurgent problems.

Some are thinking of abandoning the incumbent governments, and instead reaching out to the Islamic fundamentalists involved in the hope of persuading them to negotiate, overlooking the fact that the fundamentalists have stated time and again that they are not interested in negotiation, recognition as a political party, the democratic process, or any halfway solution such as autonomy or joint sovereignty: they want total victory.

Future targets for Islamic fundamentalists include the traditional (monarchist) Arab Gulf states, as evidenced by disturbances in Bahrain. Vulnerable Saudi Arabia, with its troublesome Shia minority, is beginning to fight back by supporting antigovernment incursions into Iran from Pakistan, while in Pakistan there is friction between Sunnis and Shias.

Most agree the struggle ahead may be lengthy, tough and casualty-prone, a test of stamina, determination and endurance, but as yet there is little sign that the Islamic fundamentalists are bound to win in the end. Apart from terrorism and local violence, they have little going for them, and their mullahs are increasingly uneasy about satellite-linked TV, which represents a damaging counterweapon.

Bibliography

Amirahmadi, Hooshang (ed.) (1993) *Iran and the Arab World* (London: Macmillan)

Azimi, Fakhreddin (1990) *Iran: The Crisis of Democracy: 1943–53* (London: I. B. Tauris).

Bakhash, Shaul (1985) *The Reign of the Ayatollahs* (London: I. B. Tauris).

Cable and Satellite Year Book (1995) (London: 21st Century Publishing).

Christopher, Warren (1985) *American Hostages in Iran: Conduct of a Crisis* (New Haven, Conn.: Yale University Press).

Cottam, Richard W. (1990) *Iran and the United States: A Cold War Case Study* (Pittsburg, PA: University of Pittsburg Press.

Grimaud, Nicole (1985) *La Politique Exterieure de l'Algerie* (Paris: Editions Khartala).

Heikal, Mohammed (1982) *The Return of the Ayatollahs* (London: Andre Deutsch).

Hiro, Dilip (1985) *Iran under the Ayatollahs* (London: Routledge & Kegan Paul).

Hoffman, Bruce (1994) *Responding to Terrorism Across the Technological Spectrum* (Santa Monica: RAND Corporation).

Iran Research Group (1990) *Iran Year Book 89/90* (London: M&B Publishing).

Katzman, Kenneth (1993) *The Warriors of Islam: Iran's Revolutionary Guard* (Colorado: Westview Press).

McCarthy, John and Jill Morrell (1993) *Some Other Rainbow* (London: Bantam).

Melman, Yossi (1987) *The Master Terrorist: The True Story Behind Abu Nidal* (London: Sidgewick & Jackson).

Momen, Moojan (1985) *An Introduction to Shi'i Islam* (New Haven, Conn.: Yale University Press).

Montazam, Mir Ali Ashgar (1994) *The Life and Times of Ayatollah Khomeini* (London and Bonn: Anglo-European).

Mosteshar, Cherry (1994) *Return to the Veil of Tears* (London: Hodder & Stoughton).

Polonskaya, Ludmile and Alexei Malashenko (1994) *Islam in Central Asia* (Lata: Ithaca Press).

Taheri, Amir (1987) *Holy Terror: Inside Story of Islamic Terrorism* (London: Sphere Books).

Waite, Terry (1993) *Taken on Trust* (London: Hodder & Stoughton).

Index

Tripoli (Lebanon)   106
Tudeh Party (Iran)   106, 126–7, 129,
    133–4
Tufeili, Sobhi   105, 107, 119
Tunis   80, 172, 181
Tunisia   12, 186, 198, 200–1
Turabi, Hassan al-   201
Turkey(ish)   12, 55, 197, 205
Turkic, language   45
Turner, Jesse   112, 120
TWA hijack   82–92, 94, 97, 105, 107,
    113–14, 118, 156
Tyre (Lebanon)   69–70, 123

UAE   76, 79
Uganda   201
Ulami, Ami   176
Ulema   28
UN   9, 22, 51, 79, 120–1, 134, 139,
    164, 171–2
UNIFIL   116
UNTSO   116
USA (US)   6, 9, 15–17, 19, 21, 27–32,
    38, 43, 48–52, 57, 59, 65–7, 69,
    71, 73, 80, 85–91, 93, 95, 98–100,
    102, 105–6, 108–10, 113–14, 117,
    120, 122–4, 127, 129, 135–6, 138,
    141, 145–7, 159, 196, 198, 201,
    203
USSR   9, 129

Vance, Cyrus   49
Vellayati, Ali Akbar   110, 113, 134,
    157
Venezuela(n)   14
Vengeance Party   103
VEVAK   15, 59, 159–60, 167, 181,
    202
Vice Squad (Iran)   141
Vienna   76–7, 155
Vietnamese   183
Vincennes   124
VVIR   42, 128, 140–1, 180

Wachsmann, Nachshom   175
Wahabi, sect   151
Waite, Terry   106, 110–12, 120
Wareh, Faik   109
Washington   2, 8, 18, 172–3
Wegener, Ulrich   152
Weir, Benjamin   101, 103–6
Weizmann, Ezer   179
Wembly Stadium (London)   11–12
West Bank (Palestine)   170, 172, 180
West Germany   3, 76, 88, 113–15,
    117–18, 152
Western Sahara   20
White House (USA)   2, 18, 87
Wilyat e-Faqir   41, 137
World Movements (conference)   162
World Trade Centre (New York)
    17–18, 20–1, 23–4, 27, 30, 32, 165
World Wide Television News   109
Wright, Peter   6

Yasin, Abdul   30
Yassin, Ahmad   166, 168, 170, 175,
    179
Yaya, Abdul Salim   184
Yazdi, Ibrahim   41
Yemen   191, 203
Yugoslavia   163
Younis, Fawaz   82, 84, 88
Yousef, Ramiz Ahmad   23, 30, 32, 165

Zagreb (Croatia)   164
Zahedan   142–3, 153
Zanzan, province (Iran)   143
Zer, Khalid   174
Zerka, Nadia   8
Zeroual, Lamine   183–4, 190, 192,
    194, 196–7
Zia, President   51
Zion(ism)   13, 69, 174, 177
Zit, Khaled   176
Zitouni, Djamel   192
Zoroastrian(s)   36